MANSON IN HIS OWN WORDS

MANSON
IN HIS
OWN
WORDS

AS TOLD TO
NUEL EMMONS

GROVE PRESS
INC.
NEW YORK

First Grove Press Edition 1986
First Printing 1986
ISBN: 0-394-55558-9
Library of Congress Catalog Card Number: 86-45257

Library of Congress Cataloging-in-Publication Data

Manson, Charles, 1934–
  Manson in his own words.

  1. Manson, Charles, 1934–   . 2. Crime and criminals—
California—Biography. I. Emmons, Nuel. II. Title.
HV6248.M2797A3 1986   364.1'523'0924 [B] 86-45257
ISBN 0-394-55558-9

Designed by Abe Lerner

Printed in the United States of America

Grove Press, Inc., 920 Broadway, New York, N.Y. 10010

5 4 3 2 1

Dedicated to destroying a myth

CONTENTS

MANSON IN HIS OWN WORDS

Introduction
by Nuel Emmons

In late July and early August of 1969, eight of the most bizarre murders in the annals of crime surfaced. The murders were committed with the savagery of wild animals, but animals do not kill with knives and guns, nor do they scrawl out messages with their victims' blood.

On July 31, 1969, homicide officers from the Los Angeles Sheriff's Office were summoned to 946 Old Topanga Canyon Road. When they entered the premises, the officers were assailed by swarming flies and the pungent stench of decaying human flesh. They found one male body, marked by multiple stab wounds, that they established had been dead for several days. On the living room wall a short distance from the body the words "POLITICAL PIGGY" were scrawled in the victim's blood. Also on the wall were blood smudges as though a panther had left its paw print.

The victim was Gary Hinman. Thirty-two years old, Hinman had been attending UCLA in pursuit of a Ph.D. in sociology, supporting himself by teaching music. It was later discovered that for additional income he manufactured and sold a form of mescaline.

On Saturday, August 9th at 10050 Cielo Drive in the plush residential area of Bel Air, adjacent to Beverly Hills and Hollywood, officers from the Los Angeles Police Department arrived at a second crime scene so gory it might well have come from a Hollywood horror film. There, sprawled throughout the house and grounds, were five viciously slain victims, all of whom had been in the prime of their lives. They were Sharon Tate Polanski, Abigail Folger, Voytek Frykowski, Jay Sebring and Steven Parent. And as in the Hinman house there was a bloody message. On the door of the home where the five had lost their lives, in what was later established as Miss Tate's blood, was the word "PIG."

3

The shocking massacre brought droves of reporters and photographers who surrounded the restricted area of home and grounds where police investigators sought clues. Nothing but the deaths was certain, yet when the reporters filed their stories, speculation filled the newspapers. Some described the deaths as "ritual slayings," others stated the killings were the result of a wild sex party, still others declared the five had died in retaliation for a drug burn. Jealousy and love triangles were also mentioned as motives. Some reporters simply stated what was known at the time; that the police were baffled about the motives for the crime and were still searching for clues in the most bizarre multiple murders ever committed in the Los Angeles area. But this was just the beginning.

On Sunday, August 10th, hardly more than twenty-four hours after the initial call summoning police to the Cielo address, the LAPD was summoned to yet another ghastly death scene: 3301 Waverly Drive in the Los Feliz district of Los Angeles, the home of Leno and Rosemary LaBianca.

Leno, forty-four, was dead as the result of twenty-six stab wounds, some of which were administered with a carving fork. When his body was discovered, the fork still protruded from his stomach, as did a knife from his throat. His thirty-eight-year-old wife Rosemary had been stabbed forty-one times. Again the slain victims' home held messages boldly printed in the victims' blood: "DEATH TO PIGS" and "RISE" on a wall, and the misspelled words "HEALTER SKELTER" on the refrigerator door. District Attorney Vincent Bugliosi would ultimately theorize that Helter Skelter explained the motive for the slayings, but for the present, everything but the nights of horror and the eight brutally assaulted bodies was a baffling mystery.

As news of the murders swept the country, newspapers, radio and television were quick to report anything associated with what soon became known to the world as "The Tate-LaBianca Slayings." The crimes and the news coverage had a chilling effect in and around the Hollywood area. Fear and suspicion gripped the homes, hearts and streets throughout southern California. Guns and weapons were purchased for self-defense in record numbers. Police investigators, pushed to find a suspect, worked long hard hours checking clues and following leads. Although several days after Hinman's death a suspect named Robert Beausoleil had been arrested, no one linked him to the slayings in the heart of Hollywood. It was not until months later, when a second suspect in the Hinman case was arrested, that some light would be shed on the Tate-LaBianca slayings.

That second suspect was Susan Denise Atkins, who would eventually be convicted for the previously mentioned deaths, as well as the death of one Donald Jerome (Shorty) Shea, a ninth victim whose murder did not surface until the killers were apprehended. (His body, a mystery during the trial, was not discovered until several years later.) Atkins flamboyantly confided her participation in the deaths to jail-house acquaintances, and described Charles Manson as a charismatic cult leader, a living Jesus, a guru possessing mystical powers strong enough to entice his followers to kill for him. Atkins' jail confidants relayed the disclosure to the police, who announced in a press conference at the beginning of December that the grisly murders of five months past were at last solved.

With Manson and several other suspects in custody, Atkins sold a copyrighted story, "Two Nights of Murder," to *The Los Angeles Times* and several foreign newspapers, and before Christmas, 1969, the world read the sensational story. It, and similar stories that followed, made Manson the most publicized and discussed villain of our time, even before he went to trial. During the trial, under the persistent attention of the media, Charles Milles Manson and his followers (now described as the "Manson Family"), would gain worldwide notoriety.

Manson was charged with being the mastermind that unleashed the animal savagery in his followers. As motive for the slaughters, prosecuting attorney Bugliosi established that Manson believed, and convinced his followers, that there would eventually be an uprising by blacks against whites which Manson referred to as "Helter Skelter," from the Beatles song of the same name. Manson was said to have ordered his followers to commit bizarre murders to accelerate this conflict, leaving false evidence to indicate that the violent acts had been committed by blacks. There was also the suggestion that Manson had chosen the Cielo Drive residence because it had formerly been occupied by Terry Melcher, a recording company executive who had failed to promote Manson's recording efforts. When Manson initiated the killings he remembered

5

Melcher's "rejection" and the secluded location of his former home, making it an ideal place for murder.

The prosecution further contended that Manson had convinced his followers a pit existed in Death Valley where he and his group would be safe during the conflict between the races. Manson predicted the blacks would emerge victorious, but would not have the mental capacity to govern properly. Once the turmoil subsided, Manson and his chosen people, having grown to 144,000, would emerge from their haven and begin building a new society more in keeping with Manson's views.

From arrest to conviction, the investigations and trials of Manson and members of the Manson Family lasted well over a year-and-a-half. Those convicted and sentenced to be executed in San Quentin's gas chamber were: Charles Manson, Susan Atkins, Charles (Tex) Watson, Leslie Van Houten and Patricia Krenwinkel (for the Tate-LaBianca murders), Bruce Davis and Steve Grogan (for their participation in the murder of Shorty Shea), and Bobby Beausoleil (for the murder of Gary Hinman). However, within a year after the group was sentenced to death, the State of California abolished capital punishment and the sentences were automatically commuted to life imprisonment. With the commutation the eight were eligible for parole consideration as early as 1978. In the fall of 1985, after sixteen years of confinement, Steve Grogan was released under stringent parole conditions by the California Board of Parole. To date, all others have been refused parole.

Most people see Manson and his co-defendants as callous, cold-blooded, dope-crazed killers. But others accept Manson as a leader and a guru with mystical powers. They champion Manson, defend him, and try to imitate the life he led before the murders. He has received thousands of letters and numerous visitors during his confinement: letters from teenagers and adults of both sexes; visits from women wanting Manson's love and attention, from seekers of advice, from would-be followers. They even offer to commit crimes for him—or rather, for the myth that has grown up around him. But the myth is very different from the reality.

It happens that I knew Manson years ago, long before there were flower children and hippies. We weren't what convicts call "joint partners," but we did share some time and space in the same institution; Terminal Island in 1956 and 1957, where I had been sentenced on a charge of interstate transportation of a stolen vehicle. At the time, he had just turned twenty-one and I was twenty-eight. The extent of our prison association was mostly based on our mutual interest in the athletic program. However, I did see in him then what I myself had been at twenty years of age: a youth among older convicts, listening to every word the hard-core, accomplished criminals said, not yet old enough to realize the agony of a life of crime.

I was released in 1957 and shortly after opened an auto repair shop in Hollywood. Manson was released in 1958. We had mutual friends in the area and because of a problem Manson was having due to an automobile accident, one of those friends told him where I was located. Though the accident was a civil matter, it was creating other problems for Manson. "My parole officer is giving me a lot of static," he said. "Either I fix the guy's car I hit, or he is going to have my parole violated and send me back to the joint. Will you help me out?" I did the repairs, fixing Manson's car as well. This incident, coupled with our having been in the same institution together, became my opportunity to record Manson's story in his own words. For, as he has often said over the past six years, "You kept me from going to jail, Emmons. I owe you. And if anyone can explain how things came to be, maybe, because you've been inside, you're the person."

I didn't see Manson again until 1960. We met at the McNeil Island penitentiary, where I was serving a sentence for conspiracy to import narcotics. Our relationship was much the same as it had been at Terminal Island—our contact was limited to the prison athletic programs, except for a few casual exchanges. I remember Manson once asking me if I knew about L. Ron Hubbard and Dianetics. I didn't and had little interest in learning, so the conversation was a short one. The time served at McNeil was time that would change my life—for the better. As you will see in the following pages, it was also time that would change Manson's life.

On my release in 1964, I wanted only to take a responsible and honest part in society. Since that time I have never infringed on the rights of others, nor have I jeopardized my personal freedom. I resumed my trade, auto repair, and later started a second career as a free-lance writer.

In 1969 I hardly noticed the Gary Hinman murder, but like the

7

rest of the world I became very familiar with the Tate-LaBianca slayings. When Manson's name surfaced in December of 1969, I was astonished—not because he was involved, but because this man supposed to have powers to manipulate others into carrying out his every whim bore little resemblance to the man I remembered.

By 1979 I had forgotten almost entirely about him, until one day a local publication carried a feature story on him. The writer had journeyed to Vacaville, where Manson was then confined, with the intention of interviewing him. Manson refused to permit the interview. The story was finally published using information from prison personnel, and it mentioned that Manson seldom responded to requests for interviews. I was then writing for a newspaper, and I felt that my past association with Manson might give me the opportunity to see him that had been denied others.

My first letter was answered by one of his inmate friends, who said, "Charlie gets letters all the time from assholes like you wanting to interview him. He ain't interested in talking to you and having it all turned around and some more lies printed. But if you want to write about a wild, crazy motherfucker, send me a television and I'll talk to you." Enclosed in the letter were two clippings identifying the person and the murders he was serving time for. Other than returning the clippings as the writer requested, I ignored the letter.

In a second letter to Manson I identified myself enough to be certain he would remember me. I then explained that if he did not want to talk to me as a writer I would come over for just a routine visit. His reply was almost immediate, if barely legible. The essence was, "Yeah, I remember you. You should have told me who you were in your first letter and I wouldn't have passed you off to Butch. I haven't been having any visitors, so don't expect too much, they say I'm crazy. But if you want to come—do what you will." When I showed Manson's letter to my wife, her reaction was, "Are you really going to see him? Doesn't the thought of it give you an eerie feeling?" She, like so many others, had read the book *Helter Skelter* and believed very strongly that Manson had the power to lure people into his fold.

The California Medical Facility in Vacaville was only a two-hour drive from where I lived. I made the drive with thousands of

8

thoughts racing through my mind, and several questions for each thought. I wondered which personality I would be dealing with: the young, soft-eyed, not-very-aggressive kid I remembered in prison, or the hard, wild-eyed villain the media always seemed to capture. But for all the thinking, I signed in at the institution with a complete blank on a line of conversation. Hell, I was wondering if I was in my right mind for even being there.

Signing in was an experience for me. Being at a prison again, even as a visitor, stirred memories of my days in confinement. My heart beat rapidly, and my hands trembled so badly I could hardly fill out the necessary visitor forms. Once inside, I had the urge to retrieve my pass, to head back out the gate and forget anything that was even remotely connected with a prison. Instead, I took a deep breath and took a seat among other waiting visitors.

After about forty-five minutes, the guard announced, "Visitor for Charles Manson." At the mention of Manson, heads turned. I started toward the visiting room. Those that weren't looking at me were craning their necks for the appearance of Manson himself. As I neared the door a guard intercepted me, saying, "No, you'll have to come this way." He escorted me to an area known as "between gates." On the way, he allowed me to stop at a vending machine for some cigarettes, cokes and candy bars.

Between gates is a highly secured area that separates the front of the institution and the administrative offices from where the convicts are housed. Two electronically controlled, barred gates face each other at either end of a twenty-five foot corridor. On one side of the corridor is a room enclosed with bullet-proof glass where at least two officers control the operation of the gates and check the identification of every individual who enters or departs. Never are the two gates open at the same time. Across the corridor from the control room are two or three rooms with barred fronts. Each room is about eight feet by eight feet with a table and four stools bolted to the center of the room.

Manson had already been escorted to and locked in the room we were to use for our visit, and while the guard unlocked the door to let me in, Manson peered out, looking me over carefully. He was dressed in standard, loose-fitting blue denim prison garb with a blue and white bandana tied around his forehead to keep his long hair in place. He had a full, Christ-like beard. At that time he was forty-four years old, but other than a strand or two of grey in his beard and hair, he didn't look much older than when I had last seen him in 1964. As the guard locked the door behind me, Manson backtracked to the far corner of the room. He looked like a frightened, distrustful animal. With his body in a slight crouch, head a little bit forward and cocked to one side, he gave me a nod and said, "What's up, man?" "Nothing," I said, "I'm just here like my letter said I'd be." With that, I placed the soft drinks and candy on the table and extended my hand for a greeting. Manson straightened his slight body, stepped toward me and took my hand. A faint smile was visible through his beard. "Yeah, Emmons," he said, "I'd have recognized you anywhere. How's your handball game?" "Hell, I haven't played since I left McNeil. How's yours?" "Fuck, are you kiddin', that Mizz Winters [then chief psychiatrist at Vacaville] and her black boyfriends have had me locked down so tight, I don't get to do nothin'. It took me nine years to get out of S Wing." S Wing is a segregated unit that confines those who are still under intensive psychological observation. "They got me in W Wing now," he added, "and that ain't much better."

The ice had been broken, but the room was filled with tension. Manson wouldn't allow me within arm's length of him, and never placed himself in a vulnerable position. He was always geared to defend himself instantly. His paranoia was even more evident when I first offered him a cigarette. "You light it!" he said. I handed him the lit cigarette, but before taking a drag, he carefully fingered the entire length of it and asked, "How far down is the bomb?" He wouldn't touch the soft drinks or candy bars I had placed in front of him until I drank from one or took a bite of candy. He would then reach for the one I had tasted, eating or drinking only after my example had assured him that it wasn't poisoned. "Are you putting on an act," I asked, "or are you really so paranoid you think I'm here to poison you?" His eyes met mine in an unblinking stare as he said, "Hey look, I ain't seen you in fifteen or twenty years. When we were in the joint together, you didn't have the time of day for me. Now all of a sudden you show up. How do I know what you got in mind? I been alive this long 'cause I'm on top of people's thoughts. You don't know how bad these motherfuckers want to get rid of me. I been livin' in their shit for ten years, and every day they send in somebody to do a

10

number on me. I been alive this long 'cause I'm aware. I don't trust you or anyone!"

At that moment, trying to change his opinion of me would have been wasted effort, but I did feel it necessary to explain why I hadn't had the time of day for him when we were doing time together. "You were eight years younger than me; I had already been through all you were going through. You and the guys you lined up with in the joint were playing games and trying to impress everyone. All I wanted was to do my time and get out. It wasn't a question of liking or disliking you." My words seemed to calm him. The intimidating anger that had been mounting in his voice vanished and he began asking about some of our former mutual friends. As it turned out, he was much more up-to-date on their lives and whereabouts than I was. Jails have a hell of a grapevine on alumni, especially if the guy has taken another fall or is still wheeling and dealing. On the other hand, if he straightens himself out, it seems the line ends and the person might as well be dead as far as other convicts are concerned.

After about thirty minutes, the guard informed us we had five minutes remaining. During that five minutes Manson brought up what I had decided not to mention on this first visit. He said, "So you're a writer now, huh? You know I've been burned by all you bastards, and I don't trust any of you fuckers to tell the truth. Whatta you think about that?" I didn't know if he was telling me to get lost, or if it was just his way of checking out my reaction. I answered, "That's all right, Charlie, I don't trust a lot of writers either. So forget I came over here looking for a story—I'm here because we've done some time together, and if a visit or two breaks up the monotony for you, I'll come back. If you'd rather I didn't, I won't." He didn't give me a direct answer, but said, "Hey, I could use some stamps and writing pads, can you handle that?" "Sure," I told him, "and if you need a few dollars on the books, I can do that too."

Our time was up, and as we said our goodbyes he stood closer to me. We exchanged a parting handshake that held a little warmth. Neither of us had mentioned the crimes. Though he hadn't said so, I felt he wanted me to continue visiting. Given time, I thought, some trust and confidence could develop between us.

I sent the writing material he asked for, along with some money

11

for commissary items. We exchanged a letter or two and I began visiting almost weekly. The next couple of visits were pretty much like the first. He didn't talk much about the outside or the past, but had plenty to say about how the prisons had changed. For a sentence or two he would be coherent—if not logical—but then he would suddenly switch subjects without completing the thought.

I wasn't aware during the six or seven visits that first couple of months that Manson had been receiving medication until one day he said, "Maybe you're some kind of therapy for me, 'cause they are cutting down on jabbing me with that needle." After that, our visits became more constructive. We began talking more about the crimes. He was evasive in response to direct questions about his actual involvement, but talked freely about "his girls," life at the Spahn Ranch, the Mojave Desert and his dune buggies. He volunteered some information about Lynette (Squeaky) Fromme and the assassination attempt on President Ford. One day, he unexpectedly asked, "You heard about Red being in Alderson, didn't you?" ("Red" was his "color name" for Fromme; several of the main girls in the family were identified by various colors.) "I have to carry that load too. I didn't tell her to take no shot at Ford. That was her trip, but like everything else, it's Charlie's fault. Hey, *Charlie's Angels* on TV is even a take-off on me and my girls. By the way, do you think I sent those kids to Melcher's house?" It was the first time he had asked outright if I thought he was guilty or not.

"You're here, Charlie," I said, "I have to believe some of it." He exploded and I got my first look at those sharp, penetrating eyes that appeared so often in newspapers and on the covers of magazines during the court proceedings in 1970. He came at me, not in a physical attack, but shouting, his face inches from mine. "You motherfucker, you ain't no friend, you're just another victim of Sadie's [Susan Atkins] and Bugliosi's Helter Skelter bullshit! Fuck you, get your ass on down the road." The guard had his keys out and was about to open the door to break up the fight he thought would surely happen, but I told the guard, "It's all right, we're just having a little disagreement." The guard hesitated and Charlie backed off and glared at both of us. He was trembling with anger. Then I saw him relax, and he said to the guard, "Yeah, it's all right, everything's under control." The flare of temper subsided as quickly as it had surfaced. Manson picked up the conversation in a

12

quiet, calm tone of voice. "You know, I been around long enough to know that if you do the crime you gotta pay, but I ain't guilty the way those pricks convicted me. So I ain't supposed to be here! At least not under the gun the way they got me. They might have made me on conspiracy, an accessory before or after the fact; that would have carried the same sentence, and I'd be doing my time without crying." Then quickly, for fear I might think he was showing weakness, "I ain't crying, understand, but these fuckers are doing me wrong." There was a moment or two of silence as his eyes bored through me in an effort to read whether I believed him or not. I broke the silence by saying, "If that's the way it is, Charlie, let me write the book the way you say it was." He smiled and said, "You cagey mother. After two months you finally got it out. But man, I don't know if I can trust you." "What's to trust, Charlie?" I asked. "Everything bad has been said about you. But your life represents all the ills in our society and, properly illustrated, it could be an example for society. You've always said, 'Those parents sent their kids to me.' Your life as it really was, without all that Helter Skelter bullshit that went down during your trials, could show why those kids came to you, and make parents take a look at themselves and their kids. There is a lot to be learned from the life you have lived. And besides, you have your own version of what happened to bring about the slayings. Let me write it."

"You know what, Emmons, I don't give a fuck about those kids out there! It's up to their parents to take care of them. Those kids and their one-way parents are what got me here. Let them take care of themselves. No—fuck it! I ain't into being no part of no book! Especially a book that makes me look like some do-gooder. Fuck 'em, they built the image, let them live with all these kids writing me letters wanting to visit me and join my 'Family.' Fuck, there was no family! Some reporter stuck that on us one time when they hassled us out at the ranch. Besides, ain't nobody out there wants to read something they might learn from. Blood 'n guts and sex is the only trip they get behind when they're spending their dollars."

I left the visiting room that day feeling discouraged. I realized I'd used the wrong approach when suggesting he allow me to use his life as an example. He hated everyone in conventional society so

13

much that he didn't want to contribute anything that might, even remotely, be of value to society.

Several days after that particular visit, I received a letter from Manson that included two letters from publications requesting interviews with him. In his letter to me he asked if I thought he should do the interviews. Instead of writing back, I went to see him the next day. No mention of the book was made, but I told him if he was allowing interviews, let me be the first. "You got it!" he replied. "But one of these letters is from a girl from a local newspaper who has been hounding me for a long time to let her come in, so why don't you check her out and maybe bring her with you." We agreed that the woman and I would interview Manson together. I spoke with her and she, in turn, agreed to certain restrictions.

During the interview the reporter asked Manson, "Why do you have so much confidence in Emmons? I mean, you have refused so many interviews, but you have allowed him to interview you." Charlie's answer held a pleasant surprise for me. "Well, me and Emmons go back a long way. He understands me. Actually he's one of my fathers, he helped raise me and he's doing a book on my life." For Manson to suggest that I had been like a father to him and had helped raise him was anything but flattering, but he *had* mentioned the book and I wasn't going to press him as to why or when he had changed his mind. Perhaps he appreciated my regular visits, perhaps he recalled the favor I'd done him; whatever the case, he was willing to cooperate.

In addition to the publication I was working for, I had made arrangements with UPI to furnish their wire service with some pictures and a release on the interview. My story did not mention that Manson had agreed to furnish me information for a book, but UPI's release said that I was writing a book on Charles Manson. I immediately began receiving letters about him. Though his crimes had been history for over a decade, Manson still attracted a startling amount of attention and interest. Most of the mail came from the United States, but there were also letters from Canada, England, Germany, Spain, Italy, and Australia. Many of them offered information for a book about Manson, all such letters suggesting that he be allowed to tell his version of his life and the chain of events that led to the slayings of 1969.

14

The material for this first-person narrative has been assembled from many interviews, corroborated by his correspondence with me and with others, despite numerous obstacles. Even after Manson had agreed to cooperate, he was not always willing to do so, and I listened to hours upon hours of repetitive complaints about how rotten the prisons and the prison system were. I was allowed the use of a tape recorder only when interviewing Manson for a commissioned article for publication. On such occasions, the institution furnished me with a tape recorder because some years earlier, after an escape attempt at San Quentin, it was believed that an attorney had used his tape recorder to smuggle a gun inside. With the exception of these limited occasions, I had to make mental notes until I could record them on tape or in writing. I spent many hours in the prison parking lot, writing down names and specific phrases that typified Manson's speech and his ideas. I frequently had to go over events with Manson several times to confirm details and correct the misperceptions created by other accounts. In some cases it was impossible to corroborate Manson's version of the facts, but the purpose of this book is, above all, to record that version.

I pieced his childhood together with help from many sources. In addition to what he told me, which contained many gaps, I journeyed across the United States to where he was born and the places he spent the first sixteen years of his life. In Indiana, Ohio, West Virginia and Kentucky I talked to those who could fill in gaps and verify what Manson said. When there was new information, I would return to Manson and repeat what I had been told, to hear his words and sense his feelings about it.

What I have recorded here as a continuous chronological narrative is therefore actually the result of a long process of discussion and re-examination of the events, checking and cross-checking of details, and re-organization of the frequent, frustrating leaps of Manson's conversation. Nevertheless, it represents Manson's recollections of his life and his attitudes toward it as accurately, consistently, and coherently as is humanly possible.

Since my first visit with Manson, more than six years have passed. During those six years, and hundreds of hours of conversation, I have experienced his hate and contempt—and he mine. I have seen tenderness, a soft side that may well have been his strength in attracting those involved with him. But never has he demonstrated any remorse or uttered a word of compassion for those lives taken in the madness he and his group shared.

When questioned about his lack of remorse, Manson abruptly changes his attitude and aggressively defends himself: "Remorse for what? I didn't kill those people! Ask the DA and all the media people if they have any remorse for sending all these kids to me, kids wanting to pick up knives and guns for me because the DA and the money-hungry writers pumped the public into believing I'm something I'm not. Shit, they built the image—and they keep feeding the myth."

The myth of Charles Manson, the publicity that made him seem intriguing, the current concern about child abuse and where the use of drugs can lead all seemed important reasons to tell his story. It seems to me the myth of Charles Manson is not likely to survive the impact of his own words. They are important testimony to the consequences of the continued use of drugs, and the account they give of his early life shows once again that all children must have love and understanding. Failing to find it at home, they will search for it elsewhere. Enticed into accepting the myth of Charles Manson as reality, many people have turned to him for help.

Manson does not exaggerate the mail, visitors and potential followers who seek his attention. I have met many of them. He has forwarded to me almost two hundred pounds of mail, and sent similar quantities to others for safekeeping and review. His statement that "some are offering to pick up knives and guns" or willing to "off some pigs" for him is verified in many letters I have read addressed to Manson.

It is frightening, and most of us wonder why they do it. Manson stated, "Look at yourselves! It isn't me or any power I have. It's the way they were treated when they were small and their parents tried to play God. All the propaganda laid out by someone wanting to feel important and get rich gave them someone to turn to in their frustration." He said it as clearly as it might ever be said.

With the exception of the introduction and conclusion, my opinion of Manson is not represented in this book. In letting him tell his story, I have edited it to eliminate repetition and digression, and standardized many irregularities of speech. Some names have been changed, even those mentioned elsewhere, out of consideration for those involved. But the ideas and opinions expressed here are entirely his. I have simply tried to record his story as coherently as possible, to convey his meaning as he presented it to me in his own words. And although it is his story, Charles Manson receives no royalties or any other remuneration from this book. His only recompense will be the chance to have his story heard. Although he has heard or read most of the manuscript, the final decision about what would be included and what would not has been entirely mine.

I would like to express my gratitude to Grove Press, especially Fred Jordan and Walt Bode, who dared, and helped, when others turned their backs.

Finally, to the Tates, LaBiancas, Folgers and other surviving family and friends, I apologize for opening wounds and stirring thoughts of those horrifying days in August 1969.

PART ONE

THE EDUCATION
OF AN OUTLAW

CHAPTER 1

O<small>N</small> A<small>PRIL</small> *19, 1971, in Los Angeles, California, Charles Milles Manson heard Superior Court Judge Charles H. Older say, "It is my considered judgment that not only is the death penalty appropriate, but it is almost compelled by the circumstances. I must agree with the prosecutor that if this is not a proper case for the death penalty, what should be? The Department of Corrections is ordered to deliver you to the custody of the Warden of the State Prison of the State of California at San Quentin to be by him put to death in the manner prescribed by law of the State of California."*

In the courtroom with Manson were three co-defendants, Susan Atkins, Leslie Van Houten, and Patricia Krenwinkel. On March 29, 1971, a jury had found them guilty of the murders of Sharon Tate Polanski, Abigail Folger, Voytek Frykowski, Jay Sebring, Steven Parent, Leno LaBianca and Rosemary LaBianca. At a later date, Manson received the same sentence for two additional murders, as did four more co-defendants: Robert Beausoleil, Charles Watson, Bruce Davis and Steve Grogan. Beausoleil was convicted for the murder of Gary Hinman, Davis and Grogan for their participation in the death of Donald (Shorty) Shea. Watson was a member of the group that did the Tate-LaBianca slayings.

—N. E.

J<small>AILS</small>, <small>COURTROOMS AND PRISONS</small> had been my life since I was twelve years old. By the time I was sixteen, I had lost all fear of anything the administration of the prison system could dish out. But convicts, being unpredictable, made it a real possibility that dying in prison would be my fate, especially when the prosecuting attorney, the media and some department of corrections officials

21

planted seeds in the minds of other convicts by statements such as, "Due to the nature of Manson's crimes he will be a marked man for other convicts seeking attention and notoriety." In hearing Older pronounce the death sentence, I realized he was doing so with the full authority of the California Judicial System, yet I knew I would never be executed by the State of California. Die in prison, perhaps. But executed by the State, no!

I was right: within a year after being placed on Death Row, the existing capital punishment law was abolished in the state of California. All those awaiting execution were automatically given life terms. For most of those on the Row, it was a new lease on life. For me there was no particular elation, only the thought of, "Now what will I have to contend with?"

My paranoia has been well-founded, for due to the nature of the crimes, the amount of publicity about my arrest and the lengthy court proceedings, the name of Charles Manson has become the most hated and feared epithet of the current generation; a cross I have had to bear since my arrest in 1969. Because of the heavy security and my isolation from the general convict population, the time spent on Death Row was the most comfortable and relaxed I have spent in the last seventeen years. But since then I have been a special case in the California penal system, and because of that I've spent my ordinary confinement dodging spears, knives and death threats from other convicts as well as having to watch every guard who gets near me.

The latest, most newsworthy threat to my life happened in the arts and crafts room at the California Medical Facility. I was sitting on a stool facing a table, working on a clay sculpture. It was one of my first efforts at any form of sculpture and I was totally engrossed with the project—so engrossed it was one of the few times since being locked up that I relaxed my constant vigil on everything that was going on around me. I didn't hear footsteps, nor was I conscious of anyone being near me until a cold liquid was poured over my head, soaking my hair, face and most of my clothing. Startled, I leaped to my feet and faced the direction from which the liquid came. My eyes were already burning from the substance (a highly inflammable paint thinner), so it was with blurred sight that I saw the assailant, a long-haired, bearded Krishna bastard, throw a burning match at my face. My hands weren't quick enough to prevent

22

the flame from making contact with the thinner, and like a bomb exploding, I was instantly a human torch. My hair, face and clothing on fire, I lunged toward my assailant. He eluded me. Pain from the flames and instinct for self-preservation didn't allow me to continue pursuing him.

I hit the floor and pulled my burning jacket over my head in an effort to smother the ignited paint thinner. Though there was a guard and several inmates in the room, I had long ago learned not to expect help or sympathy from anyone. Not that I was thinking about what others might be doing, for at the moment my head was buzzing with what to do to extinguish the flames. I realized how vulnerable I was if the Krishna bastard decided to attack me again. But first things first, I had to get the fire out. Fortunately the guy didn't come at me but just stood back and watched me struggle. I was aflame for forty-five seconds to a minute, long enough to have all the hair burned from my head and face. My scalp, face, neck, left shoulder, arm and hand suffered third-degree burns. I spent a few days in the hospital, a couple of them on the critical list.

The attack had nothing to do with who I am or what I am accused of. It was the result of a discussion on religion that took place the day before I became a human torch. The guy who threw the match is as flaky and disoriented about the laws of society as most people believe I am. Yet he, like myself, doesn't see himself as some freak with a demented personality, but as a person who was dealt a hand that couldn't be played by the rules and values of your society.

My name is Charles Milles Manson. At this writing I am fifty-one years old. If I stretch to my fullest height and cheat a little by slightly lifting my heels from the floor, I can achieve a height of five-foot-five. I think at one time I weighed a healthy hundred forty pounds, but a time or two during my confinement I have dropped as low as one-fifteen. A bulky bruising hulk I am not. But my voice can be as big and loud as the largest of men. In 1970, prior to and during the court proceedings that resulted in my conviction, I made more magazine covers and news headlines than Coca-Cola has advertisements. Most of the stories and articles written painted me as having fangs and horns from birth. They say my mother was a whore, my nose was snotty from birth and my diapers, when I had any on, were full of shit which was often seen running down my dirty legs. They would have one believe that before I was five I was a beggar on the streets, scrounging for food to feed my dirty face and fill my empty stomach. By the time I was seven, my first followers were stealing and bringing me the spoils. Before reaching nine, I had a gun in my hand and was robbing the old and feeble. Still under the age of twelve, I had raped the preacher's daughter and choked her little brother to keep him from snitching on me. At thirteen, I had a police record that would qualify me to be on Nixon's staff or head the Mafia. The dope I distributed had the choir boys strung out and stealing from the collection plate. In my string of brainwashed broads were the ten-and twelve-year-old girls of the neighborhood. To prove their love for me, they brought me the money they earned from turning tricks and making porno movies.

Isn't that the way you have me framed in your thoughts? Haven't the famed prosecuting attorney, the judges, my alleged followers, and the news media given you that picture?

Would it change things to say I had no choice in selecting my mother? Or that, being a bastard child, I was an outlaw from birth? That during those so-called formative years, I was not in control of my life? Hey listen, by the time I was old enough to think or remember, I had been shoved around and left with people who were strangers even to those I knew. Rejection, more than love and acceptance, has been a part of my life since birth. Can you relate to that? I doubt it. And this late in life, I could'nt care less! But I've been asked where my philosophy, bitterness, and anti-social behavior came from. So without searching to change public opinion, I'll relate some of my life as I lived and remember it through the guy who is writing this book. You've read everyone else's "Charlie's this, Manson's that," and their version of the Family's history, but nobody is ever totally all that is said or believed about him.

Books have been written, more are being written; movies made, and, undoubtedly, more in the making. The media have had a puppet to dangle and a dummy in which to plunge their swords. All have taken my words and thoughts, rephrased them, and published them with twisted meaning. Distortion, sensationalism and fabricated quotes were printed daily—so much so that life on earth no longer held valid meaning for me. Nor does it now. My body re-

24

mains trapped and imprisoned by a society that creates people like me, but my mind has entered a chamber of thought that is not of this earth. I have learned that to be one's self, one must never utter a word, make a sound or motion, or even bat an eye, for by doing so in the presence of another, an opinion will be formed. A self-styled psychologist will analyze you and describe you to others so that you become something other than what you are.

As I said, the media have had their day. Nobodies have become rich and influential. So-called "Manson Family" members have purged and turned, testifying for the State, lying in the courts. They have written books and sold interviews playing down their role, putting it all on Charlie. Lawyers on both sides of the fence have made fortunes through their association with the "Manson Family" trials. My feeling is, I've been raped and ravaged by society. Fucked by attorney and friends. Sucked dry by the courts. Beaten by the guards and exhibited by the prisons. Yet my words have never been printed or presented as they were said. So at this point, I have nothing to gain, or lose, by telling it the way I feel it was.

To date, thirty-seven of my fifty-one years of life have been spent in reformatories, foster homes or prisons. For the past seventeen years I have been living like a caged animal in a zoo. The cage is very much the same, concrete and steel. I am fed just as the animals are, through the bars and on schedule. I have guards patrolling my cage, making certain it is still locked and that I still live. People come to visit the institution and no matter what their other interest, all want to know, "Where is Charles Manson kept? Can we go by his cell?" And like good zoo attendants, the guards accommodate. Seeing Charles Manson in his cage, like seeing the rarest of wild animals, has made their visit complete. To satisfy my personal curiosity, I look into a mirror to see if perhaps horns are growing from my head or fangs protruding from my mouth. Unless the mirror lies, I see no horns or fangs. I check the rest of my body to see how it differs from those who stop and stare. With eyes that see, blink and stare like those who have just stopped to view, I see a body, two arms, hands and feet, and a head that grows hair in the customary places, complete with eyes, nose, ears and mouth. I'm no different from those who stopped by to give me their hated glare. Or you, who are interested in what I have to say.

25

If writers and other media people had stuck to the facts as disclosed by investigating law officers from the beginning, Charles Manson would not have been remembered. But with each writer, each book, or each television personality exaggerating, fabricating, reaching for sensationalism and adding hostilities of their own, myself and those who lived with me became more than what we were. Or had ever intended to be.

Most stories depicted me and those arrested with me as dope-crazed sickies. A June, 1970, issue of *Rolling Stone* captioned an article "A Special Report: Charles Manson—the incredible story of the most dangerous man alive." However, there were publications that speculated that the crimes weren't without underlying principles. For example, a February 1970 issue of *Tuesday's Child* said I might be more of a revolutionary martyr than a callous killer. Naturally I, and some who shared in the madness, were quick to pick up on anything that was even remotely sympathetic.

I didn't read either of the articles at the time although I heard much about them, but since late 1969 I have been reading similar headlines and seeing pictures of myself almost daily. All refer to me as the "hippie cult leader who programmed people to kill for him—the man responsible for the Tate-LaBianca slayings." They established me as some kind of mystical super-being that could look into the eyes of another and make him or her carry out my every whim. I was portrayed as a regular Pied Piper who lured kids into crime and violence.

Knowing what I am, how I was raised, and all that I've ever been, I see those stories as ridiculous. I am dismayed at the readers who lap up the lies and believe them like the Bible, but I have to hand it to the guys who created the image—the skillful writers who can suck the most out of anything and build mountains from mole hills. I really shouldn't blame the readers 'cause I kind of get caught up in the stories myself. But when I start believing I might really possess all the powers attributed to me and I try to work a whammy on my prison guard—he or she shuts the prison door in my face. Back to reality. I realize I am only what I've always been, "a half-assed nothing."

The reason for this book is not to fight the case of "the most dangerous man alive," if I am that (or was), but just to give the other side of an individual that has been compared with the Devil. And even the Devil, if there is a Devil, had a beginning.

I can't remember ever hearing about old Lucifer's mother, so I don't know if he was born or just created as a means of putting fear in the lives of children. If he did have a mother, we have two things in common. If not, our link is that we are both used to put fear in kids' minds. Anyway, I had a mother.

Her name was Kathleen Maddox, born in Ashland, Kentucky, and the youngest of three children from the marriage of Nancy and Charles Maddox. Mom's parents loved her and meant well by her, but they were fanatical in their religious beliefs. Especially Grandma, who dominated the household. She was stern and unwavering in her interpretation of God's Will, and demanded that those within her home abide by her views of God's wishes.

According to Grandma, the display of an ankle or even an over-friendly smile to one of the opposite sex was sinful. Drinking and smoking were forbidden. Make-up was evil and only used by women of the streets. Cursing would put you in hell as quickly as stealing or committing adultery.

My grandfather worked for the B&O Railroad. He worked long hard hours, a dedicated slave to the company and his bosses. He, like Grandma, lived and preached the word of God. He was not the disciplinarian Grandma was, but, like his children, he was under his wife's thumb. If he tried to comfort Mom with a display of affection, such as a pat on the knee or an arm around her shoulder, Grandma was quick to insinuate he was vulgar. To keep harmony between them, Grandpa let his wife rule their home. Poor man. In later years he was taken away from the home he supported and died in an asylum.

For Mom life was filled with a never-ending list of denials. From awakening in the morning until going to bed at night it was, "No Kathleen, that dress is too short. Braid your hair, don't comb it like some hussy. Come directly home from school, don't let me catch you talking to any boys. No, you can't go to the school dance, we are going to church. Kathleen, you say grace. Don't forget to say your prayers before going to bed and ask forgiveness for your sins."

In 1933, at age fifteen, my mother ran away from home. "Was driven" might be a better description.

27

Other writers have portrayed Mom as a teenage whore. Because she happened to be the mother of Charles Manson, she is downgraded. I prefer to think of her as a flower-child of the 30s, thirty years ahead of the times. Her reasons for leaving home were no different than those of the kids I became involved with in the 60s. And like those kids, she chose to be homeless on the streets instead of catering to the one-sided demands of parents who view things only as they believe they should be. Some day parents will wake up. Children are not dummies; a home life is a multi-directioned street, and all ways of life should be considered and understood. As for Mom being a whore, those early teachings at home prevented her from selling her body. She did have the vanity of a whore, though, and while she was never a raging beauty, she was a pretty girl—her red hair and fair complexion made her noticed in most any surrounding. She was barely five feet in height and would consider herself fat if she got over a hundred pounds. Yet despite her vanity, physical attractiveness and display of confidence, Mom was searching for her own identity and for acceptance by others. In her search for acceptance she may have fallen in love too easily and too often, but a whore at that time? No!

In later years, because of hard knocks and tough times, she may have sold her body some. I am not about to knock her. Knowing the things I know now, I wish my mother had been smart enough to start out as a prostitute. You can sit back and say, "A statement like that is about what is expected out of Manson's mouth," but to me a class whore is about as honest a person as there is on earth. She has a commodity that is hers alone. She asks a price for it. If the price is agreeable, the customer is happy, the girl has her rent and grocery money and the little teenager down the street hasn't been raped by a stiff dick without a conscience. The teenager's parents don't have a molested child going through life trying to live down a traumatic experience. The police don't have a case, and the taxpayers aren't supporting some guy in prison for umpteen years. Yes, an honest prostitute does more than help herself. She is good for the community.

On November 12, 1934, while living in Cincinnati, Ohio, unwed and only sixteen, my mother gave birth to a bastard son. Hospital records list the child as "no name Maddox." The child—me, Charles Milles Manson—was an outlaw from birth. The guy who

28

planted the seed was a young drugstore cowboy who called himself Colonel Scott. He was a transient laborer working on a nearby dam project, and he didn't stick around long enough to even watch the belly rise. Father, my ass! I saw the man once or twice, so I'm told, but don't remember his face.

The name Manson came from William Manson, a fellow Mom lived with shortly after my birth. William was considerably older than Mom, and because of his persistence they eventually got married. I don't know if it was his way of trying to lock Mom down or if it was a moral thing because there was a kid in the house. So through him I got the name Manson. But a father—no! The marriage wasn't one of those long-term things and I don't remember him. Whether the divorce was his fault or Mom's, I never did know. Probably Mom's, she was always a pretty promiscuous little broad.

When Mom ran away from a home that had completely dominated her, she exploded into a newfound freedom. She drank a lot, loved freely, answered to no one and gave life her best shot. When I was born she had not experienced enough of life—or that newfound freedom—to take on the responsibilities of being a mother. I won't say I was an unwanted child, but it was long before "the pill" and, like many young mothers, she was not ready to make the sacrifices required to raise a child. With or without me, Mom still had some living to do. I would be left with a relative or a hired sitter, and if things got good for her, she wouldn't return to pick me up. Often my grandparents or other family members would have to rescue the sitter until Mom showed up. Naturally I don't remember a lot of these things, but you know how it is; even in a family if there is something disagreeable about someone it always gets told. One of Mom's relatives delighted in telling the story of how my mother once sold me for a pitcher of beer. Mom was in a café one afternoon with me in her lap. The waitress, a would-be mother without a child of her own, jokingly told my Mom she'd buy me from her. Mom replied, "A pitcher of beer and he's yours." The waitress set up the beer, Mom stuck around long enough to finish it off and left the place without me. Several days later my uncle had to search the town for the waitress and take me home.

In saying these things about my mother, I may sound as though I am selling her short, and by society's standards her measurements

29

aren't up to par. But hey, I liked my mom, loved her, and if I could have picked her, I would have. She was perfect! In doing nothing for me, she made me do things for myself.

When I was about six years old my mom had dropped me off by my grandparents for what was supposed to be just a day or two. Several days later, I remember my grandfather asking me to go for a walk with him. Once outside the house, he became softspoken and kinder than I had ever remembered. As we walked we played games and ran races, and he would let me outrun him. He put me up on his shoulders and carried me while I pretended I was a giant and taller than anyone alive. After a while we sat down to rest. He put his arms around me and, fighting back tears, told me, "Your mother won't be coming home for a long time." I don't know if the lump came in my throat because my grandfather had begun to cry or if it was because I realized what he was telling me.

My mother and her brother Luther had attempted to rob a service station in Charleston, West Virginia. The story goes that they had used a coke bottle as a weapon to knock the attendant unconscious. They were caught and sentenced to five years in the Moundsville State Prison.

At Moundsville she lived in the women's ward of the prison, but her work assignment was near Death Row. It was her job to clean an area that included the scaffold (West Virginia was a hanging state). Mom tells a story that one day as she worked, she saw the guards escorting a man to the scaffold. Normally, on a hanging day no one but the officials and the person to be executed are supposed to be in the area. By accident or oversight, they forgot to inform Mom a hanging was to take place that day. Afraid she would be in trouble for being there, she hid in a broom closet by the scaffold. When the trap sprung, the velocity and the guy's weight caused the rope to sever his head, and as Mom peeked out the door for a first-hand view of the hanging, the head rolled right to her hiding place. She swears the eyes were still wide open and that death literally stared her right in the face.

Twenty-seven years later, when I was first placed on Death Row in San Quentin, I looked at the gas chamber. The room's two viewing windows looked like two huge eyes of death. Instantly my mind flashed to my mother, and I had a vision of her looking into the eyes of death. During that moment, I understood more about my mom than at any other time in my life.

While Mom was doing time at Moundsville it kind of fell on my grandmother to take care of me, want to or not. So there I was in the same household that my mom had run away from six years earlier. Strict discipline, grace before each meal and long prayer sessions before going to bed at night. Don't fight, don't steal, and turn the other cheek. I believed and practiced all that my grandmother taught. So much so that I became the sissy of the neighborhood.

After a few weeks at Grandma's, it was decided that I would live with Mom's sister Joanne and her husband Bill, in McMechen, West Virginia. My uncle Bill had opinions about how young boys were supposed to act, and being a sissy and afraid of everyone in the neighborhood wasn't his ideal of a male youth. I remember him telling me to stop crying at everything and start acting like a man or he was going to start dressing me and treating me like a little girl. I guess my behavior really didn't improve that much. Right now I can't remember what particular thing made him do it, but on my first day in school, Bill dressed me in girl's clothing. I was embarrassed and ashamed. The other kids teased me so much I went into a rage and started fighting everyone. Turning the other cheek, as Grandma had always wanted me to do, was forgotten. I took my lumps and shed a little blood, but in that school I became the fightin'est little bastard they ever saw. It must have pleased Uncle Bill, because from then on I wore boy's clothing.

Joanne and Bill were good people and tried to do right by me. In their home I lived what you might call a normal life, but it's hard to describe where my head was emotionally with Mom in jail and me living with a couple I didn't belong to. Hell, I don't know what kind of thoughts were going through my head then. Their treatment of me was fine. I got my ass-kickings when I deserved them and my rewards when I did something right. I was trained in proper manners and taught to wash my face, comb my hair, brush my teeth and believe in and respect God—like any other kid. But if you don't belong, things just aren't the same.

I can still remember hearing grownups refer to me as "the little

31

bastard" and the kids I played with telling me, "Your mother's no good; she's a jail bird. Ha ha ha."

One year shortly after Christmas, I got even with some of those kids who were laughing at me. I had spent Christmas with my grandparents. My only present for the year was a hairbrush. A Superman hairbrush. As I opened the present, my grandmother said, "If you brush your hair with it, you will be able to fly like Superman." Young fool that I was, I carried that brush around with me for days and was constantly brushing my hair. I'd jump off porches, anything with a little elevation, and really expected to soar in the air like Superman. I never did fly and to this day that was the only lie that my grandmother ever told me.

The kids in the neighborhood rubbed things in even more by showing me all their presents. They had toys of all kinds: wagons, trains, cowboy hats and chaps. Even now, I'm not sure if I just resented being laughed at or if I was jealous of what they had and I didn't, but one day I rounded up all of their toys I could find and carted them home with me. I stacked up some wood and threw the toys on top and started a fire. The kids were mad—some cried, others threatened me, and their parents called the sheriff. And though I wasn't taken to jail, it was my first encounter with the police. I was seven years old.

Mom was released from Moundsville when I was about eight. The day she came home is still one of the happiest days of my life. I think she missed me as much as I missed her. For the next few days we were inseparable. I was her son and she was my mom and we were both proud of each other. I loved it! I guess my mom did, too. But a twenty-three-year-old girl needs more than an eight-year-old son to complete her world. If Mom had some catching up in her life to do before she went to prison, she was really behind now. It's a lifetime too late to think about it, but things might have been a lot different if Mom had gone her way and left me with the aunt and uncle. She didn't—and I was glad.

It was some trip living with Mom. We moved around a lot and I missed a lot of school and blew a lot of what my aunt and uncle had been trying to teach me. Mom and I definitely did not live a routine life, yet I dug every minute of it. I only wished I knew if the next day was going to find me with her or pawned off on someone else.

32

If I couldn't be with Mom in the city, my next favorite place was at Uncle Jess's in Moorehead, Kentucky. My stays with Uncle Jess would vary. Sometimes I'd just be there for a week or two, other times I might stay for a couple of months or more. Uncle Jess lived in a log cabin elevated several feet off the ground by poles. Jess was hillbilly from his heart, with beard, bare feet, bib overalls, moonshine, hound dogs and coon hunting. Family could do no wrong, and Jess would protect them no matter what. But if one of the family gave him any back talk it was their ass, because he was king.

He had four daughters. They were pretty things as mountain girls go; I saw Jess bring out the shotgun more than once to send guys running down the road. The girls might sneak around, but when Jess was there to say something, they jumped. I found out why they were so willing to mind when one day I pushed one of Jess's dogs off the porch. "Son," he told me, "that hound wasn't bothering you. You got no right pushin' it around. Don't mistreat no animals." That said, he proceeded to give me a beating I've never forgotten. He wasn't much of a talker, but when he spoke, people paid attention. He sometimes warned people, "Don't take them kids off the land." He was right, for almost everyone who left the land lived to regret it or died because of it. Uncle Jess himself died on his land rather than let someone take him away from it. The law came down on Jess and his moonshine still, but Jess foxed their asses. He blew up the still—and himself.

To return to the story, before being sentenced to Moundsville, Mom had become a pretty street-wise girl, but she really learned all the ropes doing her time. She even added a new dimension to her sex life. I didn't learn about it until years later, but while she was at Moundsville some of the older dykes showed her that sexual pleasure didn't only happen between men and women. Of course, back then gays were still in the closet so Mom was pretty discreet when it came to making it with another broad. Dummy that I was at that age, I didn't mind sleeping in the other room if she had another female spending a few days with us.

With her gameness and prison education, she had all the answers and could hustle with the best of them. Trouble was, she was a fiery little broad who liked her booze and wouldn't take any shit from anyone. Consequently, we might leave a place in a hurry. I

33

remember one night Mom came running into our little old one-room apartment and jerked me out of bed, saying, "Come on, Charlie, get up! Help me get our things packed. We gotta get outta here." She had been working as a cocktail waitress at the Blue Moon Café in McMechen. One guy wouldn't keep his hands off of her. Mom told him to cool it a couple of times. When he didn't, she grabbed a fifth of booze and busted the bottle over his head. He was still on the floor when she left. "Hurry up, Charlie! I just flattened one of the Zambini brothers an' I ain't waiting around to see if he's dead or alive. Either way, I'm in trouble." The Zambini brothers were two of the town hoods and everyone was afraid of them, including Mom. We'd moved around some, but that is about the fastest we ever left a place.

The next couple of years saw us in Indiana, Kentucky, Ohio, West Virginia and probably a couple more states and who knows how many cities. By the time I was twelve I'd missed a lot of school, seen a few juvenile homes, and no longer believed all my mom's lovers were "uncles." In general, I was cramping Mom's style. Some of the "uncles" liked me and others didn't. But the feeling was more than mutual—I didn't like any of them. I guess my jealousy and resentment of those "uncles" sleeping with my mom was pretty close to the surface, and it began causing trouble between us. When I was twelve, my mom's current lover brought things to a head. Unlike Mom's usual two- or three-day romances, this guy had been around for a few weeks. One night I was awakened by the sound of their booze-leadened voices arguing. The words I remember most were his: "I'm telling you, I'm moving on. You and I could make it just fine, but I can't stand that sneaky kid of yours." And then Mom's voice: "Don't leave, be patient. I love you and we'll work something out."

Poor Mom, we'd long ago worn out our welcome with the relatives and friends who were willing to keep me for any length of time. I'd become spoiled and was accustomed to doing pretty much as I pleased. I'd been tried in a couple of foster homes but I just wasn't the image those parents felt like being responsible for.

A few days after I'd overheard the argument, my mom and I were standing in front of a judge. My mother, in one of her finer performances, was pleading hardship. She told the judge what a struggle life was and that she was unable to afford a proper home for me.

The judge said, "Until there is capable earning power by the mother and a decent stable home for Charles to return to, I am making him a ward of the court and placing him in a boys' home." At that moment, the words didn't mean anything to me. I was angry at Mom and didn't want to live with her and her friend. I wasn't depressed or disturbed. The shock was still a day away.

The court placed me in a religious-oriented school, the Gibault Home for Boys in Terre Haute, Indiana. I felt all right while being registered in the school office, but when all the papers were completed things started going wacky in my head and stomach. By the time I was escorted to the dormitory I would live in for the next ten months, I felt sick. I couldn't breathe. Tears ran down my cheeks, my legs were so rubbery I could hardly walk. Some invisible force was crushing my chest and stealing my life away from me. I loved my mother! I wanted her! "Why, Mom? Why is it this way? Come and get me, just let me live with you. I won't be in your way!" I was lonely, lonelier than I had ever been in my life. I have never felt that lonely since. I wasn't angry at her anymore. I just wanted to be with her, live with her, under any conditions. Not in some school locked away from everything.

After the initial shock, the following days weren't too bad. The Catholic brothers who ran the school were good enough to me, but they were stern in their discipline. The answer to any infraction of the rules was a leather strap, or wood paddle, and lost privileges. Since I had a problem with wetting the bed, it seemed like I was getting more than my share of whippings for something I had no control over.

At twelve I wasn't the youngest boy there, but being under five feet tall and weighing less than sixty-five pounds, I was one of the smallest. I was easy pickings for those who were inclined to be bullies. Gibault was not considered a reform school, but aside from the religious teachings it operated in a similar manner. And though guys there were not necessarily juvenile delinquents, they did share the same resentments against parents, the law and confinement as those in reform schools. I was exposed to a lot of things the average kid doesn't experience until a much older age. It never happened to me there, but I saw kids forced into homosexual acts. I was told about all kinds of ways to beat the law, and I learned how to keep my feelings to myself, because if you care too much

35

about a part of your life and personal habits, others will take advantage of it and ridicule you. Gibault taught me friends can be cruel and enemies dangerous.

Mom would come to see me sometimes, but not all that often. If she said she'd see me next week, I'd be lucky if she showed up in the next couple of months. When she did come, she'd tell me, "It won't be long before I have a steady job and a nice place to live. Then I'll come and get you and take you home with me." We'd talk about how nice it was going to be when we were back together. I was starting to grow and was definitely older in mind. I felt I could be a big help to her if she would take me home. It all sounded great and I was eager to start living the life we talked about. She'd leave and I'd run back to my friends, telling them, "Pretty soon I'll be going home. My mom said so." The next visit would be the same. "Pretty soon, Charlie," were my mother's words. I waited and waited. It didn't happen.

Sick of Gibault and tired of waiting, I ran away. Naturally I went straight to Mom's. I thought I could show her how grown up I was and how I could help her. There was no guilt trip in my mind about running away; I was sure my mom would throw her arms around me, as glad to see me as I was to be there with her. She'd take me down to the judge and tell him she was in a position to take care of us. Everything would be all right. God, was I dreaming! She turned me in and the next day I was back at the Home for Boys. But I didn't feel like a boy any longer. There were no tears. At least, none that ran down my cheeks. I didn't feel weak or sick, but I also knew I could no longer smile or be happy. I was bitter and I knew real hate.

The trip back to Gibault was a waste of gas and time. I split the very first chance I got. Goodbye Gibault. Goodbye Mom.

CHAPTER 2

I HAD LEARNED my lesson. Thanks to the memory of my own mother rejecting me and turning me in, my philosophy was trust no one and depend on no one. As for a place to run to, I felt my chances of staying lost and out of sight of the police would be better in a big city rather than a small town. Indianapolis was my choice.

Terre Haute and the Gibault School for Boys are about a hundred and sixty miles from Indianapolis. Once safely away from the school, I knew better than to try reaching my destination by way of the roads and highways. I trudged through fields and over hills, staying out of sight. I walked the railroad tracks some and hopped a freight train for a short way. I slept in the woods and under bridges. I met bums, winos and hobos, who shared their meals with me. Most people place all those derelicts in the same category, but I found there is a definite distinction between them. A bum is a guy who is down and out, maybe one who is too lazy to work and survives by begging. A wino has become so hooked on his booze that he is a social outcast, he cares for nothing but the lush and how to acquire it. A hobo is on the road because that is his chosen lifestyle. Some are honest and survive by their wits, also doing a little work here and there. Others are into doing anything that will provide for the day's needs, and stealing and lying are as natural as breathing to them. I lived and ate with these guys until reaching Indianapolis, and through them I learned an awful lot about survival without the luxuries of a house and modern conveniences.

When I got to Indy I slept in the alleys and old sheds until the night I got a bonus while burglarizing a grocery store for something to eat. The cash register change for the next morning was in a cigar box under the counter. When I opened the box and saw the money I thought I was rich and didn't even bother to cart out any of the groceries I was stealing. It was a little over a hundred dollars, more money than I'd ever had in my hands before. I rented a room in skid row, bought me some clothes, ate as much as I liked and spent the money like there was no tomorrow. A few days later I was broke and hungry. I started making my way on the streets any way I could. I'd sweep store fronts, wash windows, clean garbage cans, anything that might earn me a few cents. I'd also steal whatever I could get my hands on, and sell the goods to anybody for any kind of price. I doubt if I averaged a penny on the dollar for the value of what I sold, but for a snot-nosed kid, I was feeling pretty chesty and thought I was getting up in the world. I was getting by without starving, had my own room and was my own boss.

I had accumulated a wealth of experience and I thought I really knew what the world was all about, but my run-away from Gibault only lasted a few weeks. I had stolen a bike for the joy of having one, as well as for transportation. It was that bike that got me caught. When the police arrested me, the juvenile authorities couldn't believe that a twelve-year-old kid could be living by himself. It took them a few days to discover that I was a runaway from a home for boys. Once they knew that, they located my mom. She appeared in juvenile court with me, but she was still unable to tell the judge that she could take me back to a good home.

The judge was a sympathetic guy who really didn't want to send me to a reform school. He arranged for Father Flanagan's Boys Town to accept me. I didn't stick around long enough for the results they got with Mickey Rooney in the film *Boys Town*. No fault of the school's; I just wasn't into the discipline, and running away had become as much a part of my nature as stealing. Four days after being checked in at Boys Town, me and another guy split. We stole a car, wrecked it, pulled a couple of armed robberies and finally made it back to Indianapolis. At Indianapolis, we went to my new partner's uncle's house. The uncle was a World War II vet who was living on disability. He was also a thief, and his nephew and I fit right into his program. He was as glad we showed up as we were to have a place to stay. In no time at all he had lined up places for us to burglarize. It was kind of a one-way street, since my partner and I did all the dirty work but the uncle took the big end of the money.

We got caught going through the skylight of the third place he had cased for us. When the cops arrested us they took me to the Indianapolis City Juvenile Home. I spent a day and part of a night there. As fate would have it, the same day I was put in juvie hall, a maintenance man was doing some work around the place. He turned his back on his toolbox and I stole a pair of wire cutters. That night, after we were counted and the lights were out, I got busy with the wire cutters. In about twenty minutes' time, some thirty to thirty-five juvenile delinquents were loose on the streets of Indianapolis.

Some of the guys may have stayed on the loose for a lengthy period of time, but for me it was wasted effort. I was picked up less than two hours later driving a stolen car—I hardly knew how to shift it and could barely see over the dashboard. I was back in custody by the time the morning paper hit the newsstands with a front page spread, complete with photo, that wrote me up as the "ringleader." Instead of keeping me in juvenile hall, they booked me in the county jail. The youngest offender ever, they told me.

That was in 1948; I was thirteen years old and almost a year had passed since the day I entered the Gibault School for Boys, the beginning of my life in institutions. I had been a frightened little boy when I went there, and I had resented it with an indescribable passion, but I have to admit the administration at Gibault had the boys' interest and future as their top priority. That is more than I can say for the place I spent the next three years of my life.

The escapes from Gibault and Boys Town and my escapades on the run left the judge very little to do but sentence me to a bona fide reform school: the Indiana School for Boys at Plainfield, Indiana. And let me say, Plainfield was a real beauty! It has to have changed since I was there; too many human rights groups and concerned citizens have appeared for a place like that to continue to operate in the manner it did then. I know the school is still in operation, but I hope all the warped, sadistic bastards I met there are now dead.

While most who get sentenced to those places do need to be separated from the honest element of society, Plainfield has turned out more hard-core criminals than honest citizens. That's because of the type of person who seeks employment in prisons. For every person whose heart is in the right place, for every person who is dedicated to constructive rehabilitation, there are ten status-

39

seekers out to prove something to themselves. Some are frustrated policemen who couldn't qualify for the police force. Others are without the ambition or skills to maintain a job in a competitive trade. Believe it or not, a great many of them are there to obtain an outlet for their own perversion. Confinement and punishment are necessary in the present society, but having sadistic, perverted assholes working in an institution that is supposed to rehabilitate is the biggest bunch of bullshit going. You can't expect to straighten out an offender's life when the people in charge of him have worse hang-ups than he does.

At Plainfield I was in trouble from the very beginning. The probation officer who took me there left me standing in the hallway while he went to the administrator's office to sign me in. I had already noticed there were no fences, so while waiting I checked the front door. It wasn't locked—I was gone! My escape attempt lasted about fifteen minutes; I didn't even get off the grounds. Thirty minutes after arriving at Plainfield I had been registered, assigned to a housing unit and a work detail and charged with an escape attempt. Cottage eleven was my home and the dairy was my work assignment.

That evening, like every evening and morning, the whole institution assembled for "count," as in the military. When the count was completed and cleared, a supervisor, A.B. Clark was his name, shouted out that cottage eleven was to report to the plumbing shop. As we marched, I was thinking the whole detail was going to do some extra work. We got there, halted, and stood like soldiers on parade. Clark called out, "Charles Manson and his four best friends step forward." Hell, I didn't know what was happening but I stepped forward as commanded. Naturally "four best friends" didn't step forward. I didn't have any! I'd only been there for three hours. When no one else moved, old Clark had four detail boys from the cottage step out, then motioned us inside the plumbing shop. Tension was beginning to mount and I started to realize that I was in for something other than just extra work. Once inside, Clark grabbed me by the shoulder and shoved me toward the center of the room, saying, "Okay, Manson, drop your strides!" I asked what for. "Just get those fucking pants down, you little bastard," shouted Clark. The shop had regular work benches around the walls, but in the middle of the room was a bench that was espe-

40

cially designed for what was to come next. It was about waist-high on the average man. Bare ass, I was told to lay across the bench. I hesitated and Clark planted a boot in my ass and told the detail boys to anchor me down. Each of the detail boys grabbed an arm or leg and spread me out ass up on the bench. I was in proper position for one of two things, a fucking or a beating. When Clark picked up a leather strap, I remember feeling relieved; at least I wasn't going to get fucked in my ass.

Clark wasn't too tall, about five-foot-seven, but he was built like a fireplug and strong as a bull. The strap was made of leather, about three feet long, a quarter of an inch thick, and four inches wide, with holes drilled in the leather and a strong wooden handle. He hit the bench next to my head a couple of times to loosen himself up. I about pissed just out of fear. "Stretch him out," Clark said, and they all tightened their grip. (I found out later that if any of them let go during the lashing, they would get the same beating I was about to take.) Clark knew how to use that strap. I wanted to shout the first time he laid it across my ass, but gritted my teeth and waited for the next blow. After three more swats, the detail boy holding my right arm whispered, "Groan or cry, don't try to be tough with this motherfucker—he don't come until you cry." Clark hit me twice more on that side and, whether I wanted to or not, I screamed and the tears burst loose. He backed off and I was relieved because I thought he was through. No luck, he was just changing sides. I got an equal number on the other cheek. When Clark was finished and the boys let go of my arms and legs, I didn't have strength enough to lift myself off the bench. I just slid to the floor and lay there like a quivering puppy. When I was able to stand I noticed that none of the detail boys would look at me. But Clark had a grin on his face, and with the strap still in his hand, said, "Manson, we've been told you are a rotten little bastard, and I'm here to tell you, your ass is going to be full of scars before you leave here." It was. In fact, it still is.

I pulled my pants on. Blood was surfacing from where the strap had broken the skin and I was sobbing for breath, trying to get enough air in my lungs to control my body and erase the fear and pain. Back outside, I got in line and as a unit we marched back to the cottage. The others went to the mess hall. I was too sick to think about eating and wanted to see a doctor. But after a "fanning," as they called it, you weren't allowed any medical attention until the next day. Welcome to the Indiana School for Boys!

The next morning I went to the infirmary. They put some salve on the open welts and sent me to the dairy to work. A Mr. Fields was in charge of the boys on that detail. Fields had been told about the ass-whipping, so, nice guy that he was, he assigned me a wheelbarrow and a shovel. My job was to load all the manure in the wheelbarrow, push it up a steel ramp and dump it in a bin. With the strain of shoveling and the exertion needed to push the loaded wheelbarrow up the ramp, the cuts on my ass started seeping pus and bleeding. Fields was so sympathetic that he cracked me across the ass with a stick he always carried, and encouraged some of the inmates to take shots at me as I struggled up the ramp.

About a week later four of the bigger and older inmates cornered me in one of the feed bins. Right away I knew what they were up to. I made a dash for the door, but two of the guys grabbed me and the other two stripped my pants off. I fought like a wild man, struggling frantically. I screamed and hollered, but they gagged me so that my screams were muffled. Two of the guys held me while one tried to force his dick in my ass. The fourth guy was standing point at the door, watching for the man. I broke loose, but all four of them wrestled me to the floor and beat on me some more. Two of them had time to rape me before the guy at the door shouted, "The man is coming!" They tried to get away from the scene before Fields arrived, but they didn't quite make it. I was crying and trying to get my pants back on. All Fields said was, "You know I don't allow any wrestling. You guys get the hell out of here. And you, Manson, go wash your face and stop all your crying."

After that, Fields himself started playing games with me like I was some joint punk, available to anyone. On numerous occasions, depending on his mood, he would tell me, "Pull your pants down, Manson, I want to see if you've been getting fucked." The first time I thought he was just kidding and I walked right on by him, but he grabbed me and yanked my pants down around my ankles and made me bend over while he looked at my ass. He always did this in the presence of several other inmates. To add insult, he would pick up a handful of raw silage from the dairy floor, spit tobacco juice on it and shove it up my ass. "I got him lubed," he'd tell his pets, "so fuck him if you get a chance." The tobacco juice and silage burned and I got an infection from it, but the humiliation was worse. Yeah, Fields was a real beauty, he really knew how to care for the wards of the state and earn his state paycheck. I worked in the dairy for five months and every day was some kind of unimaginable experience.

I never was able to even things up with Fields, but I did take some of the desire out of the first guy who put his dick in my ass. That was about the only thing I ever got away with at Plainfield. One night after the lights were out and everyone was asleep, I took one of the iron handles used for cranking the windows open or closed off a window. The crank was about twelve inches long and weighed two or three pounds. It wasn't as large or as heavy as I would have liked, but it did the job. I crept down to where Mr. Stiff Dick was sleeping, eased his blanket up over his head and clubbed him several times as hard as I could. I left him there unconscious, and on the way back to my bed I slipped the crank under the covers of one of the other guys who had been in on the rape. The beaten inmate might have died, but he was lucky; security came through the cottage for a late-night count a few minutes later. In routinely lifting the blanket to make sure there was someone under the covers, the security man saw the blood and realized the guy was unconscious. He was taken to the hospital and treated for a severe concussion. Shaking down the cottage for the weapon, the guards found it in the other guy's bed. All of us were questioned. No one was charged with the assault, although the other rapist was the prime suspect.

When his partner returned from the hospital, the two of them didn't have much to do with each other. It was whispered that I had done the clubbing, and no matter how small I was, no one else at Plainfield tried to put his dick in my ass again.

I ran away constantly, not because I was such a rebel but because it was always me who was punished when someone had to be punished to illustrate a point. I didn't have anyone on the outside to tell my troubles to. No one was visiting me and I got very little mail. I was just there, and nobody gave a fuck. The fear of getting caught wasn't any worse than the fear of what the next breath might bring, so my head was looking toward the road every minute.

43

One of my escapes was planned so skillfully that I was sure I'd make it. About six guys were on early wake-up crew so that they could go out in the pastures, round up the milk cows, put them in the barn and feed them during milking time. Bed tags were used to identify them to the night attendant, who would wake them up around four-thirty. These inmates were trusted to work without supervision until Fields showed up at six o'clock. One night I stole a tag from a crew member's bed and put it on my own. The night man woke me up and out I went with the others. One of the fellows on the crew was a friend and the two of us went to the far pasture to get the cows. I kept right on going and my friend herded the cows by himself to cover for me. I wasn't missed until after Fields showed up. I had gotten off the institution grounds fast enough, but I wasted a lot of time sneaking around town trying to find a car that I could steal. Not finding one, I decided to hoof it and stay off the roads until I made it to the next town.

Plainfield is a small town bordered by a river on one side. Thinking I might be seen if I used the bridge, I decided to swim the river. When I was about halfway across, I could see people on the bank. I turned around and started swimming the other way, only to see more people on the other bank. They were guards and inmates from the school (trusted inmates helped catch other inmate runaways). My heart sunk—I didn't know what to do. It seemed senseless at that point, but I turned downstream and tried to out-swim all the people on the riverbank. Finally a couple of them dove in the river and dragged me ashore. Grinning with his tobacco-stained teeth, Mr. Fields was there to pull me up the bank.

Back at the school, a guard gave me thirty lashes with the escape strap. The escape strap was longer and thinner than the strap used by Clark. It cut a lot more and brought blood instantly. That lashing put me in bed for several days, and it was a couple of weeks before I could walk without wanting to lie down and cry.

That escape attempt got me out of the dairy cottage and away from Fields. But, fuck, I'd already been pegged as a guy to watch and the move was almost like jumping out of the frying pan into the fire. I was put in a cottage that was run by a Mr. Carr. Carr was an ex-marine, a big son-of-a-bitch whose favorite thing was to run a "jaw-line." He had a couple different versions of his jaw-line. One was to make two lines out of all the inmates in the cottage.

44

The lines were about four feet apart, good swinging distance. The sucker being punished ran between the lines, while the others swung at him with closed fists. If one of the blows knocked him off his feet, he had to get up and try to get through again. If Carr thought someone wasn't putting enough force into his punches, that guy would have to run the line.

Carr's other "jaw-line" held more personal satisfaction for him. He'd place you about twenty or twenty-five feet from him, double up his fist, hold his arm at your jaw level, and then say "run." You had to charge into that fist. If he felt you hadn't charged at full speed, he would make you do it again and again until he was satisfied. If the blows were severe enough to require medical attention—broken nose, cut lip or damaged eye—he would give you a pass to the infirmary listing the cause of injury as "slipped in the shower" or "fell while horse-playing." Carr was another guy like Fields. He'd turn his back while some of his snitching pets would try to fuck someone.

I was at the Indiana School for Boys for over three years and the only good thing I can say about it is that it had an impressive front lawn. From town it looked like a small university. But while proud parents bragged of their child's good behavior and scholastic accomplishments, I was busy watching my back and taking the shit those guards dished out. At an age when most kids are going to nice schools, living with their parents and learning all about the better things in life, I was cleaning silage and tobacco juice out of my ass, recuperating from the wounds of a leather strap and learning to hate the world and everyone in it.

When I was sixteen, I finally made a successful escape with two other inmates. The day we left, I had no more promise of going home through proper channels than I'd had three years earlier on the day I arrived. Release was obtained through merit or a court order. Mom never sought a court order, and my escape attempts and other infractions put me on the minus side of the merit system.

When my escape partners and I got away from the institution, we stole a car and headed toward California. Along the way we stole other vehicles and abandoned them, as we needed. For gas and food money, we burglarized grocery stores and service stations. We made it as far as Utah where we were arrested for being in a

45

stolen car. Since the car had been driven across state lines, we were turned over to the federal authorities and prosecuted under the Dyer Act. In March 1951 I was sentenced to the National Training School for Boys in Washington, DC. I'd had two weeks of freedom. I knew the new offenses meant a lot more time in jail but I didn't care. I was out of the Indiana School for Boys.

The difference between a federal reformatory and a state reformatory is about like the difference between night and day. On a federal level, there seems to be more concern about how you got there and what it will take to straighten out your life. At the state level—at least during my confinement—the idea was to punish the shit out of you and make you sorry you were ever born.

Even the federal inmates are of a higher caliber, a "class" group instead of the derelicts found in state joints. But guys being guys, immature, trying to prove their manhood, they still create problems for themselves. In retrospect, I have to say I have always been guiltier than most in trying to prove myself. I wanted to be one of the "in crowd" at any cost. The "in crowd" in a youth-filled institution is mostly based on physical strength—the tough guy has all the respect in the joint.

Not being a big guy, I could never impress anyone with a display of physical strength. But at sixteen, with almost five years of jail time behind me, I had all the cunning and knowledge needed to maneuver myself around any situation I didn't want to be involved in. Trouble was, I always wanted to be part of the power. So what I lacked in size, I made up for in daring. I was game for anything and saw everything that went on. I knew where all the knives were, how to score contraband, who the under-cover punks were, who to trust and who not to trust. I was smart enough not to step on the toes of anyone who might bite me.

It was important to me to hang around with the guys who had been successful and enjoyed luxuries on the outside. Their conversation was like a school for me. I was a good listener. I realized a lot of their talk was filled with exaggeration or fantasy, but they were still talking about a world I had never known. Cars, girls, school dances, parties, nice clothes and being able to come and go as they pleased. I built an imaginary world of my own from their conversations. I envied every guy who had had a pleasant experience on the outside, and tried in my imagination to substitute my-

46

self for them when they talked about it. I envied their letters and pictures from wives and girlfriends. I enjoyed sharing their plans for release and the promises of good things from their parents and friends when they got home. At the same time, I was aware that I could not relate a single moment of similar joys and dreams, unless of course I counted that day when I was eight years old and my mother took me in her arms—the day she returned home from prison.

Those were my smothered feelings. On the outside I projected arrogance and disdain for rules and regulations. I strove to prove myself to the others to be a person who had experienced everything, was afraid of nothing and could get by with anything. For a while I would actually believe I really didn't care about all that I'd missed. But then in a moment of reality, I'd be aware of never having kissed a girl. I was in reform school before I'd reached puberty. The only climax I'd ever had was from jacking-off or sticking some punk in the butt. Having a wet dream wasn't even possible for me; I'd never had the real thing so I had to finish any dream I started by hand. Still, between the stories of others and my own imagination, I had strong sexual urges, urges that got me in trouble several times. A prison psychiatrist labeled me as having homosexual tendencies. So I was supposed to be some kind of a freak. But, hey, I just went for sex the only way it had ever been taught to me. I didn't have any respect for a joint punk then and I don't now.

A lot of stories go around about forced sodomy and oral copulation in prisons and reform schools. There is some of it happening; I mean, out-and-out rape. I experienced it and I'm still ashamed to cop to it. Most of the sex is by mutual agreement, but however it comes down, those things are printed in a convict's prison record and are with him for the rest of his life. I lost a possible parole date once by getting involved with a punk. I was accused of holding a razor blade to the kid's throat while I screwed him in the ass. Truth was, the guy was an undercover queer and wanted a dick in his ass, and I didn't mind doing it to him. We both agreed that if we got caught, he could say I forced him. We got caught. I was not only listed as a homosexual, but one with assaultive tendencies. That kid knew I didn't force him, and I knew it, but I got the reputation and before long I did put a razor to a kid's throat. If you keep pushing something off on a person, pretty soon that person stops fighting the reputation and becomes everything he is accused of being. It has proven itself out over the years. You start to think, "Fuck them. If that's what they think I am, and I have to bear that cross, I got nothin' to lose in being all they think I am."

On a car-theft beef, an average kid with the average things—family, home, school, job—is usually cut loose by the parole board in a year or eighteen months. I did three years and two months in four different institutions: The National Training School for Boys in Washington, DC, Natural Bridge Honor Camp, the Federal Reformatory at Petersburg, Virginia and the Federal Reformatory at Chillicothe, Ohio. It seems none of the good of these places rubbed off on me, only the bad. My heroes weren't the movie stars or the headline-making sports figures, but the guys who got away with the biggest bank heist; the Al Capones, the Mickey Cohens, all the mobsters who defied the system that was keeping me locked up.

When I was at Chillicothe I met Frank Costello. When I walked down the halls with him or sat at the same table for meals, I probably experienced the same sensation an honest kid would get out of being with Joe DiMaggio or Mickey Mantle: admiration bordering on worship. To me, if Costello did something, right or wrong, that was the way it was supposed to be. One morning Costello and I were seated at the same table for breakfast. He was reading the morning newspaper and a new guard walked over to him and started to take the paper, saying, "You read in your cell or the library." Costello removed the guard's hand from his paper and replied, "Sonny, when I'm at home it's my habit to read the newspaper while eating my breakfast. The government has made this place my home for a while. You're here to see that I stay, not to tell me where and when I can't read." The guard hesitated for an instant, then looked around the dining room, left our table and started hassling one of the younger guys on some infraction. Anyone without the status of Costello would have been on his way to the hole after confronting a guard that way. Yeah, I admired Frank Costello, and I listened to and believed everything he said.

In May of 1954 I was finally paroled. I was nineteen, and it was the first time I was legitimately on the streets since I was twelve years old.

The parole stipulated that I return to McMechen and live with the same aunt and uncle who had taken care of me while my mother was in prison. I loved them for giving me my chance on the outside. It was through their efforts, not Mom's, that I ever got released at all.

I doubt that the average person could ever relate to the sense of freedom I felt. It was more like a dream than something good really happening to me. Each morning—no, not just each morning, but each breath was like being born again. I wanted to sing, dance and shout, "Hey, I'm free, I'm out, I'm one of you!" Hell, I didn't want to ever go to sleep. Being awake, so as not to miss a single thing that was going on in my new world, was too important. When I did go to sleep, waking up and being able to lie in bed was a treat. The smell of breakfast being cooked by my aunt, with my choice of anything I wanted, instead of powdered eggs or soggy pancakes, was as rewarding as being a millionaire. One of my biggest pleasures was just walking—in the city, in the country, going anywhere or going nowhere. Just appreciating that there were no fences, no boundaries. Being able to watch people and hear them laugh, seeing children playing in the park, looking at pretty girls in short skirts and tight sweaters. Above all, no one was demanding that I do this or that. I didn't have to keep looking over my shoulder to see if "the man" was coming, or if a bunch of inmates were up to something that I ought to check out. I was my own person. The feeling was so pure, and it was so wonderful to be free, that if someone had said to me then, "You'll be back in jail one of these days," I'd have bet my life the person didn't know what he was talking about.

Still, with all the joys of being free, it wasn't long before I realized that there is more to life in the free world than just walking around taking in the sights, especially when seven of perhaps the most important years in a person's lifetime have been spent in reform schools. In jail I was glib and aggressive and knew everything that happened from the hole to the chapel, but out on the streets I couldn't even hold a decent conversation with my aunt and uncle, let alone a stranger. All I knew was jail. I couldn't talk about what school I'd graduated from, or even gone to. There weren't any yesterdays or last months that I could refer to without exposing my past. For employment, I had to look for jobs no one else wanted. I did janitor and busboy work, weeded gardens and worked in a service station or two. I even shoveled shit and fed the horses oats at Wheeling Downs.

When it came to girls, my heart throbbed and I ached with desire but I couldn't think of the proper things to say. I didn't know the first thing about finesse, so I'd revert to some of the bullshit I had heard laid down by some of the older guys in reform school. It didn't work for me; in most cases that kind of conversation sent the girls packing instead of impressing them.

The first girl I ever made it with I ended up marrying. I'd worked all day at the race track and had stopped by a card room in Steubenville to see if I could run my day's wages into a small fortune. After a couple of hours at the poker table, I had a pretty healthy pile of money in front of me. The cocktail waitress and some of the other girls were giving me and my roll some attention. Across from me, looking over the shoulder of a coal miner, was this pretty girl who gave me an occasional smile but wasn't putting on the hustle like some of the other girls were. When I cashed in I was a big winner. I would have shared my winnings with any of those girls for a night in the sack, but a certain pride in not wanting to be some whore's trick helped me walk right by the obvious advances and single out the pretty girl I'd noticed on the other side of the table.

She had come into the place with her coal-miner father. Since he was still wrapped up in the poker game, I had no problem getting a few words in with her. She told me she worked as a waitress in a cafeteria at McMechen. We didn't make it together that night, but after visiting her at her job and dating a couple of times, we were in love.

She may not have been the most beautiful girl in the world but to me she was Marilyn Monroe, Mitzi Gaynor and Lana Turner all rolled up in one. She was a healthy, smooth-skinned Irish girl who stirred things in me I'd never experienced. I didn't get her cherry, but she damn sure got mine. The first time we made it together, I couldn't believe it was happening. Beyond concentrating on the sex act, all I could think of was, "Wow, it's happening, I'm really making it with a girl." I trembled with excitement and anticipation; so much so, I came before my prick touched her box. But that didn't kill anything for me, and when I got inside her—our arms around each other, her smooth soft body in contact with mine—I really

50

didn't care if I ever took another breath. I was in heaven and I wanted to stay. She whispered, "I love you," and goose bumps tingled all over my body. I was loving someone and she was returning my love. A huge void was being filled. For the first time in my life, I felt I could conquer the world.

We were married in January of 1955. It was a good life and I enjoyed the role of going off to work every morning and coming home to my wife. She was a super girl who didn't make any demands but we were both just a couple of kids. We didn't know how to budget our income. We were constantly broke and neither of us had the maturity to sit down and make plans based on what we were earning. Being broke and wanting things can build up a lot of pressure. That pressure grows even greater when you haven't got the money to pay routine bills, like rent, gas, lights and transportation. Sometimes we couldn't even buy groceries. It's too bad I didn't know how to handle it. Trouble was, all I knew was reform schools, stealing and not trusting anyone. The patience, the willingness to struggle and earn that normal life demands wasn't part of my make up.

I started looking for ways to get things in a hurry. With all my jail-house connections, getting back into crime was no problem. My wife also had a little bit of the outlaw tendency in her nature, so she didn't try to restrain me—not that she could have.

The larceny consisted of small time burglaries and several stolen cars. One theft was at the request of an older gangster friend: the deal was for me to steal a late model Cadillac and deliver it to an acquaintance of his in Florida. My friend put enough dollars in my hand to pay the expenses and the other guy would pay me five hundred when I got there. I stole the car and drove it to Florida. The guy at the other end took it all right, gave me a hundred, and told me to get fucked. Naturally I was pissed, but took the hundred and left. I lay low for a few hours and then doubled back and re-stole the Cadillac. Not to drive it, just to keep the guy from feeling too chesty about burning me. After a while I abandoned the car and returned home. By the time I got back word was out the gangster was looking for me. So far the law wasn't on my back, but I didn't want to come face to face with either of the two guys involved in the car deal.

My wife had been wanting to head to California even before we were married. My promise to take her there might have been the only reason she married me. No, that isn't true, but now that someone was out there waiting to even things up with me, we both wanted to leave town. I stole a '51 Mercury and we loaded in all our worldly possessions, but we still had plenty of room in the car when we headed for the land of opportunity. The trip west was a leisurely one. We'd stop in some town or city that interested us and I'd hustle for anything I could, or case a place to burglarize. If I got money, great. If not, we'd load whatever I had taken into the Mercury and sell the goods along the way.

By the time we got to Los Angeles we had a few dollars and a few items to set up housekeeping. We rented an inexpensive place to live. My wife was in the early months of pregnancy, so I went looking for honest employment and the next few weeks saw me with a variety of jobs. With the jobs, and some thievery, we weren't enjoying great luxury but things weren't too bad for us. I had gotten used to the Mercury and felt like I was the legal owner. So much so that when they arrested me in it for car theft, I gave the arresting officer a lot of shit. Because the car had been stolen in another state, the FBI took over the case. They gave me that old song and dance about coming clean on everything to clear up the books and said they would show leniency. I'm no longer sure if I voluntarily told them about the car in Florida or if they tricked me into telling them. Anyway, I did get a hell of a break when I went to court for the stolen Mercury. Mostly because of my wife's pregnancy, the judge put me on the streets with five years' probation. I still had the other charge in Florida to face. If I'd had the guts to show up in court on that charge I might have gotten another break, but I was afraid to be too trusting of the courts. Instead I hit the road as a fugitive.

I put my wife through a lot of shit for the next four months. Why she stuck with me, I don't know. We traveled a lot of miles, and we stole a lot of things to keep from being hungry or for travel money. She was getting close to having the baby and I didn't know how that could be handled on the run, so I shipped her back to Los Angeles where my mom was now living and could look after her.

Not long after sending my wife to Los Angeles I was arrested in Indianapolis. You would think I'd had enough of that city, but there I was again in the same county jail where I had started. It was easier and less expensive for the court to revoke the five years' probation than to prosecute me on the other theft, so I was returned to California and sentenced to the Federal Penitentiary at Terminal Island, San Pedro. I was twenty-one years old—no longer a juvenile delinquent. But looking back, I was never a juvenile anything, only an inmate in some reformatory. Now that I was twenty-one, it seemed only appropriate that I start my adult life in a prison with the big guys.

Terminal Island was a paradise compared to the institutions I had been in as a youth offender. The guards were there strictly for security and weren't continually hassling the convicts. And the cons themselves did their own time, without trying to run anybody else's life. It was a whole lot easier doing time with men instead of a bunch of kids who were always trying to play macho. It was so good, I didn't create any problems. Escape wasn't even on my mind. It was my intention to do my time like a saint and earn an early release. I sincerely thought that when I got on the streets again I would never do anything to put myself back in jail. I thought of those months with my wife, the thrills and warmth her body had given me, the new baby and all the pleasures the free world afforded me, and I realized what a goddamn fool I was for wasting my life being locked up.

Those first few months I went about doing my time with a positive attitude toward becoming a straight person. My wife wrote to me almost daily and came to visit as often as she could. I marveled at our new son during our visits and knew that I would break my ass to give him a better childhood than I had gone through.

But!—and it seems like in my life there has always been a "but"—before the baby was a year old, she stopped visiting. Her letters ceased without even a "Dear John." My mother brought the news. "Your wife has moved out of the house and is living with some truck driver." I flipped! The whole fucking world caved in on me. I wrote to her pleading for her to reconsider, begging her to come and see me. I needed her, loved her, and wanted to see little Charlie. Though the letters were never answered, for a few weeks I held on to the hope that her affair with the truck driver was just temporary and that she would eventually come back to me. All hope ended when Mom reported, "Your wife, your son, and her truck driver friend have moved out of the state." To this day I have never seen or heard from her or the son that came from our marriage. When I gave up on her, my attitude of wanting to be Mr. Straight left me.

My work assignment was outside the prison walls, and I decided if my wife wasn't going to come and see me any more, I was going to try and locate her. I attempted an escape. However, like so many of my escape attempts while in reform school, I was caught before I was out of sight of the prison, in the prison parking lot trying to hot wire a car.

For my attempt, I was taken off the minimum custody work assignment, which meant I was no longer allowed outside the prison walls, and given an additional five-year probation period to begin after I completed my existing sentence. It was a break from the court, but I wasn't in an appreciative mood. My marriage, the new baby and a good clean work record inside the prison had been my ace in the hole toward an early parole date. And now that was gone.

I went back to being bitter and hating everyone. I had been bitter when my mom turned me over to the court when I was twelve years old. I hated her when she refused to let me stay with her after my first escape from Gibault. The bitterness I had learned at Plainfield never left me. And though I don't blame her or feel bitter toward her now, my wife had the full brunt of my hate then.

Even if she had stuck by me and had been waiting when I got out of Terminal Island, I don't know what the results would have been, because it's obvious there is something lacking in my make up. It could have started with being a bastard son and my life with and without my mother. Maybe it was the years at Plainfield, or maybe the insanity of my uncle Jess and grandfather. I do know that until my wife left me I was filled with honest thoughts for our future together. I also know that the letdown I experienced when I realized I had lost her was a turning point in my life. I figured, screw all that honest-john bullshit, I'm a thief, I don't know anything else. I made up my mind to perfect myself in the life I had been leaning toward since I stole all those toys and burned them when I was seven years old. And what better place to begin the perfection of an outlaw than in a penitentiary, a place that was loaded with every anti-establishment offender imaginable?

I was into learning ways to beat the law besides robbing or stealing. I was already pretty adept in those areas even though I had never made any big scores and I never doubted my ability to pull off a job if I needed to go that route. What interested me now was status. Among criminals in the joint, a thief or a gunman is kind of like a blue-collar worker, whereas a pimp or a top-grade con man is comparable to a bank president on the outside, kind of a high-roller, envied by other convicts. Pretty girls and sex provide the most interesting conversation for a guy doing time, and girls and their bodies are also big business in the free world. As long as I had decided to continue a life of crime, why not pursue what appealed to me most? What could be better than having all the girls you want and letting them supply the money and lifestyle an ex-convict dreams of on the outside?

To simplify my quest to become a pimp, right there in Terminal Island was one of the nation's best known procurers—I'll call him Vic. At one time Vic had his fingers in every whorehouse in Nevada and controlled call girls in numerous other states. He was a regular godfather of prostitution. The Feds hadn't been able to bust him on any illegal activities other than income-tax evasion so I figured he really knew the score. Another thing that drew me to him was the fact that he wasn't a big guy. Though I was never consciously insecure about being small, at times I did give up on pursuing roles in life I might have challenged if I were a bigger person. Here was a guy who, like myself, would really have to stretch to reach five-foot-six in height. He was older and uglier than me, and definitely not the person one might imagine as a king-pin in a state full of whorehouses. I figured if he could make it big through broads, so could I.

Without being too obvious, I began to seek out Vic's company. I would hang around and rap to him and the guys he lined up with, the majority of them also pretty successful pimps. In most cases I didn't have to initiate any conversations; they all talked about their ups and downs as well as the procedures they applied to different girls and situations. The stories I heard about big cars, pretty girls, luxurious apartments, fine clothes and plenty of money had me thoroughly convinced: there wasn't anything better in life than having control over several women and letting them provide your every need.

One day I asked Vic point blank how he went about turning a

girl out. He laughed at me and said, "Charlie, it's been over twenty years since I've had to work on a girl for her to hustle for me. All the girls that come my way are already hustlers. But Charlie, there really isn't anything to it. Almost every broad alive, at one time or other in her life, has had the desire to be a whore. A lot of girls are wrapped up in moral ethics and would never turn out, but any woman would be lying to you if she were to deny that she didn't often wonder what a whore's life was like. For those who are reluctant, a good pimp knows how to eliminate the barriers and convince the girl that his love will be deeper than ever for her if she is willing to go all the way for him."

On my release from Terminal Island in September 1958 after serving two years of the three-year sentence, I immediately began trying to put together the life that so infatuated me while in prison. The area of my conditional release put me in the very best location possible to carry out my dreams—Hollywood, California.

What can I say about Hollywood that hasn't already been said? I saw it as the most artificial, most pretentious city in existence. I suppose that line of thinking can be attributed to the movie and TV industry since everyone in it is looking for recognition and stardom. To me it seemed as if everyone I came in contact with was greedy, narcissistic and lacking in morals. They all existed in a dog-eat-dog, no-holds-barred world. I was in my element! I was twenty-three years old and my jail-house tutoring was going to go to work for me. All I had to do was come up with that string of pretty girls and I could begin living my dream. Life should be so simple! It was all bogus bullshit, another jail-house fantasy that isn't real on the streets—but I tried to make it real.

My first problem was that I had trouble scoring with the kind of broad whose moral ethics I was capable of "eliminating." The ones who were already hustlers were with guys who had been in operation for a long time. Those guys had the class and the connections that Vic had forgotten to tell me were so important. When I finally found a girl who would go the whole route for me, I was so much in love with her that I couldn't stand the thought of some trick sticking his dick in the girl I loved. Some pimp I was.

She and I had set up housekeeping together in an apartment in Hollywood, and every day I went out hustling and stealing to bring the bread home to *her*. One day one of my joint partners who was

56

now on the streets and enjoying pretty good success as a pimp along Sunset Strip, told me, "Charlie, you're that broad's trick! What the fuck is your story? Turn that girl out!" I gave him some feeble answer like, "Yeah, I'm working on it," but knew in my mind the guy was right. The girl had me wrapped around her finger. So I fought my jealousy and possessiveness, saying to myself, "Didn't I plan on being the big-time hustler and pimp? Never mind all that love shit—Do it! Put that girl on the streets!"

That evening as my girl and I sat in our apartment, too broke to go anywhere, I made my move, telling her, "Sandy, baby, it's time for us to sit down and do some talking." "Sure, Charlie," she replied, "what's on your mind?" I went on, "We been together for weeks. You know I'm out stealing and breaking my ass to keep us in this apartment and some food in our mouths. Here we are living in an area that is loaded with all the finer things in life. Those things are passing us by. We both dig making the scene down on Sunset. You like nice things and I enjoy seeing you with nice things. Why don't the two of us really put our heads together and make us a good life in this town? It's a player's town and players only stay in an area where there is a lot of money and action. You are one of the prettiest girls I have ever seen, and I'm not the only one that thinks so. Every time you walk down the street, guys start undressing you with their eyes. Now, why don't we start taking advantage of all those rich, hungry bastards? You know I love you and want the best for you. Question is, how much do you love me? And how far are you willing to go for both of us to get on top?"

"Charlie, I'll do anything in the world for you!"

"You mean it?"

"Certainly I mean it. Tell me your plans and you can count on me."

"Would you fuck for me? Will you turn tricks and hustle your ass for me?"

"If that's what you want me to do, Charlie!"

Hell, I was geared to spend days trying to convince her to turn out. Twenty minutes after we started our conversation, Sandy was willing—almost eager.

The first trick she turned just about broke my heart. I remember waiting in the parking lot of the apartment house where it was happening. I was going through all kinds of head trips—telling my-

57

self what a dirty bastard I was. I wanted to charge into the apartment, break the door down and beat the hell of the guy whose money she was taking. I wanted to apologize to Sandy and tell her I loved her too much to ever think of her having sex with someone else. I wanted to tell her I'd keep bringing home the money for us to live on, that she was mine and mine alone. I hated myself, and most of all I hated all the guys I had ever been in jail with. I didn't blame myself as much as I blamed all those guys I had listened to while doing time in reform schools and prisons.

When Sandy came hurrying back to the car, I couldn't look at her. I could tell she was in a big hurry and I thought it was a desire to get away from the place where she had just performed—for me. When she got in the car I finally looked into her face, expecting to see tears and perhaps some of the shame I had been experiencing. Instead, she was flushed with excitement, all smiles and proud as she thrust three twenty-dollar bills in my hand. "All right, Charlie," she said, "we're on our way! It was fun—there ain't nothing to it. The john wants to see me again next week, same time, same place." I didn't tell Sandy what had been going through my mind and to this day, I don't believe she understands why I didn't enjoy her handing me the money.

That night as we had sex together, I found myself wondering if I was making it as good for her as the john had. I was a victim of the same feeling every time she turned a trick, and it was a long time before that feeling left me. But what the hell, wasn't it my choice? And after all, isn't feeling sorry, ashamed or inadequate just a frame of mind?

So okay, now I've got a girl working for me. A young inexperienced broad that don't know any more about milking a trick than a choir girl. Yet I'm on Sunset Strip playing the part with all the other pimps. Though I'm acting like I know it all, I'm listening to everything said. I learn that just the bed money isn't anything. I mean, the mark knows he's paying to get his nuts off and has agreed on the price. If the girl just screws him, the price mentioned is all she is going to get. Listening to the seasoned pimps, I found the girl has to have more talent than just fucking or sucking. She has to learn her trick and know how to reach him emotionally, get him involved so that he feels he isn't just a trick, but a special person. It's also important that the girl isn't into the business because she wants to be. The john can be made to feel like the girl is forced into prostitution by obligations, like an emergency operation for one of her children, a dying mother, or other things to make him sympathetic. Pretty soon the trick isn't fucking the girl but feeling sorry for her. Out of a sympathetic heart and a desire to show what a wonderful fellow he is, he pays more.

Sandy was not only pretty, she was smart and quick to learn. Her looks made her a desirable girl to go to bed with, but her knowledge of how to play on the weaknesses of her johns made her a real money maker.

I was caught up in wanting to be big time and to impress others. There was also the thrill of beating the law, and the chance to experience in real life all the stories that I had listened to so intensely while in jail. But just one girl in Hollywood isn't going to make you a ton of money or gain you a reputation among the pimps and hustlers, and for me, that was what it was all about. So I looked for more girls. I found a few. Mostly young, not too pretty and without a lot of smarts. Some were ready and willing to sell their asses but most were just looking for someone to be in love with. Not wanting to pass up a piece of ass or an opportunity, I would play those girls for whatever I could score from them. None were as talented as Sandy, who had really developed into a first-class prostitute. I had all kinds of problems with girls who, though willing to go through the motions of being my broads, were mostly into that life for their own thrills. About the time one was pretty well trained and starting to bring home some money, she'd fall in love with one of the johns, or some classier pimp would lure her away from me, or worse yet, she'd do some crazy thing that would bring down the heat on both of us. Aside from the problems with the police, the girl's family—if she was still in contact with them—would somehow create more problems for me. It wasn't the life I'd envisioned in my jail-house fantasies. And I can't blame all the ups and down on the girls because in my own half-assed way I was too eager to be Mr. Big. I was spinning my wheels, trying to catch up on everything I had ever missed in life. I wanted the big bucks, the flashy clothes, the new cars; I wanted to be noticed and accepted. I'd do anything to turn a dollar, and most of the time I wasn't too cool about who I took advantage of or the chances I was taking as far as staying out of the eyes of the law.

Though I was to stay out of prison for a year and nine months, I was in and out of jail several times on a variety of charges, none of which were big money scores. Then in May of 1959 I was arrested for attempting to cash a stolen government check. The check was worth $37.50. I pleaded guilty to the charge and was given a ten-year sentence which the judge suspended, placing me on probation. A ten-year suspended sentence is pretty stiff for a thirty-seven-dollar check, but considering my background and all the shit I was doing, it was a real break and I should have cleaned up my act. I didn't, even though I knew it was only a matter of time before I'd be back in prison. The idea of going back to prison didn't frighten me, and I found the life of a thief and hustler a challenge. For me being an outlaw was as natural as an attorney's son pursuing a career in law, or a doctor's child going into medicine. Most futures are established through parents and my family was made up of hobos, winos and outlaws. My homes were the reformatories and prisons. And after surviving the Indiana School for Boys, the other places of confinement were like rest homes.

So though I had a ten-year sentence hanging over my head for the slightest infraction, I didn't change my ways. It might even be said I went at things with an added zest. I began transporting the girls to conventions in other cities and states. Conventions meant a lot of lonely guys on the prowl for a pretty girl, a companion either for the night or the duration of the convention. It was fast easy money for the girls—and me. In early 1960, a pimp friend mentioned a big convention about to take place in Laredo, Texas, so I packed up Sandy and another girl and drove them to Texas. While the convention lasted, the girls worked the bars, hotels and streets. The dollars surpassed the bucks we'd been making in Hollywood for the last few weeks, so when the convention johns left town, I put Sandy and the other broad to work in one of Laredo's whorehouses. The bucks kept coming in, and I was thinking of staying in Texas for a while. But that thought came to a sudden halt when Sandy's partner got nailed for hustling. To gain her freedom, she wasted no time in telling the vice squad, "Charlie's my old man, and yes, he brought me here to work as a prostitute." Regardless of age, taking a girl across a state line to hustle her body is a no-no with the Feds so they came looking for me. I headed south and ended up in Mexico City. A gringo in Mexico isn't a

60

novelty, but some of the routes I was forced to take were pretty much of a novelty to some of the people I met.

When I first hit Mexico City, I had some dollars in my pocket so I partied and mingled with the bull fighters. I met a couple of the lesser-known matadors and spent a few days learning to use the cape and sword. Of course the bulls were only half-grown and the sword was never thrust into the animal, but even half-grown, those suckers weigh four- or five-hundred pounds and can send a guy flying. After picking my ass up off the ground a few times, I learned how to handle the cape and could stay as close to the bull without getting touched as some of those matadors. "You good, gringo," they told me. "You got all the moves, but you never be matador. You no tall enough."

When my money started running out, some of the things in the homes I was invited to also started disappearing. No one called the *federales*, but invitations stopped coming my way. I found myself in the adobe huts and alleyways on the outskirts of town. But a hustler and a thief manages to find his own kind wherever he goes, and Mexico City has some areas that would make the events on *Miami Vice* look like choir practice. I ran into some game, chilly dudes down there. Guys and broads who would cut a throat for a dime, or bury a person in an ant hill just to prove they didn't care about anyone's life but their own.

I earned some respect from that group of people by being so ignorant I didn't know where to stop. I had stolen a .357 Magnum from one of the haciendas I had visited. With the Magnum stuck in my pants and hidden from view by my coat, I was talking to a couple of thugs trying to score some mushrooms. "No, no got. Only Yaqui Indian got mushroom. They kill gringo. You loco to go to Yaqui village." I didn't believe my life would be in danger if I just showed up at their village, so I hiked out to one of them. Seeing the way they lived was like watching a Geronimo flick. With some jail-house Spanish and the kind of hand signals I'd seen the scouts use in the movies, I walked into the Yaqui camp like I belonged there. The Indians looked at me like I was from another planet.

Before I got too close to any of the huts, four bad-looking dudes stopped me, asking, "Why you come? What want? You lost?" No, I'm not lost I told them. "I want to meet Yaqui. Be Yaqui's friend. Smoke pipe with Yaqui. Maybe get some mushroom from Indian

61

friend." "Why we smoke pipe with little gringo?" they asked. "We no know you! You go now." As they spoke, they turned me around and pointed toward the way I had come. "Wait a minute," I said. "I got pesos, I buy mushrooms. I give you gift." I took a ring off my finger and handed it to the guy who was doing most of the talking. He looked at the ring and handed it back, saying, "Mushroom spiritual. Only for Yaqui." Intending to trade the Magnum for mushrooms I pulled the gun from my pants, pointing it at the guy who was talking. I said, "This buy mushroom?" The four of them backed up a step as though they expected me to pull the trigger. "Okay" one said, "you no shoot, we give mushroom." The gun looked threatening, but that wasn't the way I meant it to be, so I handed the gun to the one who said he'd give me some mushrooms. As soon as the gun was in his hands, he pointed it at me and said, "You loco, now I kill." He stuck the gun in my stomach. I just smiled at him. He shoved the gun harder and pulled the trigger. When he snapped that there weren't any shells in it, the four of them started laughing and said, "Gringo not loco. He brave man. Be Yaqui friend." I spent the night in their village and a whole group of us did mushrooms. And as their brother, I was invited back anytime I wanted to join them. When I returned to my hoodlum friends in the city with a pouch full of mushrooms, they opened their eyes a little wider and started telling everyone what a macho gringo I was.

Even the *federales* heard about the macho gringo who was a friend to the Yaqui. They told me all about it, after they arrested me. "Oh si, *Señor* Manson, we hear about you before. The United States say send you back to Texas." Two weeks later I was being booked in the Laredo jail. When it was discovered I was already on the streets by virtue of a suspended sentence, they didn't bother to prosecute on the new charge in Laredo, but shipped me back to L.A. The judge who had given me the ten years revoked the suspension and I was on my way back to prison.

Reading this far you might say, "You never tried an honest life." That isn't completely true. It's just that I don't feel the need of telling the disappointments, the rejections, the accusations I went through in trying to maintain steady employment at a legitimate job in your world. When I was working an honest job, I experienced daily the resentment of people who never failed to let me know where I had come from and where they thought I was headed. To fully describe many of those incidents would put me completely out of character. You don't want to read it, and I'm really not into seeing it written down.

I would like to say to you that I did know the difference between right and wrong, and I do know what is expected of an individual in an honest world. But where I am coming from, all that I heard when it really mattered was: "Get out of my way, kid, I haven't got time for you."

Asking me not to break the rules of society is like telling your kid not to eat candy because it's bad for him. The kid will continue to eat candy until you take it away, or until you prove why he shouldn't. You also need to provide substitutes for the candy you have denied that child. I was told often enough what was bad, but I was never given a substitute or the opportunity to try another world until I had already become so defiant and twisted, I no longer cared about someone else's right or wrong. By then I could not see enough honest faces in the world to pattern myself after. Your Bibles didn't mean anything to me. A Bible had driven my mother from her home. The people you chose to raise me beat and raped me and taught me to hate and fear. From what I have seen throughout my life, the laws of the land are practiced only by the little guy. Those who have money and success abuse every law written and get away with it.

I admit my reasoning comes from the wrong side of the tracks, but once these opinions are formed and reinforced a few times, it is hard to believe otherwise. So even if I don't shed a tear, I console myself: I had some help in becoming the person I am. Yes, I resent the system!

CHAPTER 3

I APPEALED the revocation of the suspended sentence, but not because I thought I had a chance of beating the case. By filing an appeal, I could delay being shipped off to a prison. I figured I would be able to post bond and be out on the streets until the outcome of my appeal, and with a good attorney an appeal can drag on for years. Then, if things didn't look good for beating the case, I might split to Mexico or South America. I was being held in lieu of ten-thousand dollars bail but a bond for bail is only ten percent of the total, so with a bondsman, I would only need a thousand dollars to hit the streets. I felt very confident that either my hustler friends or my girls would come up with the money for me in a few days. It might take a couple of weeks at most.

The real outcome was that none of my high-rolling friends had the time of day for me. With the exception of Sandy, the girls stopped coming to see me after a few visits and some hard-luck stories, and either went outlaw or found themselves another old man. Sandy and I had taken out a marriage license, but had never actually tied the knot. Pregnant and unable to work as a prostitute, she visited me for a month or two but soon went the way of my wife. I have never seen her or the son who was born. Anyway, so much for my control over my harem and my chances of posting bond. I wasn't in jail sixty days and both were all gone.

I spent a year in the county jail fighting a loser. I could have dropped the appeal and gotten on with my sentence but I was stubborn and defiant. My ego had been crushed when the broads stopped showing up. Screw them all! Who needed them? With all my experience of people turning their backs on me, I should have known better than to trust anyone but myself. Still, I had hoped—and was again rejected. The whole trip put me on a real hatred high. I cussed every son-of-a-bitch I knew and the government too. I wasn't about to give up on the appeal. Since the government had dropped the Mann Act charge, all I was going back to prison for was the $37.50 check. I felt it was too much time for such a petty amount. By the time the appeal was denied, I was sick and tired of the county jail. I hadn't had any visitors for the last ten months. The winos and the confinement were getting on my nerves and I was eager for a change, even if it was to be at McNeil Island.

McNeil Island is in Washington state, one of the many islands in Puget Sound. The prison is accessible only by boat and prison-owned vessels are harbored, not at the island, but at a mainland harbor. The island is only twenty minutes from the mainland, but damn, to be so close yet so far is frightening. The return trip takes years, and sometimes never happens for the guys who go there to serve time for the Feds. Most prisoners take that boat ride feeling lost, forlorn and defeated. In years past I had experienced similar emotions, but that was at the age of twelve—a thousand years ago. Now, in 1961, it was almost like returning home. Though I had never been to Mac, I was sure I would know a bunch of the guys there. With my recently-acquired experience on the streets, I wouldn't have to stand on the edge of a group listening to their tales of scores, girls and fast living. I now had a few tales of my own to spin, and with a little typical convict exaggeration I could come on as king of the road and maybe send some kid back to his cell to dream of "the life" as a pimp. No, I wasn't feeling bad at all. After a year in the restrictions of a county jail, I was almost eager.

The boat moved across the water toward the prison. Out of habit, I took complete stock of the shore lines and surroundings just in case the opportunity to slip off the island came my way. Because of the water, one of my escapes from the Indiana School for Boys flashed through my mind. I had to smile as I saw myself trying to out-swim the fellows on shore who were waiting to take me back to another beating. I pictured myself trying to swim this water, escaping from the island. Nope! Too deep, too cold and too far. I would need something that floated. It was wasted thought.

I have never been certain about the full size of McNeil because my stay there was completely within the walls of the prison itself. I say walls; actually, McNeil doesn't have the surrounding walls you might envision if you imagine a normal prison compound. The concrete and steel buildings themselves are designed to serve as barriers against escape as much as to house convicts. The entire institution is laid out so that it is possible to do a life term without feeling a ray of the sun or a drop of rain. Halls, rotundas, and tunnels connect living quarters, work assignments, education facilities, kitchen, mess hall, gymnasium, hospital, auditorium, and the administrative offices. And if a person remains in maximum-security during his entire sentence, chances are he sees sun or rain only through a barred window. Escape is a dream, not a reality.

I fell right back into the routine of prison as though I had never been let out. I knew a slew of guys. We talked the same language. Nobody looked down his nose at me. I was one of them, an equal. If you're called a bastard in the joint, it is not a reflection on your mother, simply a figure of speech. We were all from basically the same mold and resented the same things—the police, the guards and society in general.

I didn't have anyone on the outside sending me money for commissary items, but I knew how to maneuver and I kept myself provided with the essentials through wheeling and dealing in the joint. If I worked in the kitchen, I'd steal coffee or other items of food that the guys who had plenty of commissary money wanted. If I worked in the laundry, I'd starch and press the clothing for those who were willing to pay a few packs of smokes for the service. Every job I worked at had some kind of market value which I capitalized on. Additionally, I played cards and gambled. While I am impatient at most things, I had long ago learned the value of patience when playing cards for money. In some of my previous travels I had become pretty adept at dealing seconds and cold-decking, so I won more often than I lost.

The first year or so back in the joint was a breeze. I didn't have anyone on the outside I was doing hard time over. There wasn't anyone out there who gave a fuck about me and the feeling was mutual. About the only time the streets entered my mind was during bullshit sessions with other convicts, and instead of getting the blues I'd get charged up and exaggerate or tell a bigger lie than the one I had just heard. As for work assignments, I always promoted myself into a job that afforded me the easiest time, those that permitted me to hustle the needed commissary goodies. I didn't care about the programs the institution had for constructive individual development. The only thing that mattered to me was having the

66

respect of the cons I was doing time with. I was the perfect example of the completely institutionalized inmate. Fuck them, they can't stop the clock and someday I'll be back out there. That was my attitude, and in the meantime I'd just coast right on through their jails.

Then one day something happened to me, it seemed like a goddamn cloud dropped over me and wouldn't blow away. It started with a couple of my closest friends getting released. That shouldn't have mattered because in the past I'd seen plenty of guys leave who were like brothers to me. Still, I couldn't shake the gloomy mood—that fucking cloud wouldn't move on. I looked around me and hated everything I saw. I was thinking about the streets but, strangely, not about my high-rolling times in L.A. and all the girls and fast times. My thoughts were of my wife and the first few days of our marriage—me working and coming home to our little old room that only had a bed and hardly any furniture; she and I wanting to go someplace but unable to afford it, and instead pretending we had everything in the world and were making love in a palace. The love was real and it didn't matter if we had a palace or even a dime for a cup of coffee; we had each other. I had felt good about myself in those days and I realized what a dummy I had been for not toughing things out and trying harder. "Get off this bullshit," I told myself. "Get back into the swing of things." But it didn't work. I was sick of the routines. I wasn't into telling or listening to any more convict fantasies. I hated the bell that went off every morning waking everyone up. Lining up for each meal, shower line, sick line. Work unlock, school unlock. Every fucking thing in the joint is lines and unlocks and being told what you can and can't do. Man, was I sick of it. It wasn't sexual lust or a desire to be rich on the outside that was making me feel sick, it was the little things people take for granted on the outside. Who on the outside ever stops to appreciate the luxury of being able to open a refrigerator door for a drink and a bite to eat? Or being able to open a door and go outside, or at least into another room? Or being able to take a piss or a shit without being in full view of your cellmates or a prison guard? These are all very simple little things to a person in normal life, but for a guy doing time they become the very things responsible for escape attempts and violence.

I was doing hard time. The restrictions of confinement had

67

caught up with me. I longed to walk in the woods, feel the rain on my face, or the sun on my back. I wanted to stroll on a beach or stretch out on a lawn. My life, my mind, was being mutilated by concrete and steel, the clanging of barred doors, the constant drone of nothing but male voices. I felt an urgency to be away from anything created by man. Yet because I was a man, I wanted to live like one. I wanted to put my arms around a soft, smooth-skinned girl, not in lust, but just for the comfort of something that wasn't related to prison. I thought of escape but in the same moment realized my foolishness. That avenue was next to impossible. Besides, escape wouldn't give me the kind of freedom I now sought. I would still be running, hiding, living in a world that would soon put me back in confinement. I was depressed, and I wasn't just sick of jails—I was fed up with being the individual prisons had made of me.

I realized that, since my release from the reformatories, I had been my own worst enemy. I didn't feel those years in reform school were self-inflicted, and I still don't. I'd gotten shitty breaks and no help along the way. But now I was taking an honest look at myself: I didn't like my life or the outlook of my future as things were currently going. It was up to me and me alone to straighten out my act. The answer was in taking advantage of this time in prison. I should do something constructive, learn a trade to earn an honest living on the streets. In addition to that, it was important to me to fully understand myself.

I spent the next several days in a kind of trance. I went through the prison routines like a zombie programmed to walk, talk, eat and do as I was told. I didn't have a thought in my head except getting into a program that would do two things for me. One—teach me a way to provide for myself on the streets without being a thief. Two—improve my mind and habits so that I could overcome my weaknesses and resist temptations. I wanted to develop character and stop being the fool.

McNeil was an institution that afforded an inmate the opportunity to reconstruct his life. There was a good educational program, and classes in skilled trades. I was twenty-seven years old, but my education was about fourth-grade level. For the past twelve or thirteen years, I'd been camouflaging my lack of education. I had always maneuvered around anything that required reading or writing. Since I had a good memory and verbal skills, very few people realized my inability to read or write proficiently. I was serious in my desire to develop into a more capable person, but my pride wouldn't permit me to begin school programs at a fourth-grade level when the guys I was lining up with were college level. Any reading I did was done quietly, by myself. It was a struggle, but I began reading and studying in my cell.

The subject that interested me was understanding and knowing my own mind. Prison psychs had told me often enough that I had "persecution and inferiority complexes" but they never did anything to help me overcome those faults. Even if they had I doubt if I would have been receptive to their advice 'cause no one likes to think of themselves as having mental hang-ups. But since my siege of joint fever, I wanted help.

I looked into Christianity, not necessarily for someone or something to worship but for an understanding of me and why my thoughts were so negative. I started going to services with some of the other cons. I'd listen to the guys say "oh yes" and "amen" and recite Bible verses. Then outside the chapel, I'd see them stealing cigarettes from their friends, telling obvious lies or rushing to some secluded spot in the institution where they could make love to some punk. I'm not knocking Christianity, only the hypocrites. Maybe if I'd only wanted to get out, I would have played at being a Christian, but my search was for me. I was looking to improve myself without pretending.

In prison there is every kind of belief imaginable. Some are good, others are bogus. What is good and right for one person isn't necessarily so for the other guy. So I took a look at everything. I began paying attention to individuals as well as beliefs. If I saw a con who seemed to be on top of everything and in control of himself, I'd pursue his beliefs in an effort to see if I could strengthen myself through him. I began noticing the various groups around the prison, not entirely sanctioned by the administration. If I saw sincerity in the guys who were participating in group sessions, I'd find out which way they were headed. Though I wasn't black, I picked up on what the Black Muslims were practicing. I did the same with the Indians. I found them solid in their beliefs so I watched them and began to appreciate their rituals and traditions. I studied hypnotism and psychiatry. I read whatever books I could find (and un-

69

derstand) that dealt with mind development. A cell partner turned me on to Scientology. With him and another guy I got pretty heavy into Dianetics and Scientology. Through this and my other studies, I came out of my state of depression. I was understanding myself better, had a positive outlook on life, and knew how to direct my energies to each day and each task. I had more confidence in myself and went the way I chose to go, whereas previously, I had always been content to listen and follow.

As far as a trade was concerned, the institution had a variety, but most of the trade programs that interested me required lower-security custody than I had. The welding and automotive shops were outside the prison compound. The plumbing and electrical shops were inside, but the waiting lists were pretty lengthy and with all the fucking-up I had done in the past (here and in other joints—McNeil had the records), my past insincerity, and the fact that I had never completed a trade program when given previous opportunities, I was not considered. At the most, I was placed on the bottom of the list. It sounds like an excuse and a cop-out for not taking advantage of what was offered in the way of practical job training, but it's really just an explanation why I settled on music as a career.

Music wasn't a totally new thing for me. My mom, before putting me in Gibault, had let me take voice and music lessons. And there had been times in other institutions when I'd turned to music. Music is always an enjoyable time-killer in prisons. Whether you are playing or listening, it takes your mind out of the joint. Years ago a Mexican friend had taught me the fundamentals of playing the guitar and through the years it had been a comfort, as well as an escape, from the repetitive life in prison. When I wasn't eligible for one of the more conventional trades, it was a natural move for me to try and develop my ability on the guitar, perhaps someday become a professional musician.

Music in prison isn't considered vocational training or education, so the institution won't assign you to the music room like they would to a job or school program. It's considered a hobby or recreation. The practicing has to be done on your own time, after your daily work assignment is completed or on the weekends. Consequently, I sought work assignments that permitted me as much time as possible to practice my music. And while the prison

70

didn't employ music teachers, there were plenty of inmates who had been professional musicians on the streets. Some were very capable instructors. As with any other trade, learning to be a good musician requires dedication, concentration and practice. I had plenty of time. I was barely two years into a ten-year sentence when I decided music was going to be my bag. Time, practice, a lot of broken guitar strings, and numerous instructors established me as an average guitar player.

Once I got involved in music, everything seemed to fall into place for me. A work assignment in the auditorium opened up and I no longer had to work around the normal institution schedule when I wanted to practice; the auditorium housed the music room. The only setback that ever interrupted my becoming a musician involved a scene with my mother. She didn't move to Washington to be close to me, but as fate would have it, Mom moved to Tacoma and she visited me a couple of times. After I got heavy into the music trip I asked Mom if she would shop around and maybe spend a couple of hundred dollars on a decent used guitar for me. Her answer was, "Gee, Charlie, I'd really like to, but we don't have an extra dime. For me to even visit I have to steal from our grocery money." Knowing what it's like to be broke, I told her, "It's no big thing, and if you can't afford it I understand." About two months later my mom showed up for a visit with a little girl in her arms. She greeted me with, "Charlie, meet your little sister." "Wow," I said, "how in the world did this happen?" Mom explained, "Well, for the last several months we have been trying to adopt a little girl. Last month the agency informed us that they had found a child for us. Isn't she the sweetest thing?" All kids are sweet to me, but at that moment—call it a jealous rage, or maybe just the memory of what my childhood had been like—there wasn't any joy in hearing my mother's words. Especially when she told me the fees for the adoption had run well over two-thousand dollars. I flipped and said some pretty nasty things. "Fuck you and your daughter! Two months ago you couldn't afford a lousy two hundred dollars to buy me a guitar. When I was a kid, half the time you were pawning me off on somebody else. When the somebody elses ran out, you had a judge lock me up so there'd be no strings on your life. You lied to me when you said you didn't have a dime." Telling my mom I didn't want to see her again, I got up and

71

left the visiting room. It was a nasty scene, one that I have often regretted, but at the time I was so hot and mad at everyone all over again, I almost went on a roll of self-punishment. For a day or two I said, fuck that guitar and music too. But that was short lived and by the end of the week I was into music heavier than ever.

One of those who taught me a few things was a nationally known gunman of the thirties, Alvin (Creepy) Karpis, who had been transferred to McNeil when the government discontinued the use of Alcatraz Island as a federal prison. Old Creepy was a member of the notorious Ma Barker gang and had been convicted for fourteen gangster-style slayings about the time I was born. He had been in prison ever since. With over thirty years of prison behind him, the old timer might have been a humbled, shriveled-up, defeated old man. Not Karpis. At sixty-plus years, he was still in good physical shape. He had an extra-sharp mind and a quiet dignity that commanded respect from the convicts, guards, prison personnel and everyone who met him. Karpis played steel guitar, and though we weren't tuned in to the same style of music, our mutual interest in our instruments and music established a solid friendship between us. He taught me a few chords and I had the opportunity to teach him a few things. In many ways I was still a snot-nosed kid and headed nowhere, but Alvin always had more than just the time of day for me.

When we weren't playing or practicing, we spent a lot of time just talking. I liked the old man and listened with open ears to everything he had to say. He hardly ever discussed the chain of events that led to his imprisonment, but for a guy with so much time behind him, he was well versed on what was going on in the outside world. His knowledge of government, unions and foreign affairs always amazed me. Like a lot of old timers, he was always saying how corrupt the system was. But unlike the other guys who just said the words, he would pinpoint circumstances and motives behind laws and government procedures. He told me things that the CIA was doing in other countries (time has since proven he knew exactly what he was talking about). Hell, at that time I didn't even know there was a CIA.

As for his knowledge of unions, it is commonly known that Karpis had contacts with union leaders. On more than one occasion he

72

used those contacts to help an inmate prepare a parole plan by getting the inmate an offer of employment through the unions.

There were times when I would try to sell Karpis on the things I was learning through Scientology. "Kid," he would say, "your mind is your greatest friend, yet it can be your worst enemy. Don't get it any more fucked up than the world has already made it!" Another old timer added, "Never try to be something other than what comes natural. Don't tell any lies. Don't depend on handouts, make your own way in life. Never trust a politician or a wealthy man. But never let a friend down."

I had arrived in McNeil in July of 1961. I was twenty-six years old. The first fifteen months I was there, I tried to come on like I had experienced everything in life and knew all there was to know. I painted pictures—to myself as well as to the guys listening—of Cadillacs, strings of the most beautiful whores in Hollywood and a life of luxury. I played a flippant, don't-give-a-fuck role to the cons and the administration. I was constantly in and out of trouble and just plain didn't care.

But in late 1962, when the cloud settled over me, I saw myself as I really was: an immature, mixed-up person with nothing but a mouth going for him. I was without direction or a proper goal in life. In the following years I ceased to be the flippant little fool. I was sincere in my search for self-understanding and my desire to establish the capability to earn an honest living. I was serious about the music trip and felt I had my head turned in the right direction. I felt I had come a long way; I felt honest and wasn't telling any lies or even exaggerating past experiences. I looked at the future positively and was practical about what I might expect once released. My head wasn't filled with unobtainable fantasies. However, I had not outgrown my desire to impress, especially when I had my guitar in hand and was singing in front of a group. I felt confident and positive when I entertained. When others began complimenting me on my talent, I became more than a little conceited, but the conceit didn't allow me to sit back and rest on my laurels. It drove me into deeper study and involvement in a skill in which I had been recognized as having talent. I became obsessed with music. I enjoyed playing the music of recording stars, but even more, I enjoyed writing and composing songs of my own.

In June of 1966, I was transferred from McNeil Island to Terminal Island. With good time earned I was getting close to the end of my sentence, and it is normal procedure for the Feds to move you to an institution (if one exists) close to where your release plans indicate you will be living after your time is served.

The transfer was a welcome one. I was tired of the rain and fog and more than just mildly burnt-out on McNeil. I had been in Terminal Island before, and if a guy has to do time T.I. is one of the better places to be. In addition, it afforded me the opportunity to make further progress with my music. Terminal Island is only a few minutes from L.A. and Hollywood, and a lot of quality show people appear at the institution to polish the new songs and acts they plan to use on future road trips. More importantly, many of them encourage the participation of accomplished inmate musicians. I took advantage of those situations and participated every chance I got. It was good experience and I felt very professional up there on stage.

The final year of my sentence seemed to fly by. I was so busy writing music and playing my guitar I had stopped thinking about the streets. Though it was the streets and the desire to stay free that had driven me into music and helped me to overcome my other hang-ups, I was extremely content to stay right where I was. Warped as it may sound, I had become very happy and content there at Terminal Island. I had some good friends. I was accepted, even appreciated, as an individual. Other than a girl to love, or at least sleep with, I had perhaps the best world I had ever known right there in T.I. Thoughts of leaving brought back the feelings of inferiority I had studied so hard to master.

PART TWO

A
CIRCLE
OF
ONE

CHAPTER 4

I<small>T HAS BEEN WRITTEN</small> that at the time of my release from Terminal Island in 1967, I asked if I could stay. That is true. I had spent the last seven years of my life looking forward to the day when I would get out. I had dreams and plans, but as I was being processed for release, I knew the dreams would never be realized and the plans were nothing more than wishful thinking. I'd had my releases before. With me, nothing had ever been as I imagined it. There is a big difference between illusion and reality, and neither was a stranger to me. Since I had at last found a comfortable atmosphere in prison, the streets were not the place for me. My job assignment at T.I. was pleasant, I had my guitar and plenty of time to play it. There were no hassles with the authorities or other inmates. In thinking of starting all over in the outside world, all my escapes and even the legitimate releases flooded my mind. I remembered myself as a small boy, huddled in an alley trying to sleep and stay warm, yet afraid to sleep too soundly for fear a policeman might wake me up and take me off to jail. I saw myself as a man sleeping in sleazy rooms and wondering how I was going to pay the next night's rent or find food for myself the following day. I reviewed what may have been my peak—my days during the late 50s as a pimp. I remembered all the shallow thoughts of what a wheel I was, the whole time knowing I was a bogus bastard who was really afraid to take an honest look at himself. And all the desire during the last seven years for a new image and self-esteem left me. I was afraid of trying to cope in a world that I had never understood. I had my music, but I was afraid that if I depended on it too strongly, I would fail at that too. No, I did not want to go out into a world of uncertainties. For the moment I was secure, and that was how I wanted to stay.

I told the officer who was signing me out, "You know what, man, I don't want to leave! I don't have a home out there! Why don't you just take me back inside?" The officer laughed and thought I was kidding. "I'm serious, man! I mean it, I don't want to leave!" My plea was ignored.

The release procedure is a simple one. A last photo for the files. An address and instructions to report within twenty-four hours to your parole officer. If you have money on the books they give it to you. If the government is helping you with funds, those funds are to be picked up at the time you check in with your P.O. You get thirty dollars until you see the P.O. One of the institution vehicles takes you to public transportation and the driver says goodbye, and in some cases wishes you good luck. After that, you are on your own.

Terminal Island is separated from the mainland, San Pedro, by a span of water that is perhaps a tenth of a mile wide. There are two ways to get to the other side: a ferry for pedestrians and a bridge for motor vehicles. I was dropped at the ferry slip. A boat was departing but I purposely didn't try to board it. Instead I sat on a piling and watched the people, the cars and the seagulls. I tried to establish the make of the automobiles. Seven years of confinement limited my ability to distinguish a Ford from a Chevy. The seagulls swooped and dived for the garbage discarded by the people. As I watched the people I wondered how many of them had ever experienced confinement, if any of them had spent more than half their life behind bars. I was thirty-two years old, and over seventeen of those years had been spent in jail or some form of confinement.

I kept taking long deep breaths of fresh air, at the same time sending messages to myself, "I'm free, I'm on the outside. I can go where I want, I can do as I please. I don't have to get in line to eat or get out of bed when a bell rings. Nobody's going to tell me, 'Line up, Charlie,' or 'Stand up for count.'" Excitement should have been racing through me; instead there was a flat void. I wasn't scared, but felt lost and very much alone. I sat there in my ten-dollar suit; thirty dollars in my pocket, my parole officer's address and a couple of phone numbers of ex-cons who had said, "Give me a call when you get out." It was March 21, 1967. It was a bright sunshiny day, there was a brisk, air-cleaning breeze, but I was in a fog.

I must have missed several ferry crossings, and though watching everything, I was not aware of any of it. I was wondering what I was going to do after I checked in with my parole officer. A voice directed at me brought me back to the present. "Hey, fellow, you want a ride to Pedro?" It was a truck driver whose daily route took him to T.I. He was familiar with the prison and could easily spot a guy just released. No thanks, I told him and went back to my thoughts. I wasn't aware of time but I guess a couple of hours passed, and again I heard the voice. "You sure I can't drop you some place?" It was the same driver. I got into the truck and we headed over the bridge. He was a friendly, talkative guy and was curious as to what I had done time for and how long. He whistled slightly when I told him I had been locked up since 1960, and asked, "Man, how can anybody stand jail that long?" He then told me that he had once done a weekend for being drunk and had just about gone crazy. We both laughed and commented on his luck. I hadn't been in the truck for five minutes when he lit up a joint. It blew my mind how unconcerned he was about people seeing him. We both proceeded to get stoned. I couldn't believe that we were smoking pot driving through all the traffic. Christ, before doing this last bit I had lived in fast circles, and even then, a person didn't just light up where there was a possibility of being seen by a "square." I was to see a lot of changes compared to what things were like when I started my sentence in '60.

The guy invited me to his place and said I could spend a couple of days there if I wanted to. Why not? I sure didn't have anyplace else to go. He gave me a ride to the parole officer's so I could check in and then he took me home with him. When we entered his house, he introduced me to his wife. "Marge, this is Charlie." She smiled and was very friendly. She had already prepared his dinner and there were two plates on the table. Without asking me if I was going to stay for dinner, she set another plate. During dinner she asked me where I worked; before I could answer, her husband spoke up and told her I had just got out of the joint and was going to spend the night or a couple of days with them. Her smile suddenly faded and she no longer knew how to be friendly toward me. I spent the night and might have stayed for the two days I had been invited, but Marge wasn't as willing to share her home with an ex-con as her husband was. I don't mean she was rude, but I was sensitive to the tension created once it was mentioned I was just out of the joint.

The guy gave me a ride into L.A. the next morning and dropped me in front of the building where my P.O.'s office was. I went into a restaurant and had a cup of coffee while I tried to figure out what my next move should be. I had an impulse to go on into Hollywood and see if I could locate any of the crowd I knew in the late 50s. But in thinking of that group a slight surge of resentment came to me as I remembered their lack of concern when I had needed the bail money eight years earlier. No! I didn't need any of those people. Instead, I went through my pockets and took out the phone numbers of the ex-cons who had said, "Give me a call." One was a San Francisco number and belonged to a guy I had related to pretty well in the joint, so I tried his number first. My friend said, "Sure, come on up, I'll line you up for something." I then went into the P.O.'s office and told him a relative in the Bay Area had offered to help me find a job and give me a place to stay until I got on my feet, and I asked if I could go north. The P.O. agreed to anything that might give me an easier start and gave me permission to leave the L.A. area and relocate in northern California.

Frisco and the generation that now occupied its streets was something else. While in the joint, guys would mention, "Man, if you been locked up since 1960, you ain't going to believe the changes out there." And they would describe all that was happening in the Haight-Ashbury district of San Francisco and across the bay in Berkeley. For that matter, the whole generation, everywhere, would be an extreme eye-opener. I believed some of it, but wrote most of it off as just more convict bullshit. But, man, they weren't lying. Some mighty big changes had taken place since I had last been on the streets.

The friend I had called was a "rounder"; he had his fingers in everything. He made book, sold dope, hustled girls and fenced for some pretty accomplished thieves. He had connections I couldn't believe and offered to set me up in some of his activities. Eight years ago I would have jumped at his offer, but at the moment I was geared to play it straight and give my life a chance. I don't mean I was so straight I didn't want to smoke a little grass and romance a few girls, but I didn't want to start hustling and stealing things that would put me right back in jail. I did accept his offer to arrange an audition for me at one of his friend's night clubs in the North Beach area. During the audition, I didn't really let my hair down. I tried to play it cool. I strummed my guitar and used lyrics that were popular in the 50s. After listening to me, the club owner tapped his fingers rapidly in musical tempo on the bar and said, "Hey, man, you got some talent and sound fine, but you are ten years behind the times. Like the music is . . ." and in time with his finger tapping, "pa-pa-pa-pa, not daaa, daaa. Get out there and update and then drop by." The guy didn't realize how right he was in telling me I was ten years behind. And I mean in more than just music.

Before getting locked up in '60, I'd had a pretty good run on the streets, and though I knew I wasn't a big success at the things I was trying to do, I thought I was a smooth-talking mother who knew what the score was. Jail life has always kept up on what is happening in the fast lane, but hell, the things I was seeing there in Frisco, I felt I was in a horse-and-buggy trying to keep up with a jet-liner. In the 50s, to score a lid of grass you had to make a phone call or two and use a lot of discretion about who you dealt with. As for making it with a broad, a guy might wine and dine her several times before even being able to kiss a girl goodnight. Now people were like the music, very fast. And all seemed willing. Pretty little girls were running around every place with no panties or bras and asking for love. Grass and hallucinatory drugs were being handed to you on the streets. It was a different world than I had ever been in and one that I believed was too good to be true. It was a convict's dream and after being locked up for seven solid years, I didn't run from it. I joined it and the generation that lived it.

Vincent Bugliosi, the prosecuting attorney and co-author of the book *Helter Skelter*, would have the world believe I got out of prison and pledged my life to corrupting the youth of the country. Hey, those kids knew everything and did everything. I was the baby! I was sleeping in the park and calling it home. I was shining shoes for money to eat on. That is, until a fifteen-year-old kid pulled my coat. I'd seen him around for a few days as I was hustling guys for shines. One day I asked him, say, pal, why aren't you in school? He tells me he doesn't go to school. Okay then, I asked, where do you work?

"Work? What kind of a rube are you? I don't work," was his indignant reply.

"Man, if you don't go to school and you don't work, how do you get by?"

"Are you a cop?" he asked.

"Hell no, I ain't a cop. As a matter of fact I just got out of the joint and am kind of like a stranger in a strange land."

That fifteen-year-old kid bought my lunch that day and we exchanged our life stories. Less than half my age, he was the professor and I was the student. He had run away from home over a year-and-a-half before. He had been picked up by the authorities the second week after running away and was returned to his parents. His stepfather kicked him out of the house a week later. He had been on his own ever since. He was one of the smoothest panhandlers I ever saw in action. Though he slept in the park most of the time, he knew where the crash pads were and was welcome in all of them. Besides panhandling and a little thievery, he would hustle pot and acid for a couple of small-time dealers in the Haight-Ashbury district. He introduced me to the district and turned me on to my first acid trip.

The night I dropped my first tab, The Grateful Dead was playing at the Avalon Ballroom. Even without the acid, the performance would have blown my mind. All the strobe lights blinking and flashing in a variety of colors. The people in all their strange clothing looked like they were at a costume party. I flipped over the completely uninhibited routines of the musicians. And though I had never danced to that style of music, I saw that it was all motion and each person did their own thing. The music seemed without direction but created a frenzy in the listeners and dancers. Before I actually realized what I was doing, I was out there on the floor innovating to the beat of The Grateful Dead. I was wild and I was loose; I attracted attention and applause from the other dancers. The acid, the music and the loss of inhibitions opened up a new world for me. I was experiencing rebirth. Finally, in the middle of one of my dances, I collapsed on the floor.

When I awoke the next morning I was in a room with several other people. My fifteen-year-old friend had taken care of me. The people in the pad where I had crashed were a mixture of young and not-so-young, male and female. All were cordial and none were curious as to who I was or how I had gotten there. Each was just into doing his or her own thing and letting the other person do the same. I was one of them without asking or being asked; I was just there, and I was accepted. Welcome to the world.

My guitar, my voice, my song writing and my homeless state put me right at home. I was just one of thousands who called wherever they were at the moment home. My hair grew a little longer. I lugged the guitar every place I went. I played on street corners, in alleys, in houses and on college campuses. Playing on a street corner might earn me enough money to eat on for a day, but that wasn't my reason for playing and singing. There is communication through music, there are friends and appreciation. The past has no bearing and the future is not thought of, just the "now." I played for myself and whoever cared to listen. Others might join me, or I might join them in their songs. We shared and related. Doors would open—not for lucrative opportunities or success in the music world, but for friendships and experiences. If money was needed I'd hustle a bar, using my guitar and voice. I'd look into a bar; if there were numerous people in the place and no music being played, I'd approach the bartender and ask if I could play a few songs. Sometimes the bartender wouldn't go for it and told me to hit the road. If the guy gave me the go-ahead, I'd play and sing for tips. If no one was putting anything in the kitty, I'd stop playing and in my loudest voice insult the whole bar and tell them, "I just got out of prison, and me and my two partners had come by this place to rob it. I talked my partners into letting me try to earn a few honest dollars instead of robbing the place. Now if some of you bastards don't put a few dollars into this empty hat, so that I ain't a liar, I don't know how long I can keep my two partners from walking through that door with their shotguns." All the patrons would glance at the door, not knowing if I was bullshitting or not. It was surprising how effective the words were. I supported myself pretty well by doing just that. I wasn't stealing, selling dope or doing anything that would put me back in jail. I might be smoking a little grass and dropping a tab or two, but at that time, I wasn't dealing or robbing.

Or getting any sex from all those pretty little girls mentioned earlier. I was definitely conscious of them and drooled every time I got close to one. In reading about me, a person is led to believe I just moved right in and was balling every girl I looked at. But it wasn't happening. Maybe I was just too hungry and eager for it to

83

happen. The truth is, I was on the streets many days before I got my nuts out of hock. And it wasn't with one of those pretty little flower children filled with free love, but a forty-plus-year-old lush who hustled me for a drink. For all the real pleasure she gave me, I'd have been better off finding a corner, jacking off and letting my imagination carry me away to satisfaction.

My first sexual encounter with one of the young pretties happened on a rainy night in Frisco. Due to the rain, sleeping under the stars was out. I found myself a dry nook in the alcove of an apartment house and hoped like hell nobody would hassle me before I had had a few hours sleep. I had rolled out my sleeping bag and was about to crawl in when this young girl carrying a guitar stepped into the alcove for protection from the heavy rain. She wasn't dressed for the weather and was soaked clear to the skin. Her lips were quivering and her teeth chattering. For me, it wasn't a question of chivalry or lust, but a natural concern for someone cold and wet who needed warmth and a chance to dry out. So I said, "Here, get out of those wet clothes and get in this sleeping bag." She peeled off her clothes and buried herself in the warmth of the sleeping bag. I wrung out her clothes and hung them on the doorknob, then huddled up in a corner clutching my arms around my knees for warmth. She looked out of the bag and said, "Aren't you getting in?" She didn't have to ask twice. Twenty minutes later the moisture was sweat, not rain. And our bodies supplied all the needed heat. The little broad was an acid freak and not all that pretty, but she completed my welcome to Haight-Ashbury. It wasn't love, and I don't even remember her name. Love and real pleasure were yet to come.

I stayed in the Haight for some time. I can't say I had an address there, but it was home. I never rented a room or an apartment. A crash pad, a spare room, the back yard of a new friend or the park is where I would sleep. I'd catch up on baths when invited into someone's apartment. Overall the people in the district were like one big family. As a true family is bonded by blood and heredity, those in the Haight were bonded by their counter-culture lifestyles and resentment of government and society. It was a place where everyone did his own thing and didn't object to the other guy doing his. The rich, like the poor, wore faded and second-hand clothing or home-made garments. The occult was practiced almost as openly as socially acceptable religions. A Catholic or a Protestant would enter the Haight and possibly leave as a Buddhist or an atheist. Devil worship, witchcraft, sex orgies and perversion were everyday occurrences. A group of people might shed a tear one day over the slight injury of an animal, when the night before they had participated in some weird blood-letting ritual.

I have heard that Haight-Ashbury's reputation was created by "flower-children" who advocated love and peace. There were a few of those still in the district, but as a whole, that image was on the decline long before Charles Manson appeared on the scene. Other than the love and hallucinogenic drugs, I did not participate in mind trips or rituals. Nor did I get involved in all the protest concerning the Vietnam War. When approached to march or stand in front of some building in protest, I'd say, half seriously, "What war? Shit, I been locked up for seven years, is there a war going on?" The recruiter would look at me like I was an idiot and go on his way.

I observed all that was going on with keen interest, but at that time I was not into controlling anyone or being controlled. My trip was being free!

Berkeley and the University of California offered a similar atmosphere of freedom, so occasionally I would put my guitar over my shoulder and hitchhike to the campus of U.C. to spend a day or two on that side of the bay. Sometimes I would join other musicians as they played on corners or the spacious lawns of the campus. Mostly I would just find myself a quiet spot somewhere on the lawn and play and sing the music I had written. Students and passersby would stop to listen, comment on the lyrics and sometimes compliment the music. I loved it. I made a lot of friends and took pride in my accomplishments and their acceptance of me.

One day while on the U.C. campus I was strumming my guitar and humming in tune with the chords when a dog ran up to me and started sniffing at my foot. I poised my foot as if to kick the animal and a girl's voice rang out, "Don't hurt my dog." I hadn't intended to kick the pup, but when I saw the concern in the girl's face, I played a game with her: get this ugly dog away from me or I'm going to plant my foot in its ass. The girl was a slim, redheaded, straight-laced type. She wasn't pretty, but standing there in defiance of someone who might hurt her animal, she had qualities.

85

Mary Brunner was her name. She worked at the university as a librarian. I teased and threatened all the more when I saw it was irritating her. In a few minutes she realized it was a tease and laughed at herself for being annoyed. She then began criticizing my grammar, telling me, "You should stick to singing; when you talk, you come on like an ex-felon." Smiling, I said what a smart girl she was and then, hoping to shock her, I told her of my recent release from prison. She accepted my statement without displaying any emotion and quietly said, "Wow, I'll bet you're glad to be out." Our meeting had begun with a certain mutual defiance, but the conversation mellowed and we found we communicated easily. Mary had just recently graduated from the University of Wisconsin and had moved to California to "broaden her horizons." She was twenty-three years old, living alone, and as yet didn't have many friends here on the West Coast.

With some encouragement on my part, she agreed to let me fall out at her apartment for the night. My immediate thought was, "Good, I'm going to score." When we got to the apartment I was ready for sex and made a pass at her. She straightened my ass out quick. Firmly pushing me away from her, she said, "Look, I am giving you a place to sleep tonight; I'm not sleeping with you." I backed off and became a gentleman for the rest of the evening. We went down to a local restaurant and I bought her dinner. We exchanged histories, and before the night was over I considered her my friend. I slept on the couch and respected her privacy. The next morning as she left for work, I asked if I might spend a couple more nights with her. She agreed, as long as I didn't expect any sexual relationship between us. I took advantage of her hospitality. By the time she returned home from her job, I had gone to Frisco and picked up all my worldly possessions (a suitcase with three changes of clothing, a sleeping bag and of course my guitar, which had been with me the night before). When she came home and noticed my belongings, she smiled and let me know I was pushing things. Not really, I told her. I'll help you out with the rent, protect you from all the bad guys and keep my distance. She smiled and I knew it was all right. We were good companions and I kept my word about staying my distance.

Several days later I was over in Frisco and in the Haight. I had been wandering around, playing a little music here and there and in general just looking for the unexpected. While standing on a corner, I saw a young girl walking up the street. She had a back-pack over her shoulders and the lost, desperate look that was very common on the faces of new arrivals in the area. She stopped on the corner and took the pack off to rest her shoulders. I was think-ing of walking over to her to start a conversation, but before I had a chance to move, a big black guy walked up and started talking shit to her. She bent down to pick up her pack in an effort to get away from the guy, but he put his hand on her arm and lifted her up-right. I could hear his words. "Come on, baby, I'm going to give you a nice home and let you be my woman." The girl's face drained of color and she tried to pull away. As they struggled, I walked over, saying, "Hey, man, get your hands off of my sister!" He let go of the girl and started to give me some lip. I ignored him and called the girl by the first female name that came to mind: "Come on, Mary, I been waiting an hour for you; it's time for us to get home." We left the black guy standing there.

We walked down the street, me carrying her pack, and went into a restaurant. I bought her something to eat and listened to her tale for the next hour. She had run away from home ten days before. Her money was gone and she didn't know what she was going to do now. She had been told about the Haight and hoped she would meet someone in the area who would give her a place to stay until she got a job and could afford her own place. I used the black guy to illustrate the kind of treatment she could expect if she persisted in hanging around this area. I tried to convince her it would be best if she returned to her parents and that, if she wanted me to, I would hitch back with her to make sure some creep didn't pick her up. Her answer was, "If you make me go home, I won't stay there. This is the second time I left and I'm not ever going back again." Convinced she was telling the truth, I offered her the use of Mary's place.

Her name was Darlene. She was sixteen years old, small and pretty, and didn't even look thirteen. We hitched over to Berkeley. On the way I was wondering how receptive Mary was going to be to my bringing another roomie to her place. At the apartment Mary came through like a champ. She was even more concerned about Darlene being on the streets alone than I was. The two of us together tried to talk Darlene into returning home. Her answer was still a definite no.

In the following days I may have had thoughts about having sex with Darlene or Mary, but at that time I hadn't stood in a court room and heard a prosecuting attorney tell the world that I was an unscrupulous deviate who lured young girls into my lair to perform sexual orgies. So I wasn't prepared to take off some sixteen-year-old baby or rape my friend Mary. Actually I was surprised by myself. There I was, an ex-convict, a one-time pimp, who hadn't had but two pieces of ass in the last eight years, living in an apartment with two lovely girls and sleeping by myself.

A couple of days later however, Darlene was hanging around the apartment in a pair of skimpy shorts and a very revealing halter. Looking at her, I noticed stretch marks on her stomach. I pointed and said, "What are these?" Darlene glanced at the marks and replied, "Oh, that's from when I had my baby. When I was fourteen a Mexican gardener raped me." I responded, "Well, hell, girl, you're legal then. Why haven't we been sleeping together?"

"Gee, Charlie, I been waiting for you to say something. I thought you didn't want me," she said.

"Are you for real? I been locked up for a lifetime dreaming of a young tender thing like you."

Mary was at work, we had the apartment to ourselves and our romance began right then. By the time a couple of long, hungry kisses were exchanged, we were both out of our clothes and making love on the carpet in the front room. She was young, she was pretty, and she knew how to make love. And once started, neither of us wanted to stop. It wasn't rape, I hadn't kidnapped her from her parents, she wasn't turned on by drugs, and though she was less than half my age, she was years ahead of me in sexual experience. Well, that may not be a complete truth, but she did put me through a couple of moves I had never tried before.

That evening when Mary came home, I was telling her that Darlene and I had made it together and would be sharing the same room. Mary didn't make a scene but she did indicate that she thought I was taking advantage of her. "She's awfully young, Charlie. Are you sure you're being right with her?" I replied, "Hey, look, I'm only human. She wasn't a cherry and she wanted it as much as me. I didn't twist no arms. You aren't giving me any, so yeah, I'm being right with her, and myself." Darlene then spoke up for the first time. "I wanted him, Mary. He didn't force me."

I can't say that I fell in love, but this little girl was sure giving me a lot of pleasure. I thought I was satisfying her as much as she satisfied me until one afternoon when I walked into the apartment unexpectedly. I had entered the apartment without making much noise, the bedroom door was closed, and as I moved toward it to see if Darlene was home, I heard the sound of two people getting it on. My first impulse was to open the door and break it up. Instead, I quietly sat on the couch and listened to the noise of the bed, the words of passion, the sighs, the oohs and ahhs and then the exhilirated exhalation as Darlene reached her climax. I sat there burning, not so much out of jealousy, but because in our sex trips Darlene had never displayed that amount of ecstasy. Thoughts went through my mind about what an inadequate person I must be if the girl not only brought home another lover but seemed to get more out of that session than ours.

While I was thinking how I was going to handle the situation, the door opened. Darlene was the first to come out. She saw me sitting there; it startled her, she jumped and gave a small scream, almost as if she had been hit. The guy started to ask her what was wrong, then he saw me. He was a pretty big guy and I was hoping there wouldn't be a fight. There wasn't. The guilt was too strong in him to stick around for any words. He said a quick "hi" and was gone. He wasn't the least bit concerned about the safety of his sex partner. I watched the door close and then looked back at the girl. Her face was flushed and she was trembling. She started to speak but no sound came from her throat, she made motions with her hands, but still no sound. Finally, "Oh, Charlie, I'm sorry." I looked at her and played a part I didn't feel. "Sorry for what? I told you in the beginning, you didn't belong to me and I didn't belong to you."

That had been the trend of our conversation the first day she and I had made it. But when I told her that, I hadn't expected her to turn it around on me. I was really establishing an opening for myself, in case I came across other action.

Once Darlene realized I wasn't going to vent anger, disappointment—whatever—violently, she relaxed and again told me how sorry she was and that never again would she make love to anyone

89

but me. I played indifferent and said, "No big thing, baby. Just don't be bringing anyone to the pad, keep it someplace else." Once more she said, "Never, not here, not anyplace, and never with any-one but you, Charlie."

Neither of us mentioned the afternoon's happenings to Mary. It was just between Darlene and myself. That evening Darlene went to bed early, and even though it was cutting off my nose to spite my face, I had made up my mind to let her sleep by herself for a few nights. Later that evening, Mary rescued me from my self-in-flicted punishment.

After Darlene left the room, Mary, sensing the tension between Darlene and me, asked, "You two got problems?" No, no problems, I answered, she's still a baby and doesn't know where her head is at. With that, true to her habit of not prying into other people's business, Mary dropped the subject. Watching Mary move around the room, tidying up the place, I thought, "Now how come I'm not making it with her? She's my kind of broad. She minds her own business, she doesn't pry, she has an open mind and we have great communication." With those thoughts going through my head, I picked up my guitar and sang some lyrics that described my feel-ings at that moment. I don't remember the lyrics verbatim but they were similar to the following:

I am a man torn—traveling a path well worn.
A man with a struggling mind—searching for love and happiness
*   combined.*
On the campus of a university—I found a girl to love and trust—
*   but to her, sex was wrong unless a wife.*
Not being the marrying kind—I searched on.
On the streets of San Francisco—I found a wayward waif without
*   a home of her own—saddened by life.*
This wayward waif, without love, shared my must for lust.
And now in my heart are two girls—one for love and one for lust.
I am a man torn—wanting the girl I love to ease my struggling
*   mind and be my love—sharing my lust with some of her own.*
Or must I travel on—seeking another who will be both in one?
Or should I stay and forever be a man torn?

Mary had stopped moving around and was sitting down by the time my impromptu serenade was completed. She remarked, "Gee,

Charlie, coming from you, those lyrics were almost nice. You didn't say, 'I want to fuck you, baby,' like you usually do. Though you implied it." We laughed and I told her, "Some of your class and uppity culture is rubbing off on me." "I doubt that," she replied.

My song had been a kind of sexual pass at Mary, and I wanted to continue in a more serious manner, but I remembered my promise to her about keeping my distance when she had let me move in. So instead of talk directed at sex, we sat there in a comfortable and cozy atmosphere, me quietly playing the guitar when there was a lull in conversation.

For two people who were worlds apart in education and family background we had a lot of things in common, though for totally different reasons (if that makes any sense). Both of us were sensitive to the other's thoughts and didn't necessarily need to be mouthing words to paint pictures of what was going through our minds. Mary was on an environmental kick. The trees, the water, the air, land and wildlife were important to her because of her awareness of the importance of the earth and human life. I was concerned about it because I had been locked up all my life and had never been able to appreciate any of it. She wanted to preserve and enjoy; I wanted to enjoy. We were both on our own. She had been smothered and pampered all her life, and had left it all to become her own individual. While I had never had the luxury or the attention she had received, I craved the same chance at individuality. Three or four hours rolled by, of which I enjoyed every minute. Since Darlene had shown up and I was spending so much time trying to prove my manhood to her, it had been a long time since Mary and I had really rapped. Darlene had all the curves in the right places and was a pretty girl, but at the moment I was looking at a very beautiful person, a beauty that went far beyond the surface. And one-track-mind that I am, I was just on the verge of breaking my word and attempting a sexual pass at this beautiful person when Mary suddenly said, "Charlie, I changed my mind."

I knew immediately what she was referring to, but played my game: "What do you mean, you changed your mind?"

"You know," she answered, "about sleeping with you. I want you to do it to me." A smile broke on my face and she blushed, embarrassed at her own aggressiveness. Mary didn't have to repeat

91

herself. Her timing was perfect. She saved me from breaking my word and possible rejection. I didn't have to worry about getting weak in my hunger and finding myself crawling into bed with Darlene. I would be teaching Darlene a lesson without punishing myself. Also, maybe, if I really put my heart in it, I could shake that feeling of inadequacy that little girl had put me through earlier this very day. Oh, Mary, I thought, you'll never know how precious you are, a real life saver.

In a previous chapter I told of my efforts to be a pimp, and, as I said, I did eke out an existence from it for a short time. But, truth is, if you aren't already aware of it, I didn't know much about girls. I was only doing the things I had learned from the conversations of a bunch of guys in jail. I went for their lines and tried to act on what I had heard before finally discovering that they had been lies all along.

Once a pimp acquires a girl who is willing to work as a whore, he must have three qualities to hold on to her. All three actually amount to maintaining some kind of respect, the nature of the girl establishing the procedure the pimp must use. Fear and intimidation control most prostitutes, but many girls would run from this alone, so the pimp also has to provide them with something they can't find anyplace else: sexual fulfillment. He has to be the greatest stud in a whore's life, the only lover that completely satisfies her. And at all times, unless it is just a temporary working arrangement, the girl must feel she is loved by her pimp. When I was trying the game in the 50s, I was so naive I thought that simply because the girl was with me, I was the greatest stud in her life. Now I realize I had sex only to satisfy myself, and never really tried to make sure the girl had gotten the most out of it. In retrospect, I have to laugh at myself. I can't blame those girls for splitting the moment I was locked up. For what I gave them, I didn't deserve the thousand dollars for bail money.

Thanks to promiscuous little Darlene, who I had taken out of the clutches of a black pimp and rescued from a possible life as her prostitute, I had gotten one of the most important eye-openers of my life. Her affair of the afternoon told me I wasn't shit in the sack.

Now that I was about to make it with Mary, I wasn't going to be an inadequate lover. I had a point to prove to myself and I also wanted to lock Mary to me. This was going to be her party; I wanted to give her more than she could ever expect from another lover.

We kissed and embraced while removing our clothes. Instead of quickly jumping in bed, I kept control of our tempo and moved slowly, almost ceremoniously, as her blouse was removed and our lips and tongues explored each other. My lips moved over her breasts as my hands did away with her clothes, and she fumbled with the buttons on my pants. Once undressed, she wanted to move to the bed but I kept her standing with our bodies pressed close together. She was even stronger and hungrier than I was. She pulled me to the bed, wanting me in her. Instead, I slid my hand between her thighs and fingered her cunt until she begged me, "Oh, Charlie, now! Do it to me." And though I was eager to do it, I continued with my probing, squeezing and teasing until she completely left behind her sweet, innocent librarian role. Her body was doing some frantic rolling motions, as her once-gentle hands clutched me hard, trying to get me inside her. "Goddamn you, Charlie, put it in me!" she pleaded. "Do it to me now. Fuck me, please fuck me." The urgency of her body drove harder and harder into my hand, and as she climaxed I smothered her mouth with kisses. She sighed and continued a slow rolling motion against my leg and then relaxed and rested comfortably on the bed. Her eyes were closed and her face glistened with sweat. Her lips were curved in a smile that was easy to read. She opened her eyes and her smile broadened as she said, "It was good, but why didn't you put it in me?" I smiled back and said, "Because it isn't all over yet." I let her lay there for a few minutes, then suggested we take a bath.

In the tub we lathered and washed each other, dwelling longer on the sensitive areas of our bodies, playing, stimulating ourselves for more sex. When we got out of the tub, Mary quickly covered herself with a towel. I took the towel away, saying, "Look, don't be that way. Don't try to hide something beautiful. Stand up straight and be proud of your body. Here, let me dry you off." Once dry, we returned to the bed. The smell of good clean bodies was refreshing and increased our desire to go past the old dick-in dick-out sex.

Mary was not the experienced sexual partner that Darlene was, but once she overcame her self-consciousness, she was willing to try it all. And try it all we did! There isn't a thing in the book we didn't try that night, and everytime I felt her reaching her peak, I would ease off—not enough to let her lose anything, but just enough for her to get wild and frantic. After I held her there for a while, I'd do what was necessary to give her a total release.

After each one of her climaxes, and there were several, we'd lay there appreciating the contact of our bare skin.

In the beginning, Mary had been tense and reluctant to let her hands explore my body, but now as we lay there, she massaged me and caressed my testicles and penis. She talked freely about her past. I listened with very alert ears, especially when she spoke of things she had been programmed to believe were evil: sex, disrespect and the idea that there was more than one God. "Look," I said, "Here we are. We've just done everything sexual your parents and everyone else has told you is evil. Was it bad? Do you feel guilty?" She squeezed me tighter and said, "No, not a bit. I feel wonderful." About disrespect, I said, "Are those people who are demanding respect from you giving you respect? Are they accepting you as an equal? No, they're asking for what they aren't giving. Hell, respect yourself, girl. That's what life is all about. As for the one God trip, God is in everyone. Each person is his or her own God. I'm God, you're God. Believe what you want to believe and be happy."

We lay there quiet for a while until the steady motion of our exploring hands stirred us both into wanting more. I went down on her, bringing her to a peak, and then moved so that we could exchange passionate kisses. She put me inside her, and as I entered her she let out one of the most satisfying sighs I'd ever heard. Several times she was on the verge of coming, but each time, I would change my motion just enough that it didn't happen. I tantalized and teased her until she became wild, driving her body frantically against me, trying to reach the climax I was purposely delaying. I was enjoying the savagery of her lust. Even the pain of her fingernails digging into my back felt good because I knew it came from a passion I had created. When she almost screamed, "Oh God, now, Charlie, now!" we made it together, totally and completely one. Exhausted and too content to separate our bodies, we lay in our sweat, relishing our togetherness. After a few minutes, Mary

94

moved her lips closer to my ear and whispered, "Oh my God, I never knew anything could be so wonderful, so complete. I could die now, I've had my day in the sun. I love you, Charlie, I love you with all my heart." I squeezed her in my arms to acknowledge I had heard her and appreciated what she said. We fell asleep in the same position and were still in each other's arms when we awoke the next morning. [*Mary Theresa Brunner is considered the first member of the so-called Manson Family.—N. E.*]

I had meant for the night to be totally Mary's but in my desire to give her an exceptional evening I had also opened the door on a lot of things that made me feel better about myself. I felt like I had accomplished something and was just beginning to live.

When we got out of bed that morning, Mary was a different person, too. She wanted to do everything for me. She made me tea and cooked my breakfast, and before leaving for her job she asked me if I had enough money in my pockets to get me through the day. It was the first time she had indicated concern for my welfare. It was nice. She kissed me goodbye and said, "I would really like to make love before going to work, but, you little fool, you've made me too sore." We both laughed as she walked out the door.

Darlene didn't get out of bed until after Mary had left the apartment. When she did, she came walking through the room in nothing but her panties. I just looked at her and thought to myself, "You teasing little bitch, that shit isn't going to move me." She went into the bathroom and ran herself a tub of water, and once in the tub, she called, "Charlie, will you wash my back?" "Haven't got time today, baby, I got too many things on my mind," I answered back. All day, Darlene would cater to my every need. I let her do all that was convenient for me, but ignored her efforts to lure me into sex. On numerous occasions she apologized for the scene that had taken place the day before. If she realized Mary and I had made it during the night, she didn't mention it.

Some time in the afternoon I picked up my guitar and headed toward the campus. I purposely didn't get back to the apartment until pretty late, as I really didn't know how I was going to handle the situation with me and both of the girls. It was almost midnight by the time I walked in. Darlene had gone to bed and Mary was there waiting for me with open arms. Our conversation was light, but intimate. We were soon in bed together. The sex wasn't as prolonged as it had been the night before, but I made sure Mary was well satisfied before I released myself. In the morning I stayed in bed until after Mary went to work. As soon as Mary had closed the door, Darlene came into the room. She was jealous and wanted to know what was going on. I refreshed her memory as to who had made it with another first, and repeated that she didn't belong to me and I didn't belong to her. She started to cry, professing her love for me. I assured her it was all right to love me, but let me be my own person—then she could always remain her own person. A few minutes later we were locked in an embrace and exchanging kisses that led to another terrific session. This time I applied my total consideration toward Darlene. I stimulated, taunted and teased. I located all her sensitive spots and was conscious of what pleased her most. I controlled my ejection until I had brought her twice. During her second climax I came with her, and after a few minutes pause we started all over again. We were about four hours in the sack. Not all of it screwing, but talking and enjoying our nudity. During our intercourse, I brought forth all the sounds from Darlene I had heard through the door two days before. And with those sounds, there was a brighter shine in Darlene's eyes. She also, at least verbally, accepted the fact that she would be sharing me with Mary.

That evening I met Mary at the library and we walked back to the apartment together. On the way I told her I had balled Darlene again. Mary was silent for a few moments and then asked, "Does that mean you love her more than me and now you are through with me?" "No, Mary, love's got nothing to do with it. What it means is, I love you, but I don't belong to you, nor you to me. I do not love Darlene, she is just a body, a body that I like having. I've got some catching up to do, and as a matter of fact, I'd like to fuck that girl right there," as I pointed to an attractive girl passing by us. Mary said, "Wow, Charlie, I don't know if I can handle that. Are you always going to be that way?" "To tell the truth, I don't know," I said, "but it is the way I am now. For what it's worth, I do love you and would hate to think of ever losing you. That probably doesn't seem reasonable to you because of your upbringing, but if you can forget all that bullshit that has been handed down to you through the years from your parents, which they heard from their parents and so on, it's not such a big thing to live with." She said, "Charlie, you're too much. I can't say how I'm going to handle it, we'll just have to wait and see."

I had expected Mary either to kick my ass out of her apartment or give me an ultimatum like "me or Darlene." When the two of us got back to the apartment, the girls were a bit distant with each other but very polite when a word was a must. As for myself, dirty bastard though I may seem, I enjoyed every minute of the arrangement. Both girls seemed to want to please me more than the other did. So for a few days, I balled Mary at night and Darlene by day. The three of us went places together; I was proud of myself and my two girls. Mary handled it very well and never asked me to stop my thing with Darlene. Darlene, on the other hand, was constantly asking if I loved her more than Mary, if sex with her was better, and so on. She never stopped wanting to be the only girl in my life. After a couple of weeks, when I still would not place her above Mary, Darlene told me she was going home. I gave her bus money and took her to the depot. I don't think she really returned to her parents' house, but she did leave. I never heard from her again until after my arrest and conviction. She wrote and asked me if there was anything she could do. This many years later, I still get an occasional letter from her. [*She is married and has three children and is living in northern California.* —N. E.]

Neither girl was ever conscious of it, but the sexual relationships we were going through made me feel more comfortable about myself than I had ever felt before. I had learned from experience that sex is more than a stiff dick in a hot box. From beginning to end, it is a mind trip. The power of sex isn't all I learned from those girls. The two of them, from completely different backgrounds, gave me a fair glimpse of the generation that was so dominant in the 60s. While some were running from bad homes and traumatic experiences, others were leaving good homes because of their disenchantment with the restrictions of their parents' code of morality. They were all searching for a way of life that would allow them self-expression and acceptance among those they chose to be with.

And me, well, I had left prison and hit the Haight like some hungry puppy—or like a lonesome dog. I was searching for someplace and someone to belong to. But thanks to Mary and Darlene, I made one of the most rewarding discoveries of my life. I learned that a hungry puppy can get some attention and a few scraps from a nice person, but if the puppy keeps begging, pretty soon he becomes the property of that person and has to perform for every piece of meat and pat on the head he receives. It's "Sit up, stand up, roll over, speak" before getting something to eat and a comfortable place to stay. When the pup is trained, the relationship is one of master and obedient servant. Well, I'd been someone's puppy for most of my life. I'd been following and begging and losing more ground than I ever gained. For thirty-two years, or at least as long as I had been conscious, I had been playing the game all wrong. Those few days, the sex trips and the turn-around those girls did when I stopped kissing ass and came on with a different attitude, took me right out of the puppy dog syndrome.

Before the relationships with Mary and Darlene I had been hanging around the Haight and making my way with my music, but I lacked the self-confidence to leap right out and consider myself an equal. I was still somebody's bastard kid with too much of a bad background behind me to ever feel like I really belonged. After those encounters with the two girls, I became a very confident person. I was aggressive, adventurous, and felt I understood the minds of most of the kids that flooded the streets.

In 1967, Berkeley and the Haight-Ashbury district of San Francisco were havens for me and real places to learn. They provided an opportunity to mingle in and observe all kinds of culture. It was a fascinating trip, and for an ex-con it was almost unbelievable. To "red-blooded Americans" they represented dens for corrupted souls, but to me, it was like the Garden of Eden. My musical talents made me something more than a bum, and some even considered me an artist. A lot of invitations and opportunities came my way that might never have happened without my guitar. My prison background was never a factor and my prison education—the years of conniving, conning and devious ways—put me a step or two ahead of most people living in the districts.

I liked the city but I did not like a constant diet of city life. I enjoyed the trees, the open space and the adventure of traveling. I might be at Mary's or in the Haight when an urge would prompt me to hit the road. I would leave for a day, a week, or longer. I might go north to Mendocino along the coast, or seek the mountains and the beauty of the trees, or I might head south toward the beaches or the desert. Sometimes I would just plain hit the road, headed nowhere, strictly for the excitement of travel and meeting people and the challenge of the unexpected.

I hadn't been able to afford a car since my release from prison, so all my early traveling was done by hitchhiking. During that time it seemed as though most people who gave the hitchers rides were looking for adventure themselves, some deviation from their normal living habits. When the drivers asked me the stereotypical questions—"Where you headed? Where you coming from? How long you been on the road? What do you do for a living?"—what I told them depended on how I judged the person who had given me the ride. If the person was a quiet type and just doing a hiker a favor, I'd tell things pretty straight. If the person was a talker it didn't matter too much what I said, I'd just let him or her ramble on. If they showed prying curiosity about my life, I might try to impress by reeling out a string of fascinating experiences—some lies, some truths. If the driver was too smug I'd try to shock him and tell him I just got out of prison and was on my way home.

On many occasions, my destination depended on where my ride was going. It wasn't unusual for me to be heading back to Mary's apartment in Berkeley and end up in Sacramento, Reno, or some other place if the ride suggested I go along with them. If a lady or a pretty girl was giving me a ride, I might say, I'd like to go wherever you're going. Sometimes it would work and sometimes not, but what the hell—nothing ventured, nothing gained. For me, just out of the joint, everything was an adventure and I didn't want to pass up any opportunities. I was fast discovering that a gift of gab and a touch of intrigue could go a long way in getting people to pay attention to you. A lot of people were into acting out a fantasy just for the thrill of a new experience, especially with a stranger who they would never see again, and who would never be able to tell tales. I discovered that being bold, what some people might call uncouth, put me next to a lot of things I enjoyed, things which might have gone right on by if I hadn't had the gall to suggest them. That isn't to say I hit on everyone who ever gave me a ride. It isn't too difficult to tell whether the person is open to suggestions or not. For the record, I struck out a lot more than I scored. But scoring or striking out, hitching was the only means of transportation I had. And hitch I did, until a soft-hearted ride made my first set of wheels possible.

I was headed south and a heavy, bald-headed guy gave me a ride in his pickup truck. He was kind of a religious fanatic, so naturally he wanted to save my soul. By the time we got to where he had to turn off he had decided I should share dinner with him and his family. Being hungry and having no schedule to keep, I figured, what the hell, I could listen to his preaching for a while. He lived in San Jose, and I not only had dinner with him and his family, I spent the night. We discussed the Bible, said a few prayers and sang a few religious songs. I admired the piano that accompanied our singing. I left with an invitation to revisit his home any time I was in the area. More importantly, because I had admired their piano the night before, he told me the piano was mine if I wanted it. He may have thought I'd never be in the area again to claim the gift, but I very much wanted that piano. I had another reason for return-ing: he had a beautiful young daughter, and by the looks I was getting she was just as interested in me. The fellow's name was Reverend Dean Moorehouse and his daughter was Ruth Ann. Dean's house became a regular stopping place; his door was always open to me.

One time while in his neighborhood I saw a Volkswagen van. It was like seeing a girl and all of a sudden getting big eyes for her. I had to have that van. With maybe twenty-five or thirty dollars to my name, I knocked on the owner's door and began negotiating. When the discussion was over, all I had to do was deliver Dean's piano and the van was mine. Dean, true to his word, gave me the piano, and we used his pickup truck to haul it over. I drove away with my first set of wheels since my release. The van was not only transportation, it was a home on wheels that afforded me a nomadic lifestyle.

Those first weeks in my new van were among the happiest of my entire life. Mary and I fixed it up so that it was a regular little whorehouse on wheels. I don't mean broads were turning tricks in it, but it was a love pad. It was no problem to stop anywhere, with anyone, and make love for a few minutes, hours, or even days if I wanted to. I took pride in sharing it with other people who didn't have a place to sleep—sometimes just for the night, other times for as long as we enjoyed each other's company. That van gave me a way to travel, a place to sleep and a feeling of ownership.

People admired it: the fad of the times was not new and shiny things, but used and convenient items, and in the circles I traveled in, a van or a bus was the desired mode of transportation. That vehicle fit me in every way.

For the first time in my thirty-three years of life, I was current with fads and lifestyles. I wasn't a misfit, somebody's bastard child, or an ex-convict that people didn't want around. And this situation existed not only in the Haight, but all over America and other countries as well. The flower children and the hippies were accepted as part of the times. My chest was probably puffed out bigger than it was supposed to be, but damn, there was joy and excitement to just being around a whole generation of people who saw me as an equal. That little bus and what it represented had a lot to do with the excitement I felt.

Now that I had the means and style fitting the standard of the times, I had some traveling to do. There were places to see and experiences to live—that is, if I stayed within the boundaries that govern an ex-convict still under the supervision of a parole officer. But what parole officer would deny a man the opportunity to visit his mother? So with a little lie on my tongue, I told my parole officer I'd like to make a trip to Washington and visit my mom for a few days. I did have thoughts of maybe locating her, but truth is, I was more interested in revisiting some of my old convict friends who were living in the Seattle area and just traveling around. The parole officer gave me permission, so when Mary and I headed for Washington, I was totally legal.

In the summer of 1967 the highways were loaded with hitch-hikers, especially along the coast route. The beaches, the mountains and all the beauty of nature were a magnet for those people, mostly kids, who were searching for something, or simply escaping from homes where they were abused or neglected, or felt unwanted. Naturally, the coast route was the way we headed north. If you're a nature lover and appreciate the beauty of wooded mountains as they meet the shore line of a huge ocean, there is nothing like the drive up Highway One along the north coast of California. Prison walls make for a bitter, ugly world, but they also make a person really able to appreciate nature: the clean fresh air, the free-flowing rivers, the unconquerable force of ocean waves. Driving up the coast that summer, I really got caught up in thinking no one should ever be confined or controlled by other people. No one

101

should have the trees cut or the rivers dammed. I was into being free. Although not a believer in God the way a lot of people believe, I felt if there was indeed a creator of heaven and earth, that creator meant for all things to live and die in their natural state. Animals shouldn't be hunted and nature shouldn't be disturbed, even destroyed, to benefit the whims of mankind.

In Mendocino County there are three small towns, Albion, Casper, and the town of Mendocino. In decades past, Casper and Mendocino were seaport towns, supply harbors where sailing vessels and the old steam trading schooners stopped to take on supplies and wood for fuel. While the towns no longer had any sea trade, they did maintain a traditional nautical appearance, providing tourists and travelers with a glimpse of life from a previous century. Albion was a community where hunters, woodsmen and fishermen had lived in times past. In the 60s, those towns and similar communities became havens for the same kind of seekers who flooded Haight-Ashbury—except that these people were into the environment, nature, religious practices, and individualism even more than those who congregated in the Haight. Most were honest and their word was as binding as any legal contract. Some were artists who were content to use their talents for individual satisfaction, surrounded by nature and serenity. Others sought the areas for religious practices that were frowned on by conventional society. Communes and occult groups were not uncommon in the surrounding hills and beaches, but there were also those who camouflaged themselves as artists or religious searchers, using their secluded retreats to grow pot or manufacture hallucinogenic drugs.

The time I spent in those three towns and others like them while enroute to Seattle was an eye-opener, and more of a learning experience than those first few days after my release from prison and introduction to Haight-Ashbury. Mary and I picked up a lot of hitchhikers, shared a lot of meals, smoked plenty of locally grown grass, experienced the effects of mushrooms, dropped a few tabs and enjoyed a lot of sex. I got my first look at commune living, which in most cases isn't all sex orgies or domination by an individual trying to pass his beliefs off to everyone, but more usually a group wanting to live in harmony by their own standards. I don't deny the existence of communes that thrive on shared or group

102

sex—that trip initiated me to the joy of balling more than one chick at a time.

By the time we reached Seattle, we had been on the road for almost two weeks on a drive that would normally require less than twenty hours of driving time. With each passing mile, every new face, each conversation and incident along the way, I saw a world that was made for me. All my years in prison had opened my mind up to everything those kids wanted out of life. That period I spent searching to develop my mind at McNeil put me in perfect harmony with all those seekers who had broken away from society's traditional teachings. Actually, I had the sense of being a step or two ahead of some of those who were still experimenting and searching. For once in my life, I wasn't resentful of all those years in jail: the association with my many fathers and brothers in prison had groomed me for exactly the kind of world I was now living in. I had the answers for all the hang-ups and frustrations of those kids fleeing their homes. And for the most part, everything was answered by, "Be your own person, love yourself, but let go of your ego. Don't be influenced by material things. Nothing is wrong if it feels good and satisfies you. Live for now, forget yesterday and don't think too much about tomorrow. Love is for everyone, to be shared."

My philosophy was real to me and it was accepted by almost all who listened. Everything I said seemed to impress those around me. It didn't matter that I was an ex-felon, or that I could barely write my name. What mattered was that I could make those I talked to feel comfortable with themselves. My music and my words affected lots of people. Right or wrong, the fact that those people were searching and listening was a reflection on the flaws of their parents and the establishment. And this many years later, I don't see things getting any better.

One of the first guys I called when I got to Seattle wasn't an old convict friend, but a counselor who had helped me out a great deal at Mac. For an authority figure in the joint he was unusual; he wasn't caught up in playing God and had always treated me as an equal. So I thought I might tell him I appreciated his interest and help. I may have had a yen to show off some, for in addition to Mary, a couple of other girls had been riding around with us for the last few days. If he was the partying kind, he was welcome to try his luck with my two new friends. As it turned out, he wasn't into inviting me to his home, but gave me that old coffee-shop routine. When he answered the phone, I said, "Mr. Adams, this is Charlie, Charlie Manson, remember?" A short silence and then, "Oh yeah, how you doing, Charlie?—and where are you?" I told him I was in town and would like to come by and see him. He hesitated and then said, "Look, Charlie, I'm about ready to leave the house, so why don't I meet you in town, say the Greyhound Bus station, in thirty minutes?" He walked into the bus station, Mr. Clean in his shirt and tie. The girls and I, looking like hippies, set him back a step or two. It was amusing to see him ill at ease when in our past association he had always been poised and confident. We had coffee and about twenty minutes of conversation, then he said he had to leave. I remember thinking, "You smug prick, you didn't really give a shit about me. You were just playing the part to earn your paycheck."

I also had the number of a Hawaiian friend who had worked in the barber shop at Mac. "Pineapple" we called him. Pineapple had opened up a barber shop after he had gotten out and was playing things pretty straight—the biggest charge of his life was when the warden of McNeil came into his shop for a haircut. Though he wasn't free to spend a day or two with us, he was into smoking a joint and having a drink. He had eyes for balling one of the girls but time and his wife didn't allow him the opportunity. I can't knock the guy for squaring up, but between him and my former case-worker, I knew I was living the best of the different worlds. Pineapple knew what had happened with a lot of our old joint buddies and he had a permanent address, so through him I had a way to contact some guys I might want to be in touch with later.

Now that I was in Seattle I gave some thought to seeing my mother but the telephone directory came up blank. I remembered the name of the restaurant she had worked at years before, but when I went by there no one remembered her.

Because of Mary's job and my parole officer, our trip back to the Bay Area was much faster than our drive north. Also, to pacify my parole officer, I had to be thinking about something that would show a means of support. I got a couple of one-night stands in some off-beat clubs in the Tenderloin in Frisco, and with a little

104

panhandling and a dollar or two earned in dope transactions, money wasn't a big problem—other than the van and gas for it, I wasn't into material things. But what I wanted most was to get on with my music, to get recorded and shoot for the moon, and it wasn't happening in Frisco. So I explained to my parole officer that I had some studio contacts in L.A. and received permission to head south for a short period of time. I wasn't lying, for one of my Terminal Island partners had said he would open the door for me with a recording friend of his.

Mary was holding down her job, so I headed south alone. There were just as many hitchhikers, and almost as many girls thumbing as guys. Before reaching San Jose, I stopped for two girls who were headed for Santa Cruz. Santa Cruz wasn't along the route I had intended to take, but the girls were young and pretty, so what guy in his right mind wouldn't go a few miles out of his way to accommodate?

The girls, we'll call them Jane and Stella, checked out the van as soon as they got in and commented, "What a crazy pad." Seeing the guitar, they asked if I played it. I told them I was on my way to Hollywood and a recording session. Five minutes later we were as tight as lifelong friends and well on our way to being stoned on their pot. Soon Jane was driving and Stella and I were in the back getting it on. We'd been at it for about half an hour when Jane pulled the van to the side of the road and crawled in the back with us. She had her clothes off in no time and wrapped her arms around me, pulling me away from Stella. Stella wasn't ready to let me go. The struggling got good and we had an hour session that satisfied the hell out of all three of us. The big trucks going by at sixty miles an hour and rocking the little old van didn't do a thing but add movement to our love-making. The truth is, though I had thought of making it with them when I first picked the girls up, it wasn't me who made the first advance. Stella opened that door by saying, "Pot makes me horny as a motherfucker. How about you, do you think you can bring me?" The world had really changed in seven years. And a van was the only way to travel!

Unfortunately, the girls had obligations in Santa Cruz and were unable to make the trip to L.A. with me, but we made arrangements to get together at a later date.

When I got to L.A. the studio contact was out of town for a few

105

days so I didn't get to see him. To kill time I hit a few spots in Hollywood along Sunset Strip where I used to hang out in the 50s. As I walked in and out of the bars that were my old haunts when trying to make it as a pimp, I thought of Sandy and the son I had never seen. Occasionally while at Mac, I would think of her and get a little bitter. There was no bitterness now, just the thought of how nice it would be to say hello, to ask how her life was going, and to see a son I'd never laid eyes on.

After seven years not many of the old gang were still around. Perhaps it was just as well. I still had bad vibes about sitting in the county jail waiting for one of those solid partners to come up with the money. Pimps, like whores, have a short life span. I don't mean longevity, I mean remaining in one place. The police usually get on to them, and staying in one area is a sure way to end up in jail. Another reason is that a guy who lives from a broad often uses other people without repaying favors, and his friends get tired of giving. That could have been the reason no one came to my rescue when I needed the bail money in 1959.

Failing to locate anyone, I drove down to the beach cities where I was sure to find the type of people I'd met since getting out of prison. Venice was a smaller version of Haight-Ashbury: pot, acid, and people wandering in search of something. Something they wouldn't recognize if they found it. Runaways, dropouts, kicked-outs and fantasy-seekers, all in need of a friend and a direction in life.

One evening I parked the van and was walking around looking for the unexpected. Or maybe it was the expected, I'm not sure, but there she was: a young, freckled, redheaded girl sitting on a bench. I stopped several feet away and checked her out. She was shapely and about eighteen. The light red-brown freckles and long red hair seemed very appropriate for her fine features, which at the moment showed a combination of hurt, anger and sadness. In a book I once read part of, the author said I approached this par-ticular girl and used the words, "I am the God of fuck," and lured her into my van. I'd like to say that author is a fucking liar. As are a lot of other writers. But back to the girl.

I sat down a short distance from her. She gave me a glance but hardly acknowledged my presence. When I spoke, it was with con-cern. "You look like you have problems," I said. "Is there anything

106

I can do to help?" She looked at me for a moment and said, "It isn't anything that I can't handle." "Okay," I said, "if you're sure I can't help. I just thought you might need a friend." With that I got up and left. By the time I reached the corner she was right behind me, saying, "Wait, where are you going, can I come along?" The girl's name was Lynette Fromme, sometimes known as Squeaky.

We walked the streets for a while. I told her about myself and the things I was into. She shared some of her past. By the time we had walked a short way and talked a lot, she was ready and willing to head north with me. There was no immediate sex trip. With her sharp mind and sharper tongue, she was more capable of intimidating me than me her. Intimidation was never part of our relationship. When we did get around to having sex, it was because we both wanted each other.

Lyn wasn't the norm of the neglected or abused children who ran away from home. Her reasons for being on the streets alone were very similar to those that had caused my mother to leave her parents' home. Where my mom had left because of a dominating mother, Lyn was escaping from the dominance of her father. Like her dad, she was a strong-willed person and the two constantly clashed. In clashes between child and parent, the child is seldom the winner, so after finishing high school Lyn moved out of her parents' home. She was supporting herself and attending college. Then, at the request of her parents, she moved back in with them. On the day that I met her she and her father had had what she termed "a one-sided argument," he summing it up by demanding she abide by his rules or get her butt out. In need of a friend and a place to stay, at least temporarily, she had gone to her boyfriend's place, but the boyfriend was not at home. The park bench and the sad face I saw were part of a lonely, forlorn girl's dilemma.

Fate had it that I be present when her crisis was at its peak. From that day to the present, our association has been one of mutual understanding. There has never been a need for extended conversation between us. Call it vibes or mental telepathy, but a glance or movement has always seemed to provide instant and accurate communication of what we wished to say.

We lingered in the area for a few days waiting for my studio contact to return. After several calls he still wasn't around and, partly because of Lyn's urge to get on with her new life, we headed

107

back to Berkeley and Mary's apartment. Mary and Lyn became instant friends. There was no petty jealousy or competition. Having the two of them without any dissension confirmed some of the thoughts that had been going through my mind since making the trip to Washington. I wanted my own little circle.

In visiting the communes, I had thought, why shouldn't people be able to live as they choose? As long as they aren't stealing, hurting others or infringing on other lifestyles, why should they be denied their preference? Anything would be better than what existed in places like the Haight and Venice, where habit-forming drugs, crime, violence, perversion and greed now dominated what was originally good.

With Mary's place as a kind of headquarters and permanent address for the benefit of my parole officer, I was pretty free to move about as I wanted. Since I was a musician, travel and job changes were expected, so if I was in Frisco today, Mendocino tomorrow or Santa Cruz next week, my parole officer had no cause to get upset. If I wanted to travel a long way south, north or even back east, all I had to do was say I was following a lead on a job or advancing my music career. The search to find my mother was also a good reason for a lot of moving around. On each trip, short or long, I met new faces. Some became permanent companions and played heavy roles in things yet to come. Others were just acquaintances. I had some of the most fabulous experiences a person could ever dream of. That is, until maybe mid-summer of 1969. So while there are hundreds of people, and maybe even more experiences, I could mention, I'll stick pretty much to those who traveled with me when everything was fun and games and rode with me when things got evil and ugly.

Charles Manson (fourth from left, front row), perhaps seven or eight years old, at a family gathering in Kentucky.

Main building of the Indiana School for Boys in Plainfield, Indiana. Manson spent three years here, from age thirteen to sixteen, and knew it as "Painsville." (Nuel Emmons)

The dock at McNeil Island Federal Penitentiary, where Manson served five years beginning in 1961. It was here that Manson first thought of becoming a professional musician in order to escape the life of petty crime he had been leading. (Nuel Emmons)

Manson in his twenties.

Spahn's Movie Ranch, just outside of Chatsworth, California. Manson arrived there in 1968, and he and members of his circle lived there intermittently until after the Tate-LaBianca murders. (Michael Haering/*L.A. Herald Examiner*)

George Spahn, owner
of Spahn's Movie Ranch,
with Cathy Gillies.
(Michael Haering/
L.A. Herald Examiner)

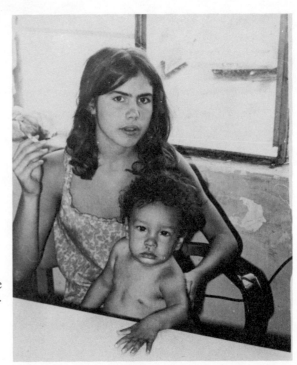

Ruth Ann Moorehouse
with her child.

August, 1970. Still able to relax at Spahn Ranch are Ginny Gentry, Catherine Share, Sue Bartlett, Danny DeCarlo, Sandra Good, Lynnette Fromme, Chuck Lovett, and Ruth Ann Moorehouse. (Michael Haering/*L.A. Herald Examiner*)

The Barker Ranch, in Panamint Valley, California (near Death Valley), which Manson envisioned as a permanent home for the group and where they fled after the Tate-LaBianca murders. (Michael Haering/*L.A. Herald Examiner*)

The area behind the 28-acre Spahn Ranch is pockmarked with small caves like this one, which the group used for protection against imagined enemies. From left: Danny DeCarlo, Catherine Share, Mary Brunner, Chuck Lovett, Ginny Gentry, Cathy Gillies, Lynnette Fromme, Sandra Good, and Ruth Ann Moorehouse. (Michael Haering/*L.A. Herald Examiner*)

Lynnette Fromme, Sandra Good, Mary Brunner, and Ruth Ann Moorehouse in a supermarket garbage bin, one of their main sources of day-old fruits and vegetables. (Michael Haering/*L.A. Herald Examiner*)

During the police raid on Spahn Ranch, initiated on suspicion of auto theft.

Some of the weapons confiscated in the raid.

December 1969: bearded, in chains, and dressed in a jail jumpsuit, Charles Manson is taken to Independence (California) Court House, as a suspect in the Tate-LaBianca murders. (Michael Haering/*L.A. Herald Examiner*)

Linda Kasabian being escorted to the Hall of Justice in Los Angeles. She was given immunity for her testimony against Manson. (Michael Haering/*L.A. Herald Examiner*)

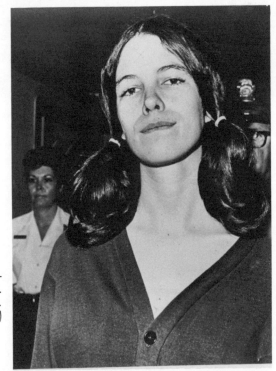

Leslie Van Houten at the Tate-LaBianca murder trial. (Michael Haering/*L.A. Herald Examiner*)

Sandra Good as she
looked in 1982.
(Nuel Emmons)

Susan Atkins at the trial with
her attorney, Richard Cab-
allero. (Michael Haering/*L.A.
Herald Examiner*)

Charles "Tex" Watson,
at the trial.
(Michael Haering/
L.A. Herald Examiner)

Bruce Davis

Susan Atkins, Ruth Ann Moorehouse, and Lynette Fromme sitting outside the court-house in Los Angeles. The "x" each etched on her forehead in imitation of Manson was a symbol of their protest against the trial. (Michael Haering/*L.A. Herald Examiner*)

The entrance at Vacaville Medical Facility (in Vacaville, California) where new inmates are admitted. Charles Manson was confined here from 1976 to 1985. (Nuel Emmons)

Manson being interviewed in 1982 for television, wearing the shirt hand-stitched for him by Squeaky Fromme and Sandra Good. (Nuel Emmons)

Manson, about 1984, with the swastika he cut on his forehead visible.
(Nuel Emmons)

Charles Manson, age 51.
(Nuel Emmons)

CHAPTER 5

MARY BRUNNER and Lynette Fromme were the beginning of what other people later referred to as "The Manson Family." Personally, I had long ago lost the desire to be any part of society's normal family atmosphere. My mother was dominated so severely by her parents that she fled into the unknown for relief, and then she only played at having a family of her own. I'd had two mates and two sons, one child never seen and the other known only as an infant. Of course, splitting up that scene had been pretty much my fault, but because of it, "family" to me was an empty word. Had it just been my experiences that soured me on the meaning of family, my views might be different, but every kid who ever stepped in my van had bad family relationships. I know too many righteous-appearing fathers who thump on their old ladies, beat their kids, play at incest, chippy with any strange broad who gives them a look, and yet thrive on the role of a family man, the king of respectability.

I see wives and mothers as a more dependable lot than fathers, but over-all, the vanity of a female, that need to be pretty, loved and accepted, wins out over being a devoted wife and understanding mother. Many, like their husbands, thrill at outside romances. For the convenience of their own pleasure, both mother and father cheat their kids out of knowing the true meaning of family. So Mary and Lyn were not "family," but the beginning of a circle of people who voiced their own opinions and played out their desires with me. That was true of anyone who entered our circle, especially those who stayed with me through the summer and fall of 1969.

At that time I didn't see myself as wanting to control anyone or be a leader. I didn't want to pull a person away from what he or she desired or enjoyed. I didn't want to save souls, nor did I want to corrupt anyone. I simply felt that if I ran across someone at a cross-

109

roads in life I could lend a helping hand. I had a need to be with people who wanted love and understanding. Because I had experienced so much shit in my life, I felt my advice could help and strengthen some of those lost children.

Where the girls were concerned, I admit wanting to make it with anything that wore skirts, but not if it meant rape. For every girl I have ever made it with, there are ten times as many I have helped without thinking about sex. As for men, it was just as important for me to do good by them, but guys have skills for survival that a lot of women don't and consequently I came into contact more often with girls.

Writers have said that all I wanted was to manipulate everyone I met. Not true! That all reflects back on the same old crap. If a guy has a bad record, nothing good he does is ever mentioned or looked for. It has been laid down that every breath of fresh air I inhaled was fuel for evil and corrupt thoughts. Hey, in 1967 when all my travels began, I had a heart crying for love. And there isn't much doubt about my craving some attention and wanting to be accepted. These are all things I had in common with the kids I met, and perhaps the total explanation of why we ended up together. I wasn't the culprit who lured them away, as everyone wants to believe. Never did I force anyone to join me, stay with me or succumb to my will. Things that were originally good and meant always to be good somehow got turned around later.

As for the rap and programming previous accounts have said I laid out, sure, I talked a lot to the kids, but mostly in answer to their questions and confusion. The only thing I had to draw on was my own past and my own version of a better way to live, which had always been to forget what you have been: Don't live in yesterday's world. Don't put too much faith in what tomorrow is supposed to bring, for it seldom happens as planned. Don't lock yourself too close to any one person, for if you do, you're sure to be hurt. If you want to share with other people, share what you have. Don't hide behind emotions and what others, such as parents, have programmed you to do. Get your head out of material things, for it only puts you in competition with greedy, power-conscious pigs. Wipe your own ass, do your own thing and ego be damned.

That wasn't something I preached on every corner, only to those who wanted to ride and linger in my van. Different strokes for different folks—a lot of people would stay for a day, a week or longer, and then be into moving on. If that was their pleasure, far be it from me to deny them the other things they sought.

However, being the center of attraction, the one everyone leans on, the advisor, the authority and the hub that turns the wheel, can sometimes have an adverse effect on a person. You see it every day among wealthy people. It often happens in charitable organizations, in religion, in those who govern, those with physical strength, and those who receive even the slightest bit of authority. Given a little taste of power, personalities often change, and someone who was once humble and righteous becomes a tyrant, so caught up in status that the original good becomes bad. Unfortunately, it happens without conscious awareness. It kind of creeps up on you, and before you know it, all that strength and power inflates the ego to the point where a person starts struttin' and thinking his shit doesn't stink. All my life I've hated those pious bastards who, because of their position in life, delight in controlling other people. And now that it's too late to set back the clock, it ain't hard to see how I got around to being everything I hated.

But back then, four or five months after my release from prison, I was living a fantasy come true. I had the feeling of being above anyone's power to ever lock me up again. Sure, the pot and pills we used were technically against the law, but they were so common, a person felt almost legal if he wasn't actually selling. Other than nailing a few under-age broads who were already giving their bodies to whoever they fancied, I kind of had the feeling of being a good samaritan because I was helping a lot of those kids on the streets. On more than a couple of occasions, if kids were down and out and had decided they would rather go back home, I took them back to their parents.

I did have a lot of association with several of my old jail-house partners, some of whom were still very heavy into guns, holdups, and anything at all to make a dollar. What they did away from me was their business—I was enough of a con not to talk about them—but when I was around I made it very clear my bag wasn't robbing or hurting anyone for the sake of a dollar. If they dug me or the girls who traveled with me, guns and all the bullshit that goes with guns were out. For the record, there is one instance when an ex-partner of mine gave me his whole arsenal, two pistols and a carbine, which I took and dumped into the bay. The guy had given them up willingly enough, but he was a little pissed that I had dumped them in the bay when they could have been sold for two or three hundred. My answer was, "Look Danny, if I'd have sold those guns, they'd have been used just like you were planning to use them."

I'm not sure if it was happening when I first hit the Haight, but as the months went by and I got deeper into what was going on there, I could see the district getting ugly and mean. One night I came out of a friend's pad on Lyon Street. I had parked the van on another street a couple of blocks away. It was a cold night and I was moving pretty fast when I rounded the corner of the street where I had parked, so fast that I almost collided with three guys beating the shit out of someone. Just as I pulled to a stop, one of the three shoved a knife in their victim's stomach. He fell to the sidewalk and didn't make another sound. I backed away and the three guys started to make a move on me. "Hey guys, I didn't see a thing. You don't need to take me out," I hurriedly said. They gave me a look, glanced at each other, and then one of them said, "Okay, split, sucker—and remember, you haven't seen anything." I turned and left—under the circumstances I didn't mind having to circle the block to get to my van.

On another occasion, Lyn, Mary and I were walking up the street, and I noticed a policeman about five yards away, behind us. Suddenly a big commotion broke out in front of us. Six guys were in some kind of hassle, yelling "motherfucker" and "you dirty bastard," when a gunshot ended all the conversation and a guy fell to the ground. Everyone started disappearing. I turned around to look for the cop just in time to see his back going around a corner. Fuck, if everything was getting so bad that even the cops didn't want to hang around long enough to do their jobs, Haight-Ashbury was no place for me and my girls. We started spending less and less time in that part of Frisco.

A few weeks after we got the van, Mary either got fired or quit her job, I'm not sure which. But with none of us holding down a steady gig, there were no strings or limitations to our travel. I had to check in with my parole officer, but he was all right and went along with most of what I told him. Somehow in the fall of '67—I think Lyn was the instigator—we ended up spending some time in a pad in Santa Barbara, a place some of the people we met in our travels turned us on to.

Santa Barbara is not all that far from L.A. and the three of us would cruise down there pretty often. On one of the trips, we went by a pad in Manhattan Beach that belonged to a guy I had done some time with. He already had a visitor, a girl of about twenty-one. She wasn't a prizewinner for beauty but, like Lyn and Mary, she had smarts, and the more I talked to her, the more she interested me. Her name was Patricia Krenwinkel, and she also lived in Manhattan Beach. Before leaving, she gave us her address with an invitation to stop by any time. "Any time" was just a few hours later.

She shared an apartment with her older sister, a hard-core heroin addict. Pat was no cherry in dope or sex, but she resented her sister's dependency and all the activity that goes on around a dope fiend's pad. Pat's trip, besides a secretarial job she didn't like, was a little pot and sex in the dark. I spent three or four days with Pat at her apartment while Lyn and Mary took care of some other things.

On the surface, Pat was full of self confidence. At one time she had been pretty deep into the Bible and believed that everything in the world was as mom and dad described it. When Pat was seventeen her parents divorced and the real world started exposing itself to her. After attending high school in L.A., she went to Mobile, Alabama, for a semester at a religious school. She wasn't into staying any longer and returned to Manhattan Beach to move in with her sister, whose activities added to her total disenchantment with what she had thought growing up was all about. From our first hours of conversation, it was easy to see she didn't believe in herself as much as she wanted others to believe.

Pat's sister was in her own little world, and even when she was home it seemed like Pat and I had the place to ourselves. We played and listened to a lot of music, stayed pretty well stoned on pot and made love. The pot and the music were a natural stimulant for passion, but when it came time to undress she had to have the lights out and be under the covers. I was sensitive to her inhibitions and began things her way. Pat had hang-ups about her body, which was actually a very good body but, in her eyes, covered with too much hair.

I wanted to tear down those things that stopped her from liking

113

herself, so I was extra tender and careful. Sex can be a little bit of everything. It can be low-key and tender, or sensual and violent. There are those who delight in a certain amount of pain, and there are those who, if hurt, lose the edge of a climax. On this first night with Pat I wanted more than a sex trip, I wanted to free her mind of those hang-ups as well. Nothing was hurried. I didn't come on hungrily and savagely, and I was totally conscious of what my movement and words brought forth from her. We spent five hours in conversation, sex and complete fulfillment. Before we went to sleep, Pat put her head in my lap and cried, telling me, "Charlie, you've given me a new world. Anything you do has to be right. Take me with you wherever you go."

That was the last time I ever saw Pat cry, and her self confidence became more than skin deep. She left Manhattan Beach with Mary, Lyn and me in the little van. She didn't even stick around long enough to pick up her last paycheck or sell her car.

In the next few weeks we just about wore the van out. Between four people—sometimes more—living inside it and all the miles we traveled, it was an amazing vehicle. Thank you Dean Moorehouse.

I gave a lot to the girls in the way of attention and conversation. Just three or four months earlier the talk would have been bogus convict bullshit, but the more I got into laying it out and realizing all that I was saying, the more I saw it working. And the girls were giving me as much as I was giving them—not just passion trips, but new thoughts about life. The four of us had so much harmony and love, the words became honest and real to us all. We shared more than simply doing things together. We looked at things through the same eyes, thought as one, lived as one. We were all one.

I had a lot of pride in those girls, and to say I didn't want to show off because of our togetherness would be a lie. So, speaking honestly, some of the traveling we did was not to see a new place or a search for an experience, but to show off my good fortune, and maybe make some of my old partners envious of me. With all my talk about getting rid of the ego, I guess I couldn't live by all I preached. The desire to put myself where I knew a lot of other guys wanted to be never did cease to exist in me.

From Manhattan Beach, the four of us headed north. We stopped

114

in Santa Barbara long enough to gather any gear we had at the house, and then went on to Frisco to spend a few days dropping in on different people around the Haight. We went on a few acid trips and partied a lot. It is amazing the amount of attention one guy and three girls pick up when they enter a place. A guy alone with car trouble can sit on the side of the road for a week and nobody will stop and give a hand, but let there be a girl and you get plenty of help. With three girls, people are so anxious to stop and give you a hand that they have wrecks. Walking down a street or going into a party, restaurant, or nightclub, you immediately get some attention. And in the right spots, if you can play a little music and the girls join in, the party becomes yours. With things shaping up as they were, the party was mine everywhere we traveled.

From Frisco, we took the coast route up through Mendocino, Eureka, Oregon and into Washington state. For money, we'd cut a few weeds, mow some lawns, wash a few dishes or haul someone's garbage off to the dump. That is, if we got desperate we'd take those routes. For the most part, playing music in a park or on a street corner provided pretty well for us. If we got really desperate, Pat still had her dad's gas credit card. In the areas where grass was being cultivated and pills being manufactured, the growers and manufacturers were pretty generous. Sometimes, for a couple of hours of music, we'd not only leave with enough grass and pills for a few weeks, but all the connections needed to score any time we wanted. It wasn't unusual for one connection to open the door for us further on up the road.

It was on this particular trip that we first met Bruce Davis. Bruce was from Louisiana, had a couple years of college behind him and had come west a year or two prior to our meeting to live it up with the hippie generation. He was about twenty-five or -six, and he'd done jail time. Nothing like the time I had done, but enough to relate to some of my past. He'd had a passing interest in Scientology and was a good musician. I liked his company. The girls had become so much a part of me, talking to them was like talking to myself, so though he didn't travel with us all the time, it was nice to have another guy around when he did.

Five people traveling in the van was no problem, but when you consider the five of us had all our worldly possessions tucked away, tied on the roof or hanging from any available space, things got pretty crowded. Using that vehicle for a home was like five people trying to set up housekeeping in a phone booth. During the summer traveling up and down the coast in California had been comfortable enough because if too many bodies were around, the weather permitted sleeping outside. But up there in Oregon and Washington, things got damp and uncomfortable in the fall. So we headed back south.

There were some guys I wanted to look up in Nevada, so instead of taking the coast route we traveled inland. When we got the Reno area, I headed for Mustang Ranch, hoping to locate an old prison buddy. Mustang Ranch was one of Nevada's legal whorehouses. When I got there, it wasn't a house at all, but several large mobile homes assembled in a love pad spacious enough to accommodate rooms for at least twenty girls. The fees started at twenty dollars and quickly rose to five hundred depending on the pleasures and time wanted by the customer. The parking lot was open, but a cyclone fence with an electric gate kept out unannounced guests. Passage beyond the gate was controlled by an inside switch, permitting only those who had been observed by the madam or house man. Naturally I went in alone. Once inside, all the girls that weren't active at the moment were called into the lounge for my review, and there were some way-out girls for selection. Five or six months earlier, I might have emptied my pockets and sold all my possessions just to get lost between the legs of some of those girls; now the whole scene was amusing, and I was enjoying the fact I wasn't one of the needy customers. "No, no," I told the madam, "I got a whole world of girls out there, I just came by to see a friend." The madam sent the girls back to their rooms and told me my friend wasn't around.

I spent a few days around Carson City looking for old pals and earning a few dollars. I sat in on some poker games, testing my old skill as a joint card shark, and got lucky without having to cheat. We left Nevada with a lot more money than when we had arrived.

Back in California, just outside Sacramento, we saw the answer to our cooped-up existence in the van. With some skillful negotiating, some dollars from Carson City, and the owner's pleasure in eyeballing the girls, we traded our little van for a spacious school bus. Sacramento was a hang-out for a lot of the people we knew from the Haight, so we had a lot of places to fall out while we converted our school bus into a home.

A friend of mine was also living in Sacramento. Besides being a jail-house acquaintance, he had been a friend and working partner when I was trying to make it as a pimp in the late 50s. He was one of those guys I looked up to in the joint, and even when we were working together on the outside I was inclined to follow his advice. He used to tell me: "To your face, everyone is your friend, but if you really want to test a guy's character, turn your back on him for a few minutes around your old lady. If he don't try to fuck her, he is a pretty tight friend. But if the guy tries to make it with the girl the minute you turn your back or get locked up, cut the guy loose. He ain't no friend." For all my friend's advice, every time I turned my back on him or got locked up, he was one of the first to try nailing one of my broads. But I liked the bogus son-of-a-bitch and enjoyed his company. There was added enjoyment when I dropped in on him with those young pretty girls. When he saw how they busted their asses to make me comfortable, he made no bones about wishing he was in my shoes. He kissed my ass to get closer to the girls, and my head may have grown a little bigger because of it.

Living in the bus was like going from a one-room cabin to a mansion. It was our house, our studio, our love pad, as well as our transportation. It soon became one of the most popular vehicles along the coast. Everyplace we stopped, someone wanted to join us. Countless people had experiences in that bus they will remember as long as they live. Freedom, love, and music were our thing, and understanding—each always willing to honor the feelings and thoughts of others—tightened our circle.

My music reflected the happiness of our lives. Everything was coming together. With that thought in mind, I remembered the studio contact who'd been out of town when I was in L.A. I again tried contacting him. When things are going good, it seems like more good things fall into place. He accepted my call and said: "Sure, come on down, we'll give a listen and if there's something there we can set up a session."

I told my P.O. what was happening and he made the arrangements for parole supervision to be transferred to southern California. Before heading south we spent a few more days around the Haight, and Susan Atkins came into the picture. I was in one of those old houses in the Haight where it was constant party time. Normally, it was the type of place where people are in and out between acid trips and loud music, but on that particular day the activity was at a minimum. Several people were sitting around a room, smoking good, mellow grass. I was playing the guitar and singing. The door to the hallway was open and from time to time people from other rooms would stop at the open door or come inside to listen. Susan, who later became Sadie to all of us, was one of those uninvited but welcome guests. After I put away my guitar and all the other people were gone, Susan introduced herself to me, saying how much she loved listening to my music. I politely thanked her and the conversation continued. A few minutes later we were up in her room making love. The scene with Susan wasn't finesse and persuasion, but a battle of the bodies to see who was the strongest and the more talented of the two. I wasn't about to let no broad out-do me, so I gave her all she wanted and more. Her big thing was to be on top, not just in position, but in rhythm and control. She wanted to dominate and she was an exciting challenge, but when it was all over she was as limp as a rag, whispering, "Charlie, Charlie, Charlie, oh my God."

In the course of our earlier talk, I had mentioned I was heading south for a recording session. Before I left the bedroom, Susan had asked to come along. She brought two of her girlfriends, Barbara and Ella. Both were pretty girls and just as game for anything as Susan was.

As we started for L.A., the mansion on wheels was getting smaller. Bodies and possessions were everywhere, but there always seemed to be room for one more. And the particular "one more" I wanted was the preacher's daughter, young, innocent Ruth Ann Moorehouse.

Shortly after I traded Dean's piano for the van, I had lured Ruth Ann into visiting Mendocino with me. There she provided me with perhaps the most memorable and rewarding experience of my life. While the whole scene may seem gross and immoral to some readers, I have never felt anything but gratified for taking a gift that was denied me in my youth.

To be in Mendocino with me, Ruth Ann had to run away from

118

home. So we decided I would say goodbye to her and her folks, she would stick around the house for another day and then meet me at a place not too far from her home. That done, we drove to Mendocino. During the trip to the coast, we were very much like father and daughter, she full of curiosity and questions about life and everything she saw, me answering and explaining. At the coast she got a big thrill out of running barefoot along the beach, and I thrilled at watching her. I admired the beauty of her body and her youthful energy as she chased the out-going waves.

When she tired of her play along the beach, it was natural to go inside the van to dry off and relax. On entering the van, the father-daughter relationship became one of boy and girl, youthful lovers out for their first experience with sex. You can resent my making that statement, but at that moment the significance of what was about to happen erased the difference in our ages. I was as young as Ruth Ann, and the act was even more meaningful to me.

I didn't push any grass or pills on her. I wasn't forceful or demanding. Once inside the van, I put my arms around her and kissed her lightly on the lips. She responded with equal affection. We exchanged kisses and embraces with mutual emotion. I treated her like the most delicate flower on earth. My love and desire for her was expressed with all the sincerity in my possession. She didn't struggle against my kisses or my hand at her breast, nor did she pull away when my hand slipped inside her panties. All her responses indicated she wanted me as much as I wanted her. When I started to remove her panties, she made the slightest effort to escape and said, "But my daddy . . ." Before she could say more, I whispered, "Forget your daddy. I'm your daddy. Doesn't this feel too good to be wrong?" She let me remove the panties and the rest of her clothing and lay there watching me as I removed mine. We went back to the soft passionate kisses, my hands exploring her body.

I can't say what was going through her mind, but I felt like I was sixteen and she was my first girl. She had been a cherry, and for that instant I was a virgin who had just made love for the first time. We kept going until both of us thrilled in one of life's greatest pleasures.

It hadn't been dirty or forced but simple, clean and beautiful. At thirty-two years of age, after a marriage, many girl friends, and

119

countless sex encounters, that thirty minutes of passion in the arms of a fourteen-year-old girl put me a little bit closer to liking a world I had hated since the very early years of my life. Some might think I should feel shame, but I didn't then and I don't now. None! You sent me all those children in the 60s who went through hell with me, yet she is the only one I took from you.

While we were at Mendocino, Ruth Ann's parents had reported her as a runaway. The police picked her up and in an effort to dissuade them, I got booked for interfering with an arrest. Dean and his wife came to get their daughter and I was put on the good preacher's "don't come around" list. But when a guy wants something, he doesn't follow all the rules. When I thought about moving permanently to L.A., I realized I wasn't above looking into the mouth of the lion if there was a possibility of stealing away the young cub. Besides, I wanted to show Dean what his gift of the piano had transformed into.

When we arrived in San Jose, the preacher's welcome wasn't warm and inviting, but the good reverend soon saw the bus full of kids as a captive audience to whom he could pass on the Holy Word. With a full congregation before him, Dean went into his spiel. Pat, Mary, Lyn and Susan were well-versed in the Bible, so Dean's preaching was not falling on unschooled ears, but those girls had their own ideas about Biblical concepts and they had Dean's head spinning. They provided counter-opinions to everything he said, and the poor man couldn't afford to make even the slightest misquote, or one of the girls was sure to call him on it. But Dean revelled in the challenge. As he tried to convert the people who rode in the bus, I took advantage of his ignoring his immediate family and whispered our plans to Ruth Ann.

At the time, I'd have liked nothing better than to tell Ruth Ann to get her things ready and leave with us, which is what she wanted to do, but she was still just fourteen and already on probation for running away. Taking her with us would have been inviting police trouble. Instead, I told her, "We're going to southern California, so we won't be seeing you for a while." She broke into tears and said she wanted to leave with us now. Until she was older, or the situation different in her home, I explained, there wasn't any way she could go without creating a lot of problems for me and the others.

120

Lyn also spent some time comforting Ruth Ann. In the process Lyn had told her: "Right now, you're so young that almost anything your parents tell you is law, but if you married someone your parents wouldn't be able to tell you what to do. Anything you decided after that would be up to you."

A few weeks after we left, Ruth Ann married a bus driver and became her own person. Shortly after the marriage, she left him and joined us in L.A.

Though we had pulled out of San Jose without the reverend's daughter, we'd no sooner gotten to southern California than up pops Dean Moorehouse. How he found us is still a mystery to me, but I guess a black school bus full of girls isn't the hardest thing in the world to trace.

We had stopped at a friend's acid pad. I was pretty stoned and enjoying a trip. All of a sudden there was Dean and another guy with something that looked more like a cannon than an ordinary pistol pointed straight at my head. Dean's friend aimed the gun while and the red-faced, raging preacher told me what a rotten, child-raping bastard I was. It seems that after we left San Jose, Ruth Ann couldn't dry her tears. Her father asked why she was crying, and was told: "Daddy, I love Charlie. We made love together and I want to be with him." Dean overlooked the "we made love" and came after me like I had beat the girl and raped her.

His threats sounded anything but religious. Dean wanted some ass, and I think if I'd seen him coming, I'd have found some place to hide. Talk is what I wanted, not an argument with that pistol. As calmly as I could, I had one of the girls get Dean and his friend a soft drink while I listened to him rant and rave about what a low-life I was. He threatened police, castration and beating my ass to a pulp. His temper finally seemed to subside and when he reached an almost normal tone of voice, I said, "Look, Dean, this is between the two of us. Why don't you have your friend put his gun away and go for a walk so you and I can straighten our problem out?" Dean nodded his head in approval, so his friend put away the gun and left the house. I handed the preacher a tab of acid and said, "Here, this'll keep your blood pressure down." He paused, gave the pill a blank look and downed it with a sip of Coke. Then he continued telling me what my life was going to be like when I got to hell. As the acid started taking effect, I started talking. "Look, Rever-

121

end, it ain't like I did something nasty to your little girl. I only did what goes through your mind every time you look at a pretty girl. Now you're a preacher, so you know it's just as evil to lust for something as to do it. Hey, I only did what you would like to do. And you can't blame me or that girl. If you'd spend more time paying attention to your family and doing what you preach to everyone else, that girl wouldn't be looking for some way to get out of your house. Man, don't you see, with all your religious convictions, you're not giving your daughter a chance to live her own life. Kids grow up fast these days. They got to have space. Space that ain't smothered by parents who are locked into yesterday . . ."

By now the acid was sending Dean into a world he'd never seen. I wasn't sure how he was going to react, but for the moment I felt I had escaped violence. Not to press my luck, I suggested he get in his friend's car and head for home. He left without further argument. And though he came looking for me weeks later, it wasn't for his daughter's sake, but for more acid to join a world he had always preached against.

Several weeks before we decided to come south, I had met a lady in Frisco. She was a trippy broad, about forty-five years old, who experimented with everything. When I met her, she was pumped up about devil worship and other satanic activities. I didn't attend a lot of the places she invited me to, but we often discussed the good and bad sides of different beliefs. As a result of our acquaintance, she had given me a standing invitation to visit her home in Topanga Canyon. I was in L.A. waiting for some action on a recording session. We needed a place to park the bus for a while, so we went looking for her house. Taking Topanga Canyon Boulevard, we came to a two-story house with a peculiar winding staircase, which one of the girls quickly dubbed the "Spiral Staircase."

I don't know much about the history of the place, but long before we arrived there, it had become a meeting place, a party house, a freak-out pad, and for some, a hideout. Its isolated location served a lot of purposes for a lot of different people and, like the lady who owned the place, some far-out, spaced-out, weird people were frequent visitors.

The day we first drove up, we were innocent children in comparison to some of those we saw during our visits there. In looking back, I think I can honestly say our philosophy—fun and games,

122

love and sex, peaceful friendship for everyone—began changing into the madness that eventually engulfed us in that house.

It was a kind of "house of transition." Those who lived in the mountain communes, practicing things that would not be tolerated in the cities, would use the house as a place where they could shed their commune attire for more acceptable city clothes. Not only did they change clothes, they took on new personalities as they went into the cities to do business, recruit followers, or simply re-live what they had originally left. The mixture of people, the variety of beliefs and practices and the assortment of drugs would have shaded any of the parties in Haight-Ashbury.

On the other side of the coin, there were those who lived in the city and walked the straight and narrow by day—people with beautiful faces or charming personalities, people who made great contributions to society. They came in the dark of night, visiting the Spiral Staircase to indulge in what they preached against by day. There were nationally respected celebrities, a prominent sports figure or two, some of the influential and wealthy, and on occasion, some who wore the cloth and preached the word of God. It was a strange house, but one to learn in; a place where mental sickness and mass confusion were the best one could expect.

Normally, I am a person who picks up on vibes. Acquaintances, decisions, the songs I write and the music I play are all reflections of the vibes I feel. Though I was welcomed to the house by hearty hugs, good music, and passionate kisses, I had bad vibes about being there and staying longer. Yet I stayed. And though I would often leave in the weeks to come, I would also return.

Each time I returned, I would observe and listen to all of the practices and rituals of the different groups that visited the place. I'm not into sacrificing some animal or drinking its blood to get a better charge out of sex. Nor am I into chaining someone and whipping them to get my kicks like some of those people were. Still, through the drugs and listening to the ways a particular leader or guru maneuvered his people, some of their rap may have become embedded in my subconscious. Planting fear in their people is the way a lot of leaders keep control. At the time, love and doing our own thing was what held us together and that's the way I wanted everything to be, but at a later date, the things I was exposed to at the Staircase may have come back to me.

To those who live within society's moral code, the house might have resembled a movie scene of a massive party at a dope fiend's pad: music playing, often blaring, sometimes soft and sensual; strobe lights blinking, or hardly any light at all; guys and girls everywhere, seated on couches, chairs and pillows, on the floors and on the beds; marijuana joints being passed around; tables showing long lines of coke; pills and capsules of all colors, each providing a different high; long-haired, bearded guys in weird clothes with exaggerated lengths of gold and beaded chains; scantily-clad girls, obviously drugged, willing to have sex . . . If the movie switches scenes at this point, it has only scratched the surface of the parties at the house in Topanga Canyon. Needless to say, when Charlie Manson arrived with a dozen young, pretty girls, all eager to experiment and play, I was an immediate favorite.

The girls and I entered the house as a group, and as a group we maneuvered through the crowded rooms, pausing here and there to listen to a word or introduce ourselves to those who indicated they would like to be friends. Some did and some didn't, depending on what state of mind a drug had left them in. There were one or two familiar faces and they quickly approached me, mostly for introductions to some of the dozen girls who were always near. Once we had toured the entire house, understanding and accepting all that was going on, some of the girls, with my nod of approval, began sampling the drugs, sticking mostly to LSD.

Earlier, the lady of the house had handed me a small vial filled with pills, saying, "Welcome, Charlie, here are some special treats for you and your friends." So with four of the girls still at my side, I found an area on the floor where we could all sit. Rather ceremoniously, we formed a circle and sat with our legs crossed in Indian fashion. I handed each of the girls an LSD tab, and like Indians passing a peace pipe, we shared a Coke to down the pills. It was potent stuff. In a matter of minutes, the five of us were drifting off in separate worlds.

Acid, depending on quality and amount taken, is not always a pleasant trip, but it does always provide a hallucination that goes far beyond the realm of everyday thinking, surpassing the most vivid of imaginations. Among other things, acid can reach into the subconscious to bring forth the experience of deeply-smothered

124

thoughts, long-forgotten dreams, real or imagined incidents that happened long ago.

To illustrate what I mean, I'll backtrack to the days when I was at the Gibault School for Boys. One stormy night, a day or so after I'd had a visit from my mother, I was going through one of the loneliest periods of my life. Lying there in bed, my sorrow and self-pity were so strong I couldn't help but cry. To keep the boys who slept on either side from hearing me, I got up and moved to a window some distance from the nearest bed. I looked out the window into a dark rainy night. I stood there for a while crying, wishing for a life different from the one I was living. The more I thought and wished, the more I cried. Finally I knelt and prayed to God with the strongest emotion possible for a boy of twelve. My prayer may have seemed selfish because every word was for myself. Not for riches and other things a kid might pray for—I asked that someone love me enough to need me.

My prayer finished, I stayed at the window watching the rain beat against the glass and wondering if there really was a God up there, and if so, whether he heard me. Thunder sounded and a flash of lightning brightened the sky. I pressed my face closer to the window just as another flash lit the sky, and on the other side of the glass I saw a vision of Jesus. He said no words, just gave me a slight smile and an encouraging nod of his head. I went back to bed with a secret and my face was dry of tears. By morning I was not sure if my vision was just a dream or if I really had stood at the window. Perhaps it was just the strong imagination of a boy who wanted things to be different. Not wishing to be looked on as a nut, or laughed at as a fool, I have seldom mentioned that night, but for the longest time, I knew something good was going to happen for me. When weeks, months and years went by with nothing improving in my life and no love, I ceased to think of that night at all.

The vision came back to me at the Spiral Staircase. I had often taken the acid route and was familiar with the valued awakening of senses that allows a view of a world that begins where this one ends. I had in the past felt vibrations of cosmic force and revelled in psychic phenomena, yet the trip I was about to undergo would give me the deepest penetration into awareness, extra-sensory per-

ception, confrontations with devils, travels in divinity and association with multiple deities I had ever encountered.

I was a boy and at the same window. I was no longer kneeling,
but standing next to a man in a long white robe. His was not the
face of Jesus in my vision, but the atmosphere seemed holy. Our
feet touched nothing but air. His hand was on my shoulder and he
did not speak, but deep amplified echoes voiced a message as
though out of the skies: "Now, Charles, these are your loves and
you are their need." The message rang in my ears, and the words
vibrated through every pore of my skin, giving my body an
awareness of what was registering in my mind. Still suspended in
air, I looked out over a sea of faces, faces full of love and trust,
faces looking at me. The words faded and the robed man drifted
away. And as he did I was no longer a boy but a man, and myself in
a white robe.

The vision left me. I glanced at my clothing and there was no
robe. I searched for the sea of faces, but saw only four girls with
glazed eyes on trips of their own. All of us were still sitting Indian-
style in a room of people just as spaced out as we were.

I realized the image had been nothing but a trippy result of the
acid, yet, as I looked around the room, all the faces were open
books. I could enter their minds or bodies if I chose to. Seated
across the room much like some Buddha, a giant of a man had not
taken his eyes off the girls or me since we had taken our positions.
He stared with contempt and anger. Why, I didn't know. I resented
his stare, and as my thoughts registered the resentment a staggering couple on their way to another room overturned a heavy floor
lamp, putting a gash in the man's head. I smiled and looked away,
feeling very much as though I had delivered the blow.

Sadie was in the doorway between rooms dancing topless. The
doorway gave her the attention of people in two different rooms,
the one where the music was being played and the one we were in.
It was the closest thing to center stage that Sadie could find. When
my eyes first focused on her, she had had her back to me, but as
though I had called her name, she turned, paused in her routine,
and gave me a questioning look. I smiled and nodded my head as
though approving, and she resumed her dancing, trying to be the
most seductive girl alive.

The four girls and I sat there in a world of our own, communicating without the use of words. I felt a twinge of thirst; Lyn, without speaking or being spoken to, went to the kitchen and returned with a glass of water. I drank my fill and Mary started to rise and return the glass, all in silence. My thoughts were: "Mary, you are carrying my child, so relax and let Pat return the glass." Mary relaxed and remained sitting on the floor. Pat reached for and returned the glass. I leaned forward and placed my hand on Mary's stomach. Mary had become pregnant by me in the early months of the time we had spent in northern California. Beneath my hand her skin was transparent and through her flesh my eyes saw the five-month foetus that was clearly a male child.

The experiences and perceptions that seemed to be achieved through the use of acid made it and other mental stimulants a very substantial part of our lives. While being under the influence, certain things became so pronounced and real that I couldn't help but believe in them long after the drug had worn off.

With the abundance and variety of drugs available in the Spiral Staircase, time was never a factor. Of course, if you were one of those "straight-by-day" types you had to hurry home in time to reappear as a model citizen, but time had no relevance for the rest of us, who were not pretending and lived in the full swing of the lifestyle we had adopted. If your pleasure was to continue a high that was starting to subside, a move to the nearest container provided all that was needed to keep the high intact.

That first party was one of the very few times I allowed myself to get so wasted that I lost a handle on what was happening or even whether it was day or night. At some point—it could have been the same night or next night—I found myself sitting alone in the bus. I was sweaty and on the funky side so I filled a pan with water and gave myself a whore's bath, using a large white beach towel to dry myself. Clean and dry with the towel draped around my shoulders, I was running a comb through my hair when a topless, barefoot Sadie entered the door of the bus. She hesitated and looked at me and the towel covering most of my body. Her feet were dirty, and the pan was still full of water, so I said, "Here, let me wash those dirty feet." And I did. Directly behind Sadie was a guy, also shirtless and barefoot; I'm sure Sadie had him in tow for sex. After I washed Sadie's feet she turned and washed the feet of her friend. Sadie later spoke of that scene as some kind of religious

127

experience for her. She has insisted: "Charlie was dressed in a white robe, and I had so much love for him, I thought he was Jesus." Except maybe in jest, no one else ever said that shit. If a white towel, some very dirty feet and some words from a dope-taking, ding-a-ling broad can lead a bunch of people into believing a guy is some kind of God, I feel there are a lot of people in this world who are crazier than most would like to believe I am.

If privacy was what Sadie and her friend were looking for, I wasn't going to take it away from them. I left the bus and started back, but I had taken only a few steps when several of the girls came from the house. They had some new acquaintances with them. All quickly turned me around, and back in the bus we went. Twelve girls and five guys add up to an uneven seventeen, but we were without conscience or inhibition and full of drugs, defiance and curiosity about the challenging thrill of sex. We didn't have any problems at all.

The balling, partying, oral-copulating, heterosexual, homosexual, masturbating orgy that occurred in the bus that night was not initiated or programmed by me. I won't deny that for some of the girls I was instrumental in erasing the previous inhibitions that at one time would have prevented them from engaging in such a scene, but I did not originate that one. In fact, to me it was like a red light flashing, like, "Hey, stop! Things are getting out of hand here." Without some kind of control, pretty soon I'd find myself standing in the middle of the road watching the ass end of the bus getting farther and farther away from me. I had to start using more discretion, at least when we were in someone else's territory.

Jealousy is a hell of a thing, and I ain't going to cop to ever being jealous of any of those kids. Individually, they could always go any route they chose, but as a group we couldn't pull up to some pad and be used. Though the orgy had included only four who were not part of our group, I saw that there would be more outsiders next time if things didn't tighten up some. Pretty soon the girls would become victims of more than just being sex objects. If outsiders moved in so easily for sex, they could just as easily start maneuvering some of the girls into heavier shit—like chains, whips, blood-drinking, animal death and even human sacrifice. It was a hard-core multiple-devil worshipping bunch of people who passed through the doors of the Spiral Staircase. I had picked those girls up from the streets because they were looking for something. I didn't want any of those self-styled priests, priestesses and gurus using the kids or me. So when those early changes started happening in our lives, I took charge. It wasn't that I was trying to play leader—I had a feeling of responsibility. I wanted them to love and to be free to go on, just as I wanted my own life to continue as it had been for the last several months. At that time, not in a million years could I have been convinced that things would turn out bloody and bad.

CHAPTER 6

I THINK by now it is obvious that being shy isn't part of my makeup. I do come on pretty strong, but boldness and aggressiveness is sometimes just an effort to hide fear, weakness and doubt. And while I am reluctant to cop to it, the fact I'd been out of the joint for seven months and hadn't made a move to kick off my dream of making it in the music world suggests I wasn't as loaded with confidence as I pretended. I believed in my talent and ability, but knowing how hard it is to break the ice, I'd been living with the fear that a hasty recording session might close a door on me before I really got started. Then too, in past years, I'd had my burns and disappointments when I put too much faith in a convict's word. So though I was pretty good friends in prison with the guy who provided the Universal contact, I was halfway afraid he was blowing smoke when he said he could introduce me to a guy who would arrange a recording session. I thought his friend might not be anything more than some clerk or glorified messenger boy.

Still, I had come to L.A. on the strength of that phone call. As it turned out, the contact was a man big enough at Universal to have his own clerk and several messenger boys. The first meeting with him wasn't a session, but more to get acquainted. I was impressed by his position at the studio, and by the time he heard me play some music, he was so impressed with me he arranged for a full-fledged recording session. The recording date was set up for two days down the road. In the meantime, he wanted to know all about me, my lifestyle and all the things I was into. It was astonishing to him that I was living in a bus with twelve girls. Right away he wanted to know what my hold over them was. "No hold," I assured him, "we're just a few people who happened to hook up and each of us is our own person. The girls do what they want to do and so do I. It just happens they dig looking out for me, and for the

130

good they do me, I return an equal good. If you're interested in meeting them and seeing for yourself how we live, you're welcome to visit with us."

The Universal guy was interested, but rather than have him see the things that went on at the Spiral Staircase, I scheduled things so that I could come by the studio and pick him up. Because I wanted things to be smooth, I thought of postponing the day's meeting until I could put myself and the girls in more impressive surroundings. But, "Fuck it," I thought, "this is me and this is the way I'm living." When I parked across the street from Universal the following day, the exterior of the bus, though scrubbed and clean, was still a pretty seedy sight. I paid very close attention to his reaction when he saw our home on wheels, and when he displayed an amused smile, I was glad I had chosen to stay with things as they were. Once inside, the amused smile was replaced by a look of amazement. With Lyn at the helm, the crew of girls had broken their asses cleaning and decorating the interior. And their game at impressing someone was just beginning.

With the burning incense, the hanging tapestry, and the wall-to-wall sleeping and living arrangement neatly in order, the living area looked like something out of the *Arabian Nights*. For an added touch, eight pretty girls—some had been left elsewhere—had placed themselves in comfortable and enticing positions. When I started introducing them to my new friend, I was amazed at their poise and cordiality. As soon as we sat down, one placed a cold beverage in our hands while another brought out hors d'oeuvres. I was handed a lit cigarette. One girl massaged my neck and shoulders while two others got out my guitar and carefully polished it before returning it to the case and placing it in an overhead compartment. The way they catered to me, I was afraid they were overdoing their little act. The attention given to us made it seem as though man was king and woman his servant, and the effect on our guest was great. He spent considerable time with us, and by the end of the recording session he really thought I had the right hold on life.

After the recording session, our new-found supporter thought we could get something on the market immediately, but he was not the final voice. Others at Universal thought more work and arranging was needed before recording for the market. I was not disap-

131

pointed, since my initial session had shown a lot of promise and there was a standing offer from Universal for another shot when I "rounded things out more solid." I was also introduced to a lot of the bigwigs at Universal, and as a result of our conversations about my religious beliefs, philosophy of life and outlook on the future, I was offered the opportunity to act as a technical advisor on a religious film they were thinking about producing.

I associated with a lot of celebrities, whose names, for their sake, I will keep to myself. I can't pull the covers off anyone who hasn't been associated with me in previous writings, but I do wonder why more of my associations with some of Hollywood's elite didn't surface. In that respect I think we are back to society's old double-standard bullshit. Some people, regardless of how dirty their hands are, have the juice to smother things and appear lily white, while those without juice are made to look dirty if they are only in the vicinity of bad happenings. I could authenticate experiences with some of those in Hollywood that would make the sexual practices I enjoyed look pure and innocent.

For a period of time, I had the run of Universal. Naturally, when possible, I shared some of that with the girls. Before too long, Charlie, his way of life and his girls were on the let's-get-acquainted list of many of the not-so-straight idols of the movie world. We were invited to private parties in Beverly Hills, Malibu and other exclusive areas. A lot of the movie people shot up heroin, smoked opium, free-based and snorted cocaine. As much as the girls and I were into the hallucinogenics and marijuana, hard, habit-forming drugs were not our thing. We had long ago chucked our inhibitions about sex, but chains, whips, torture and other weirdness were not part of our routine. Until mixing with the movie set, performances were not us either.

One guy at Universal (I'll call him Mr. B) latched on to me shortly after I first showed up around the lot. It was no secret that I was an ex-con, and all he wanted to talk about was the sex available in confinement. Not being a dummy, I just flat asked him, "What is it you want, a dick in your ass or in your mouth?" He wanted both, so after that I visited his dressing room on a regular basis. That was long before the gays came out of the closet—everything was still hush-hush.

But it didn't end there. One day he said, "Charlie, will you come by the house tonight? I want you to meet my wife." Sure, I told him, how many girls do you want me to bring? "No, no girls. Come alone," he replied. I'm game for almost anything, so showing up alone was no problem. When I got there I was introduced to his wife, who had been in a couple of minor roles on television. She was a pretty brunette, thirty-five or forty, and very shapely. He was dressed in a pair of satin pajamas and she was in a sexy transparent pink nightgown. In the beginning the two of them were nervous and conversation was tense, but by the time we smoked some very potent grass and drank some wine we were relaxed and horny. She and I were on the couch and he was sitting in a chair watching us. She had her tongue in my ear and was unbuttoning my shirt, so it was a natural move on my part to place my hand between her thighs. She began removing my pants. I really expected Mr. B to come over and start giving me some head, which I didn't want to happen because I wanted the broad. To my joy, B remained in his chair with his hand on his own dick and Mrs. B and I got it on. She did most of the maneuvering and I was just along for the ride—after all it was their party. The only noise in the room had been Mr. B's sighs and grunts, but at the peak of orgasm, Mrs. B broke the silence by saying, "Bite me, bite me." Since I was in her from behind I couldn't reach her neck or shoulders, so I bit her a couple of times on the back. They weren't skin-breaking bites, but they were hard enough for her to get the sensation she wanted, and left teeth prints that would last a few days. After a few minutes she rolled us over and I was on top of her. It was time for B to make his move, and he did. Now, taking it in the ass ain't my thing. I told about getting raped when in Plainfield; well, ain't no dicks been in my ass since. When B made his move, I thought I was going to have to bring this party to an end, but instead of trying to nail me, he started licking Mrs. B's toes and legs and working his way up to us. When she and I made it he pushed me aside and buried his face in her crotch and jacked himself off. I got a lot of satisfaction out of making it with a TV actress while her movie-star husband got his rocks off and a lot of laughs thinking how long their fan clubs would last if our little scene could be aired. As I walked out the door, B slipped five one-hundred dollar bills in my pocket. It was a scene we repeated several times with a few different twists before my stay at Universal ended.

133

The film I was consulting on had to do with the Second Coming of Christ. On occasion, I would have rap sessions with a couple of writers. I'd lay out how I interpreted the Bible, where I thought the world was headed, my belief in reincarnation, and what I thought would balance out the world. The writers would take a lot of notes and then bury themselves in structuring the material into a movie script. Sometimes we would meet once or twice a week and then maybe not at all for several weeks.

With that type of schedule, the bus and anyone who cared to come along did a lot of roaming around, but we always seemed to return to the Spiral Staircase. My bad vibes about the place never did leave me, but the challenge of arguing philosophies and beliefs with those who visited the place kept bringing me back. It was also a testing station for me. Those leaders of communes and occult groups and rich bastards from the city all had eyes for my girls. Their efforts to lure my people away from me allowed me to see where the love and loyalty was. When not one girl ever left me to join one of those groups, I started to realize the strength of our togetherness. Other people started noticing it too, and we often left with more people than we had when we arrived.

Dianne Lake was the first. Dianne, who we later called Snake, was a pretty fourteen-year-old who had been living with her parents in a commune up in the hills called the Hog Farm. With her, it wasn't a question of escaping from abusive or stern and restrictive parents, nor was it sex, for in their communal lifestyle at the Hog Farm, Dianne had seen a lot. She had her parents' consent to make a trip into the desert with us, and after spending some time traveling in the bus she did not want to return to her previous life.

Bobby Beausoleil was a handsome twenty-year-old who, due to fast living, was far from being a kid. He'd been on his own for several years. A great musician, he had been involved with the movie industry and he always managed to be living with more than one girl at a time. He and I had a lot in common. Though he didn't travel with us immediately, he eventually became very much a part of our circle, and it was through him that Cathy (Gypsy) Share, Leslie Van Houten, Gary Hinman, Kitty Lutesinger and a few more became part of our group.

The first day Bobby showed up at the Spiral Staircase, I thought I saw too much vanity and conceit in his make up to ever like him,

134

but when I heard him play his guitar and sing, I had a lot of respect for his ability. The two of us could jam and improvise in perfect harmony, always anticipating the other's moves. Universal had mentioned the need for more accompaniment and background to my music, so, if for no other reason than to get together to play music, I got Bobby's address. He and one of his girl friends were staying with Gary Hinman, and it was through Bobby that I met Gary.

After a lot of traveling, we finally shook the Spiral Staircase and came up with a place of our own. We needed it! Twenty people traveling in a bus can be an adventure, and although the bus gave us a fair amount of comfort, even a gypsy needs some kind of head-quarters. You can live without fresh hot and cold running water, electricity, a shitter that you can fart in without everyone looking at you and the other conveniences of a house, but goddamn, it's nice to stretch out every once in a while. The place we moved into was not all that far from the Staircase. It was more an oversized cabin than a full-size home, but since our sleeping arrangements were mostly mattresses on the floor, there was plenty of room for all of us.

On occasion we would catch some overflow from the Staircase or friends, but unlike the Spiral Staircase, we weren't open to everyone for extended visits. If someone knocked and we liked them, fine, but if not, there was no invitation to stay.

One night, like most nights, we were sitting on the front room floor talking and playing music. A warm glowing fire in the fireplace furnished both heat and light. The girls, pretty little nymphs that they were, were either nude or very scantily clad because of the comfortable warmth of the fire. A knock on the door brought Brenda (Nancy Pitman, a girl who had just recently joined us) to her feet. At the door was a small kid, about seventeen or eighteen, who was looking for the fellow who used to rent the house. When he saw Brenda's bare breast he did a little stuttering before his words were intelligible. She asked him in, and when he saw the rest of the girls, he didn't have the presence of mind to formulate speech. I was amused as he tried not to be obvious in checking out asses and tits. "Uh, uh, I, I, I was looking for Jay. Uh, uh, he used to live here," he finally managed to say. To help the kid relax I asked his name and then introduced him to all those in the room.

135

His name was Paul Watkins but we called him Little Paul. He had been on the road for several years and said he had visited several communes, but the way he couldn't take his eyes off the nude bodies, I wasn't sure he'd ever seen a girl in the raw before. His interest and ogling made him human and I was enjoying his efforts at trying to be a cool cat, so I asked if he wanted to sit down and join us. He did, and with a little nod of my head, Brenda and Snake motioned for him to sit between them. They passed him a joint and before long he was as high as the rest of us. I think he was in more of a fantasy land than he had ever dreamed possible. The grass took effect, the rhythm and lyrics of good music started us toward sensuality, and he found himself with two girls caressing him and removing his clothes. He spent the night and left the next morning, but returned a couple of months later. At first a part of our circle, he later became a Judas.

My association with Universal eventually ended with nothing accomplished. My second recording session never materialized, nor did the Second Coming of Christ flick get off the ground. The writers and potential producer came up with the idea of having Christ, in his Second Coming, be a black man. I couldn't buy that concept, so my juice at the studios went the way of the flick—shit canned.

There was a time or two while working with the writers at Universal when I envisioned myself as a talent capable of handing out enough material to make a first-class movie, one so successful it might give me some recognition and enough dollars that I didn't have to be constantly on the hustle. When our disagreement severed the relationship, I had a taste of disappointment. To console myself I reasoned, "Fuck 'em, who needs them? I'm not into all that material bullshit anyway." So we uprooted and hit the road for a while.

As far back as 1955, when I was driving the stolen 1951 Mercury along Route 66 and passed through the Mojave Desert for the first time, the spacious, sparsely populated land there had moved me. On recent trips with the girls, I had felt the urge to see more of the desert than could be seen from the main highways, but so far I had only seen it as everyone else does, from the most traveled route. In the spring of 1968, I began making trips to areas of the desert seldom seen by tourists, little towns like Shoshone, Tecopa, Panamint Springs and others so small they don't rate an acknowledg-

136

ment on most maps. The smaller the town, the more earthy and likable were the people who lived there. Even more to my liking, we could get so far off the beaten path that we were seeing places only visited by property owners, prospectors or some recluse seeking escape from people, laws and protocol. I was a long way from being a recluse, for certain parts of my make up demand I have someone around me, but I did want to escape the laws and protocol. I thought the desert was the place to start establishing some permanent roots. If more of those who shared the bus with me had appreciated the desert as much as I did, we would have moved there long before we did. However, at that time, most of the kids saw the desert as being too desolate, and too far from some of the pleasures they still enjoyed. So instead of immediately settling anywhere, we continued to roam around, calling the bus our home. For a break from the constant travel, we would sometimes spend a week or two in a friend's home. On some occasions we simply moved into an unoccupied house without the consent of the owner. Surprisingly, some of those stays would last several weeks before we were told by owner or police to get our asses out of there.

On April 1, 1968, Mary gave birth to our son Valentine Michael Manson. Her hospital bed was a mattress on the floor of a shack we were staying at in Topanga Canyon. I played doctor in delivery, cutting and tying the umbilical cord. The girls, now fifteen in number, were her nurses. I was proud of "Pooh Bear," as we called him, being the product of my loins, and he was the center of attraction and joy of our group. We thought he should be raised without the traditional mother-father set-up. We would all share responsibility for him. He would be spared the hang-ups usually handed down from parent to child, allowing him to grow without being subjected to narrow, one-sided opinions. He could achieve manhood with love and understanding. His head would not be full of doubt, nor would his nature be warped by complexes instilled by selfish, dominating parents. He would know love of heart and freedom of mind denied most living humans. And we in turn would learn from our child who did not know hate, jealousy, greed or ego.

Having a newborn baby in our midst did not alter our lifestyle. If there was a change, it was that Pooh Bear gave us all the opportunity to express and practice the opposite of the flaws the kids

137

saw in their parents. As a group, the kids felt parents and society smothered them, used them and denied them. They felt parents and society in general sometimes meant well, but were too caught up in their own lives to inspire their children properly. Pooh Bear and other infants in our circle would have it better. We all felt we were contributing to a personality who would eventually make for a better world.

Pooh Bear traveled everywhere the black bus went, with fifteen or twenty people looking out for him. On one occasion he was the cause of an arrest in Ventura County. We had parked the bus and set up camp in a wooded area. Sheriff's officers came by and hassled us. They booked me and a couple of the girls for having false identification cards. Mary was booked for breastfeeding her twenty-day-old child in public. The traveling and partying we did had accustomed us to being hassled by the police, but normally a few smiles from the girls would have the cops telling us to play it cool and travel on down the road. That day, the girls weren't into smiling and the word "pig" was tossed around, so when one of the cops saw Mary's bare boob in Pooh Bear's mouth, he came up with some law that prohibits such a thing and Mary was booked along with the rest of us.

Our numbers were growing so fast that the bus became too crowded for comfort. When people aren't comfortable, dispositions turn sour and trivial incidents become cause for major arguments—especially with a bunch of headstrong young females. Truth is, there were times when I wanted to revert back to the good old comfortable days when it was just Mary, Lyn, Pat and I, but every time I thought about who should go, I'd find a reason for having that person around. The answer was to get a place large enough for all of us, one that was off the beaten path so that city people and the law weren't in our faces all the time. The desert still looked good to me. It was looking better to some of those who didn't care for it in the beginning, but there were still those among us who didn't like the thought of desert living.

Sandra Good provided the answer. Sandy was one of the latest additions to our group, the picture of what most poor kids dream of, a pretty college coed who at twenty-three had the world by the ass. In San Francisco, she was part of the social set. Wealthy, divorced parents gave her everything she asked for—that is, everything but genuine love and companionship. Despite the material things she could have for the asking, she was searching for a chance to belong. She had flown down from Frisco just for a night of excitement and some friends brought her to our house.

The night she visited us, I remember her as being more than a little stuck on herself. She was dressed in slacks and a blouse that came out of the most recent fashion magazine, and her earrings and jewelry went with the make-up on her face. She was a beauty more suited to some plush restaurant than the floor of the shack we occupied.

The surroundings weren't the most comfortable for her. Without her knowing, I spent a great deal of the night watching her and observing her reaction to what went on. The rest of the girls were in jeans, body shirts, or loose fitting blouses, no make-up and only a ring or two for jewelry. As I played the guitar and sang I watched her attempt to remove her earrings and make-up without attracting attention. She looked at the other girls to see how they wore their hair, and inconspicuously ran her hands through her own hair so that it would fall naturally, like the rest of the girls. I thought to myself, "She may be stuck on herself, but she isn't above wanting to be like those she is with."

We whiled away the hours playing music and smoking dope and others would occasionally leave the room to go to the bathroom. Sandy did not move, but as more time passed, I watched with amusement as she squirmed, held her breath and did everything else that might relieve bladder stress. Finally, I handed my guitar to Bruce and let him play while I took Sandy by the hand and walked her to the bathroom. "Here, honey," I told her, "it's flattering you like my music, but no one should sit it out so long as to wet their pants." I got one of the most relieved and grateful looks I've ever seen. When she came out of the bathroom, we didn't return to the room where the music was being played but went for a walk. The walk resulted in some conversation, a lot of sex and our getting to know each other. Sandy dropped out of all her social circles and became one of us. One of the strongest! And through an acquaintance of hers staying at the Spahn Ranch, we found an open door that eventually allowed us to locate there.

Spahn Movie Ranch is located just above Chatsworth, California in the Simi Hills. Though only a thirty-minute drive from the

139

heart of Hollywood, you leave the hustle and bustle of city living far behind when you drop off the freeway onto the ranch property. In addition to two main ranch buildings and miles of land where movie-land cowboys, outlaws and Indians played out dramas of the Old West, there was a mock-up of an old western town. Along a boardwalk were buildings designed to be the saloons, cafés, hotels and jails of the horse-riding, gun-slinging days of the wild and woolly west. Over the rise from the make-believe town were some old outlaw shacks where rustlers and black-garbed villains fought losing battles against the sheriff's posse or the hero of the film. Seeing the place for the first time, and realizing its potential for accommodating our needs, I thought, "This is it, this is where we belong."

The place was owned by George Spahn, a worldly man in his eighties who could sit for days spinning yarns about his association with those western movie legends of the past: Will Rogers, Tom Mix, Hopalong Cassidy (William Boyd), Roy Rogers and Gene Autrey fell from his tongue so easily that you had to believe George's friendships with them were as strong and real as life itself. I'm sure that during the era George spoke of, his ranch was in great demand by the movie industry, but like George himself, age and time had created a lot of changes. He now owned fifty or sixty riding horses and all the tack needed for customers who came for a day in the saddle. The ranch and the make-believe western town were nothing more than background and conversation pieces for those renting the horses and were badly in need of repair. To maintain the corral and stables and care for the horses, there were six or seven guys around who listed their place of employment as the Spahn Movie Ranch, including Shorty Shea, Juan Flynn, John Swartz and Steve Grogan.

Near-blindness kept George from moving around very far from the front porch of his ranch house, so he wasn't always on top of what went on any distance from the house. But despite his blindness and lack of mobility, old George was a long way from being anybody's fool. And he wasn't senile. He was still a pretty shrewd horse trader, and knew and understood people better than a lot of those who make their living analyzing others.

My original visit to Spahn Ranch had two purposes, to check the place out, and to find Sandy's friend who lived there working as a

140

mechanic. Because the bus needed some repairs, I went out to see what he could do in the way of fixing it. The guy spent a couple of days working on the bus and I had plenty of time to wander around the ranch and meet some of the people who lived there. The more I saw of the place, the more it appealed to me. Though close to a freeway, it was secluded and private, and near enough to the city that we could still bounce in and out for any music connections I might come up with, or if some of the kids just wanted to be around the bright lights.

The particular dwelling that was most suited to our numbers was the main ranch house; not the one George lived in, but one some distance from George's place and the western movie set. At the time some hippie guy named Kaplan, his family and several others were living in the place. Kaplan seemed to be pretty well established around the ranch and was in the good graces of old George, so maneuvering him and his group away from the place I desired was out of the question. At least temporarily.

Sandy's friend finally got the bus in running condition and I left Spahn's without approaching George about letting us move in—I knew I'd be back. Several days later I was on George's front porch giving him my best pitch on why he should let us locate on his ranch. I had two of the girls with me, primed to play friendly but innocent roles. When I drove into the ranch yard (not in the bus but a borrowed car), George was sitting on the front porch. About four stairs led up to the porch level, at the bottom of which I stopped and said, "Mr. Spahn, I'm Charles Manson and I'd like to talk to you about renting some space on your property." Old George replied, "Well, son, we can talk about it, but you'll have to come closer, I'm as blind as a bat. Can't see a damned thing, but that don't stop my talking or thinking. Step right up here and let's hear what you got in mind."

The girls and I stepped up on the porch, and George raised himself out of his chair and offered his hand in greeting. Behind his thick, tinted glasses, I could see eyes that were open and moved like normal eyes, but instead of moving his hand toward mine for a customary handshake, he just lifted his hand in the general direction of my voice. I moved my hand to his for the introduction, and as I introduced each of the girls, he faced their voices and waited for their hands to locate his. I thought he wasn't as blind as he

141

pretended when he placed his left hand on their shoulders, giving each girl an intimate squeeze as he shook with his right. I thought that this cagey old bastard used his bad eyesight as an excuse to cop feels, among other things. But later incidents proved George was almost as blind as he said he was. After a few words of conversation with each of the girls, George got back to me. "Okay, son, what can this old cowboy do for you?" "Well, sir," I said in my friendliest voice, "I'm a musician and for the moment me and four or five others in my group are living in a bus that has been converted into a traveling home. We need a place, a permanent place we can call home. Thing is, right now we haven't much money, but all of us are willing to do some work around your ranch to balance out for a place to stay. The girls could clean your house and cook for you and us guys could do whatever needs being done around your property." "Well now," he said, "I got a cook. Pearl comes around and does my vittles and cleans the house. But maybe she'd like to take a breather once in a while. I got some hired hands that look after my horses, but maybe they could use some help in keeping the place up. Where did you have in mind staying?" "Well, the big ranch house is more to our needs, but I notice someone is living in it. If they should happen to move on, I'd like to work something out with you on that house." "Now, son, Kap and his people have been here a while, so if I was you, I wouldn't be counting on that house. Got two old rustlers' shacks over the hill, but they ain't got conveniences. A body would have to rough it livin' in them." "Hey, Mr. Spahn, we're use to roughing it. For now those places would be fine, and we'll sure please you with our work," I replied. "Call me George, son. We'll talk about the chores after you get situated."

I hadn't been honest with George about our numbers, but I figured we'd be out of sight of the ranch house and he wouldn't realize how many of us were around. The old shacks gave us privacy and a foot in the door. With a little time, old George's obvious interest in the girls could be catered to sufficiently so that by the time the full number of people were brought to his attention, he'd be appreciating us too much to want to send us down the road. And if we played our cards right, it wouldn't be too long before we would be living in the main ranch house.

The next day, with Pooh Bear and eighteen others—four guys

142

and fourteen girls—a dozen of whom lay out of sight on the floor of the bus, I quietly drove past the main ranch house and parked the bus next to one of the old rustler shacks. The girls, enthusiastic about a place to spread out, quickly got to work with soap, water and scrub brushes. By evening the shacks were spick and span and very livable. A nearby spring, candles, lanterns, a wood stove and an outdoor john gave us all the conveniences needed.

Not wanting to overplay my hand with George and his hospitality immediately, I explained to the kids George wasn't aware that our group was as large as it was, so for a while, everyone was to stay close to our area and not be exploring or making our numbers obvious.

My deceit lasted about three days. The first ranch hand that got over our way saw all the young girls and quickly spread the word to his partners that there was "a whole canyon full of young pretty girls over by the outlaw shacks." By day four, the outlaw shacks were the most popular area around the ranch. But it was just for looking; no touching. I'd made it clear to the girls to play it tight instead of loose, but that didn't stop the cowboys from looking and wanting. As far as old George being upset, Lyn and Sandy had already spent some time cleaning his house and giving him plenty of attention, so when I told him that there were a few kids around who were just passing through and wouldn't be staying too long he didn't object. With the deceit bared, I felt a lot more comfortable, actually more comfortable than I had felt in several weeks. The surroundings and atmosphere were relaxing. We had a place where everyone could do their own thing, with or without the group. We not only had space to live, but a place to grow—and grow we did! At one count, more than thirty-five people who were later called part of the Manson Family lived there at Spahn Ranch, and many times that number passed through. Those first months at the ranch held some kind of magic. Love, togetherness and fulfilling each other's needs bonded us as one. True, our lives were everything parents and society preached against, but that was the reason those kids were there in the first place. The dope, the sex and all the avenues we traveled were nothing more than rebellion against a world that preached one thing but failed to provide an example of it. The whole trip in the 60s—all the protests, the drop-outs, the runaways, the flower children, the hippies, the drug addicts, and yes, the murdering outlaws—was the product of a society that spoke lies and denied their children something or someone to respect. And unfortunately, society remains the same.

There was a time, along with the hate I felt for a world that had shit on me, I hated myself for not being able to live by the rules of society. But the deeper I became involved with those kids, the more I hated the world they came from. And the more I hated the world that had driven them from their homes—the world I had come from—the more I began to like myself. I started believing I had some of the right answers in my head. But believe me, none of the answers that filled my head included murder!

Previous writings have portrayed me as the dominant force behind all of the wrongs that went on while we were living at Spahn Ranch. Although I don't deny responsibility for the majority of the things that did result from our life and beliefs at Spahn, I'd like to make it clear that when twenty people are living together in a sharing situation, one individual's thoughts and games wear out and other members contribute. Not all the thoughts and games played at Spahn and in our travels were mine.

Eighteen of us and a newborn baby moved onto the Spahn Ranch property. The only perfect person among us was the infant Pooh Bear. The rest of us had our quirks, good sides and bad sides, individual thoughts, dreams and imaginations. Living in movieland's make-believe, we began to play-act at making those thoughts, dreams and imaginings become real, if only for the hour or two we spent pretending the cameras were focused on us. If Sandy, Mary or any of the other girls wanted to play at being the Queen of Sheba, Holy Mary, or Tempest Storm, we all played characters to fit their whim. If one of the guys, including myself, had a desire to come on as King Richard, Pancho Villa, Lucifer, Elvis the Pelvis, or Jesus Christ (which may have been my favorite role), everyone joined the cast. Pretending occupied our time and our minds and, aided by some dope, the play-acting became so real that sometimes long after the scenes were over, the feeling of really having been that person lingered so strong it became real life.

The main ranch house we wanted eventually became ours as did the dwellings that made up the movie set. With so much space at our convenience, and without the police in our face every time we farted, some way-out things began happening there. The place be-

144

came a mecca, a natural oasis for people who wanted to let their hair down and chuck their inhibitions. There were so many people and so many experiences that it would be impossible, or at least a life-long effort, to write them all down.

Not all of our activities were that pleasing to old George. There were a lot of ups and downs, but we managed to live on the ranch from the spring of 1968 until the roof fell in on us in late 1969. The length of our stay there can be attributed more to George's fondness for the young girls than from my conning. He was especially attached to Lyn, dubbing her "Squeaky." It has been said I planted Lyn in George's house for my own ulterior motives, but that isn't so. Lyn thought George would be more comfortable with a younger and more capable person, so she became a steady cook, housekeeper and companion to him. In assigning herself to that role she was perhaps selecting one of the more comfortable living conditions around the ranch. She could also keep me posted on what went on between George and others who might have resented some of our activities and our living at the ranch. If, as some have said, she slept with George to further enhance our position there at Spahn, that was her desire and her business. Not mine! Still, because Lyn had initiated it, and because having someone around George was to our benefit, I saw to it that one of the other girls filled in when Lyn wanted a break or had the urge to travel.

In addition to the work the girls did around the house for George, the rest of us did anything we could in the way of keeping the place repaired. We shoveled a lot of horse shit, groomed some of the horses and on George's busier days we helped all we could with his customers. For the most part, those labors paid George for allowing us to live on his property. There was no fixed rent, but when we had money, we gave some of it to George.

For all the space and pleasures at the ranch, I would still have the urge to travel. Something inside me was always gnawing at me to look over the next hill, check around the next corner, look into the other guy's game or just spread myself out so that I didn't miss anything. Sometimes, in getting away, I would be just like those people who came through the Staircase and made their changes. I'd put on another face and hang around the city for a while. Or, with yet a different face, I'd head over to Las Vegas or back up to north-

145

ern California. I'd go alone, or with just one or two of the girls, or maybe with just one of the guys. Often, even if I left the ranch with someone, I might send them back alone, or I might just get out of the vehicle we were in with a "see you later," and go searching for the unexpected. On these excursions, it was like going with the wind. I didn't know, or wasn't concerned about where I would end up. Sometimes I'd get involved with a bunch of bikers, sometimes with some religious nuts, surfers, hobos, actors or musicians. And if I liked any of them, I'd tell them to look me up later at Spahn Ranch. Some I'd see again, some I never laid eyes on since.

It was on one of those impromptu trips that I first met Dennis Wilson, the drummer for the Beach Boys. I had stopped by a friend's house in San Francisco to replenish my supply of grass. When I started out of the place, another guy was on his way in. My friend kept me from leaving, saying, "Hey, Charlie, you two ought to meet. You're both into music. Dennis, this is Charlie Manson, he sings and plays the guitar. Charlie, say hello to Dennis Wilson of the Beach Boys."

It goes without saying I was glad to meet someone who was on top of it in the recording world, so instead of leaving, the three of us sat down and did a joint together. When I left I had Dennis' address and an invitation to stop by when I was in L.A.. I left a similar invitation with him.

Shortly after that particular trip I stopped by the address on Sunset Boulevard that Dennis had given me. Christ, the place was a mansion. On about three acres of land with a swimming pool, servants' quarters and the whole works, it was the ultimate display of money and success. Prior to visiting Dennis' house, I was well aware of the Beach Boys' popularity and achievements, so of course I respected their capabilities. But now I was standing in the middle of all the riches and power that can result from just being able to write and play music. I envied the son-of-a-gun. Not for the material things that surrounded me, but for the recognition and status that allowed a person to live in such surroundings.

When Dennis asked me in, I simply gave the interior of the house a casual glance. As impressed as I might have been, I wasn't about to seem ga-ga over his possessions. However, when he took me on a tour of the place and we reached the room where his equipment—drums, mikes and speakers—was set up, I was so im-

146

pressed I couldn't help but compliment him on the room and all the goodies it held. The room was almost a complete studio and anyone into music and a place for good sounds had to be appreciative.

Dennis was a hell of a guy. For all his success and wealth, he still enjoyed the simpler things in life. Sure, he put on airs and played the role of a Hollywood success story. He'd make appearances and play whatever part the occasion demanded, but inside he was a rebel and had long ago tired of catering to the whims of a public who wanted him to be the "All-American Boy." He still loved his music, but he tried to escape from the demands of his agents, the travel and the appearances, every chance he got. He wasn't looking for a way out, just time and space to let his hair down and be out of the public eye. He was the dream of ninety-nine percent of American youth, but he was just as lost, just as wanting, just as in search of something as those kids with me. So it was kind of natural Dennis and the rest of us hooked up.

Dennis opened the doors of his house to us, and as much as his business agents would let him, he opened his pockets. Others have painted pictures of us moving in on Dennis like a bunch of vultures. We never did move in. Some of us stayed there for days at a time, but always with an invitation. He also spent some time out at the ranch with us. He liked his booze, grass and cocaine. Acid was a sometime thing with him, but girls were a constant desire. As a celebrity in the music and movie industry, he could have girls of all ages, shapes and sizes just for the asking. But in the circles he traveled in, most wanted possession and marriage. The girls with me wanted neither from Dennis. So for all the good he gave and shared with us, we gave and shared with him. He was no fool and was his own person when accepting or giving. He gave what he wanted and took what he wanted.

The good times with Dennis lasted for well over a year. In that time he and I worked on several songs together, two of which made it onto an album the Beach Boys recorded. He even gave me some gold records that had been presented to him. Along with the music, there were always parties and gatherings that saw two different worlds coming together: the rich Hollywood set from one part of Dennis' life, and us, with no material values, from the nonconforming side of his life. Through Dennis and some of those gatherings, I met a lot of people with solid connections, including Terry Melcher, Gregg Jakobson and several others who liked my music enough to want to record and market me and my material.

Dennis himself thought I was some kind of wizard when it came to playing and writing music. Next to him, the guy who was most impressed was Jakobson. Jakobson was a little bit of everything around the music scene: talent scout, agent, sometime producer and promoter. He was almost as interested in my talent as Dennis, but he was also attracted to our way of living. In addition to wanting to do my songs for tapes and records, he had plans of filming us. He was fascinated by the spontaneous episodes of our life, the love, the togetherness and the ingenuity we had for survival with or without the dollars most people depended on. He wanted to do a documentary film on us in our natural surroundings with music as the main focal point.

Terry Melcher is the son of Doris Day and head of a recording studio. More than anyone else, he had it in his hand to pick us up and put us in the music world. He did give us a little attention, a lot more than was brought out during the trials and in other books that have been written. He and Jakobson arranged for a couple of recording sessions and, in looking back, I guess the girls and I blew it. Melcher and the people who were doing the session had their ideas of how they wanted the recording done, the girls and I had our idea. We clashed, and nothing was accomplished, but that relationship lasted right up until August of 1969.

As long as I was still trying to get into a music career, Melcher and Dennis and Jakobson were people I liked being around. When things were really desperate out at the ranch and some money was needed, Melcher was a touch. For the prosecuting attorney to say I sent those kids after Melcher is total bullshit. Why would I? He gave me money, lent us his car and credit card. Melcher was all right and I had no bad feelings for him.

Among the people who were not celebrities I met while visiting Dennis was Charles (Tex) Watson. Originally from Texas, he'd been in California for a couple of years and hadn't made much out of his venture to the Golden State. Most reports on Watson overlook his activities in California before he became associated with me. The two years he spent using drugs and pushing dope, burning everyone he came into contact with is forgotten. What has mostly

148

been established is that, prior to meeting me, he was the pride of Copeville, Texas: an exceptional student, ace athlete and perfect picture of the All-American Boy. But for the moment, that's neither here nor there. How we met is more to the point.

Considering Dennis Wilson had a mansion on Sunset Boulevard, owned a Rolls Royce and a Jaguar and was one of the better known celebrities in the area, it seems a little absurd that he would be hitchhiking. But, as I said earlier, Dennis was kind of a rebel. So, as it happened, both his cars were laid up, and instead of taking a cab or calling someone for a ride, he was thumbing it home from wherever he had been. Watson, driving an ancient 1935 Dodge pickup, stopped for the hitchhiker and got the reward of his life when he found out it was Dennis Wilson of the Beach Boys. When they got to the house, Wilson, always gracious, asked Watson to come in for a while. Several of us from the ranch were in the front room playing music. (Dean Moorehouse, who had shown up several weeks earlier and had been given a job around Dennis' home also happened to be there.) There was some grass and hash around so naturally Watson was welcome to join us in singing and smoking. Hours later he left with Dennis' invitation to visit anytime he wanted. After that, we saw a lot of Watson. Before meeting us, his popularity among his old friends was on a downhill slide because of drug burns and a habit of never paying his bills. A few weeks later he couldn't pay his rent and was facing eviction, and Dennis allowed him to move into the mansion. The guy was such a freeloader that pretty soon even the big-hearted Dennis sent him packing. Not too long after Dennis cut him loose, he showed up at the ranch, broke and hungry, with nowhere else to turn.

By mid-1968 almost all the cast of characters with the exception of Kitty Lutesinger, Linda Kasabian, Leslie Van Houten and Stephanie Schram, were living at Spahn Ranch. And by now, because of some marijuana busts and other minor charges, the police had visited us a time or two. Some reporter covering the scene elected to refer to us as the "Manson Family," so that is how we were known to the world.

At the ranch were Paul Watkins, T.J. Walleman, Brooks Poston, Bruce Davis, Tex Watson, Bobby Beausoleil (sometimes), Mary Brunner, Lynette Fromme, Pat Krenwinkel, Nancy Pitman (Brenda), Sandra Good, Cathy Gillies, Ruth Ann Moorehouse, Dianne Lake, Steven Grogan, Susan Atkins (Sadie), Juan Flynn and maybe ten or twelve others who didn't share in the publicity. We were thirty or more people, kids mostly, really without reason or purpose. I had dreams and expectations of making it in the music world, which I felt confident would begin materializing in just a few more weeks. But my individual goals didn't give purpose to the whole group. So what we had was a bunch of kids loaded with energy and a lot of spirit, but totally without goals for the future.

My rap had always been, "Yesterday is dead, there is no tomorrow, only now!" Now is the most important time in anyone's life. But I was discovering that to be content with now, you have to have a vision, a plan, or at least a hint of what tomorrow might bring. For myself, and maybe one or two of the others, the anticipation of a future in music gave me direction. But I realized that some goals for the future had to be established to keep the kids happy. For the moment I didn't have the answer. But, even if I had to fabricate a meaningful tomorrow, I felt I would come up with an agreeable direction for all their energies.

In the meantime we continued the make-believe games, music, drugs and making love. Our eating habits were pretty well controlled by what some of the nearby markets discarded from their shelves and produce bins. We didn't eat meat, so that eliminated the most expensive part of the grocery bill. If we had someone near a garbage bin in the early morning hours when markets receive their shipments, we could get slightly bruised fresh vegetables and other produce only slightly older than what a customer buys over the counter. And if two or three bra-less, short-skirted girls are going through a garbage bin, a male produce clerk can put some surprising things in the bin for them. Bakeries also have a problem with merchandise going stale, and the girls fast became the best non-paying customers for day-old goods. Beverages, rice, noodles, potatoes and seasonings are about all we ever had to purchase, and we ate as well as most people did.

In the mornings and throughout the day, each individual was pretty much on his or her own as far as eating was concerned, but for the main evening meal, it was get-together time. We had discussions, with input from everyone. Suggestions, plans, and desires would be openly expressed. If it was at all feasible, the rest of us would try to see to it that every suggestion was acknowledged and

150

every desire fulfilled. It was during these rap sessions that the true feelings and character surfaced the plainest, since seldom, at this time of day, was anyone under the influence of drugs. All thoughts and words were presented and considered with a clear mind. From these conversations came things like: "Charlie, I think we should spread our love all over the world." "I liked living in Mendocino better than here." "I'd like to check some things out in England." "When are we going on another long trip in the bus?" "Tell us about the time you lived with the Indians in Mexico." "Squeaky, can old George still get a hard-on?" "You know, if my mom and dad didn't fight so much, I'd still be living at home." "Hey, you know what would be a gas? If we could put enough LSD in the city's drinking water to turn the whole city on. Wouldn't it be fun to see the whole town freaked out?" "Sadie thinks she's got the clap. If she does, that means the rest of us are going to be coming down with it. And if that happens, I'm going to kick her face in."

Sometimes the kids were so honest arguments would ensue. Sadie did in fact have the clap and she did get shoved around by some of the girls, but she claimed she'd gotten it from Clem (Steven Grogan). Clem said, "No way," but by the time word was spread, almost every one of us had to have treatments. Hell, with our lives, who was to know who got what first. For that matter, if one of the girls came up pregnant, it was a guess as to who the father might have been. But over all those evening meal conversations gave me clues about what would best satisfy the majority. So hell, if someone wanted to check out England, we'd send him on his way. Bruce did go to England for a few months. The little girl who said she'd still be home if it weren't for the fighting her parents did was really saying she missed her home and wasn't all that happy being away from it. I had a private talk with her and assured her I'd take her home if she wanted and maybe talk some sense into her parents. She elected to stay with us. The idea about spreading our love all over the world was appealing to me and started some thought churning in my head. The preference of Mendocino over Spahn Ranch wasn't out of the question either. I put the girl who expressed that desire in the bus with whoever else wanted to go along and sent them north. In sending them, I had the thought of groups of us being located in a lot of different areas as a means of meeting more people and spreading our love. Also, I

151

thought in spreading the group out, some of them might discover what it was they wanted in life and develop some direction.

Pat, Susan, Mary and the baby Pooh Bear, and two other girls took the bus and ended up at a little town, Philo, in Mendocino County. Letting them go up there without one or two guys along was a mistake. Five girls alone in a small town was trouble. The house they rented was immediately dubbed "the witches' house" by the school kids. A short time later they were arrested for turning some of the local kids onto acid—that's the neighborhood and police version. The girls say that a gang of high school guys forced their way into the house, threatened them and forced them into having sex. To keep from getting beaten the girls gave the boys some acid, at Susan's suggestion. The guys went wild and started tearing up the house and totally destroyed the bus. The cops showed up, arrested the girls and cut the guys loose. Mary's baby, Pooh Bear, was temporarily put in the care of some foster parents. And instead of spreading love, we got ourselves on the shit-list of the Mendocino County authorities.

Before everything was cleared up, we'd had a very costly learning experience. We learned that any further ventures creating new places for expansion should be done with girls *and* guys. Cost-wise, besides the bus that got torn up, we had to make two or three trips from the ranch to Mendocino, and on one of those trips the motor of the bus we had just bought blew up, leaving six people stranded outside San Jose.

But even some bad has good. The good came when T.J., Clem, Tex and Ella were hitchhiking back to the ranch. They were picked up by a girl named Juanita driving a new travel van and by the time they arrived back at Spahn, they had Juanita convinced she should spend some time with us. Juanita dug our lifestyle and jumped right in on all our activities. The van became ours and in addition, she contributed over ten thousand dollars to our needs.

The money was needed, because a lot of things at the ranch seemed to turn to shit after the arrest of the girls in Mendocino. The cops were hassling us, George was on again, off again about us staying there and I was starting to feel the pressure of responsibility for so many lives that were going nowhere. Juanita's chunk of money gave us some slack. A few dollars went to George and he liked us again. We got the bus fixed and back on the ranch. Even

152

though I wasn't into material things, I saw the value of a dollar and all the tensions it erased. That also made me see the need to turn our heads toward something that would earn us a few dollars so that, until we were well settled in our own world, we wouldn't have to be at anyone's mercy when we needed something.

About the same time Juanita showed up, I was pumped up about checking out some property in the desert that Cathy Gillies' grandmother owned, Myers Ranch. With the bus now in good running condition, twenty of us headed out there. The traveling wasn't rough until we got to the town of Trona, where the pavement turned to gravel. We had to double back south on a rutty old road that shook the hell out of the passengers and put the bus to the test. The heat and the rough ride were getting to some of the kids, but personally, I enjoyed every minute. The farther we got from civilization the better I liked it. Finally Cathy pointed to an old rutted space that had once been a road and said to turn down there. After a quarter mile of slow moving while some of the kids moved rocks and boulders so the bus could progress, we gave up trying to go any farther on wheels. Cathy told us it would take about two hours for us to walk the rest of the way.

If you want to learn something about personalities and depth of character in people, take them on a laborious journey in the desert. It was around five o'clock in the evening when we decided we would have to hike the rest of the way. We weren't prepared for hiking, but by wrapping things in sleeping bags, paper bags and boxes, we managed to outfit ourselves with the needed items. To impress us, Sadie stacked herself with the biggest load and started off out in front of everyone. Clem was right behind her with an equal load. The rest of us strung out in single file and headed up the canyon looking more like overloaded grocery shoppers than hikers in a hot desert with five or six miles of rough terrain to cover. Five minutes after we started our trek, Sadie and some of the other girls were shifting their ill-prepared loads around. It was obvious they weren't going to get much farther before some improvements in the load distribution would have to be made. Sure enough, minutes later items began to drop and the rest of us behind would have to recover them and add them to our own load. At the end of the line little old dependable Squeaky trudged along, quietly picking up what the others had dropped. After an hour, we

153

stopped for a breather and redistributed our loads. Dispositions were far from jovial. Even some of the guys voiced regrets about coming along.

Two-and-a-half hours later, a leg-weary, arm-tired, hungry and grouchy group of people got their first look at Myers Ranch. I think Cathy and I were the only ones smiling. The others were too tired to appreciate it. But there it was, a fair-sized dwelling surrounded by unexpected green vegetation, a nice little oasis in the middle of nowhere. The house had a large front room with a big fireplace, two bedrooms, a small kitchen and a back porch with an attached bathroom. It was more than just an old miner's shack and a hell of a lot better than some of the places we had called home before. But at that moment those weary hikers didn't care if it was a castle or a hog pen, they just wanted relief from the weight of the packs and someplace to rest their tired bodies. After a quick meal of canned fruit and candy, the whole crew sought the comfort of their sleeping bags.

The next morning I quizzed Cathy as to how receptive her grandmother would be if a bunch of us moved into her desert home. Cathy was a little uneasy about so many being there, and we decided to look at the only neighboring ranch, about a quarter of a mile back. The Myer house and surroundings were the best, but I didn't want to get Cathy in a cross with her grandmother, so I decided to speak to the owner of the second choice. Little Paul and I hiked back to the bus and drove to Indian Springs where the owner of the property, Mrs. Barker, lived. We found her, like old George, sitting on the front porch half asleep. Paul and I walked to the porch and introduced ourselves. I wasn't laying out any bull—I told her truthfully a group of us would like to stay at her ranch while we were putting together some arrangements for musical recordings. I also mentioned I did some song writing for the Beach Boys and, to add credibility, I gave her one of the gold records that had been presented to Dennis. She didn't object to our living there if we took care of the place.

Paul, I think, shared my enthusiasm for the desert. "Wow, ain't this great Charlie?" he said. "Man, people can really get their acts together out here. This desert air makes you feel so alive, you could conquer the world. Goddamn, I'm glad we found this place! The 'man' (the police) ain't around to be fucking with us. Ain't no neighbors tryin' to get you to conform to their ideas. Look out there, there ain't a car, a house or another living human being in sight. Fuck, man, this is heaven!" Paul was right, because for me, it was the one spot on earth that came close to being my kind of heaven. There were no fences or boundaries. The only restrictions that existed were the mental and physical limitations of the person who lived there. Like Paul had said, the "man" wasn't around to hassle us. We could be like the first born on earth. Society's rules and demands didn't reach way out here.

Unfortunately, I knew that not all the kids were into our being here as much as I was. Yet I felt if they had something to believe in, a life to look forward to, it wouldn't be long before every member of the group would be able to appreciate what the desert had to offer.

The Barker Ranch wasn't as large as the Myers place. It had a small front room, a bedroom, a big kitchen and a bathroom. There wasn't a fireplace or any electricity. All heat and cooking would come from the oil-burning stove in the kitchen. But, like the Myers place, there was plenty of water and a lot of green vegetation with some shade trees. Like the Myers place, it was an oasis.

The property was a victim of years of neglect and the uncontrolled growth of grape vines that had been planted years ago, so the next few days were spent fixing up the place to accommodate our needs and pleasures. The whole group enjoyed it. Nothing was urgent, so all the work and exploring around the place was done at a leisurely pace in the early morning hours of the day. By the time the sun hit its peak, most of the kids were in the spots they had found to be shady and cool, and we had siesta when the sun was at its hottest.

The evening meal, later in the evening because of the heat, was like it had been at Spahn's, a family affair with everyone expressing their views and throwing out suggestions. During one of the first meals we had at Barker's, one of the girls asked, "Geez, we're out here away from everything, it's too quiet, too dead, what are we going to do with all our time?" "Do?" I answered, "I'll tell you what we are going to do. We have love, the strongest kind of love, and with that love we are going to put some purpose, some direction in our lives. We are going to practice and play music until we are perfect, so perfect that when we go into the city, we can make

155

the best recordings ever. And we'll be the best, all of us! And beyond just music, we're going to find ourselves, know our souls, understand our hearts and learn from our children." (Susan had given birth to her son Zezozoze Zadfrack while we were still at Spahn, so he and Pooh Bear were with us.) "We are going to cast aside our remaining egos, rid ourselves of all the crap our parents threw down on us, quit reflecting our mothers every time we open our mouths. Be ourselves. We will have no leaders, no followers, just our individual selves. Individuals so strong with each other that all of us will be one. That's what we are going to do. Can everyone agree to that?"

While giving my spiel I had the full attention of everyone there, and not one set of eyes looked away from me. For the time being, everyone present accepted the desert as the place to be.

Before a month passed, we knew every rock, gully, bush, spring and old mining claim within miles around the ranch. We became familiar with everything that grew and lived in the desert. We learned that in the daytime rattlesnakes and other varmints shift to the shady side of a rock or bush, so it was safest to pass on the sunny side of what might be a lair. At night, you stayed away from the part of the rock that received the most sun during the day, since at night the snakes used the warmth of the rocks as heating pads. Nothing was foreign to us.

In my lifetime, I've been around every form of drug in existence. I've never had any use for heroin, opium, cocaine or anything else that makes you an addict, although I've always been strong on grass, hashish, LSD, mushrooms and just about everything that gives mind trips. But a couple of the most profound experiences of enlightenment came to me when I was not under the influence of anything. Anything, that is, except the heat of the desert sun and, perhaps, the fear of death.

One such experience happened about three or four weeks after we had moved onto the Barker property. I woke up very early one morning a little on the listless side and not totally content with myself. I wasn't looking forward to the hour when the kids would be awake and moving around. There wasn't anything heavy on my mind, nor was I angry. It was a simple urge to be alone and away from voices, questions, and opinions.

156

I could have walked a hundred yards in any direction from the house and had all the privacy I needed. Instead, I filled a small canteen with last night's cold coffee, stuck half a loaf of bread in my jacket pocket and walked outside in time to see the first rays of the morning sun peek over the Panamint Mountains. The first two hours of my solitary hike took me to a point where I could see out over the basin of Death Valley to another range of mountains. The walk in the crisp early morning desert air was invigorating, and by the time I sat down to tear a chunk of bread from the loaf and take a sip of the cold coffee, my surly mood had vanished. As I sat there looking out over the flatland and trying to gauge the distance to the next range of mountains, I was giving credit to the pioneers and all those who traveled without motor-driven machines. And I thought about the Indians who once dwelled in the desert without modern tools or equipment.

I felt the kids and I, living the way we did, were a lot closer to nature than most of society, although we depended on the modern conveniences more than we liked to admit. Hell, rough roads, temporary power failures and a busy telephone line had often caused complaints and aroused anger. I was amused at myself and the kids, who, even in our rebellion against society's rules, depended so much on what man had to offer. We could hate and resent all we wanted, yet we were spoiled, soft and incapable of doing so many things. What would any of us do if all of a sudden we found ourselves out in the middle of the desert with no transportation, food or water? Would we survive?

I took another look over the basin at the distant range of mountains. It didn't seem they could be over ten or twelve miles away, but I knew the distance was actually more like sixty-five or seventy miles. From where I sat, it took me about forty minutes to reach the edge of the basin. When I got there, I sat down and slowly finished off the bread, took several more sips of the coffee and placed the canteen on a rock. According to the height of the sun, it was about eight-thirty in the morning. I started to lay my jacket on the rock beside the canteen, but reconsidered because, even though the day promised to be a hot one, evenings in the desert can get pretty damn cold. And what the hell, even the Indians had warm garments.

To this day, I don't know why I decided to cross that plain.

157

There wasn't anyone around to impress, I wasn't loaded on anything but fresh air, and I wasn't on the run from a reform school.

With a bandana tied around my forehead to keep the sweat out of my eyes and my hair in place, the thongs on my moccasins tied snugly and my jacket tied around my waist, I began a steady, easy trot across the desert. It was never my intention to get to the other range of mountains. What I had in mind was to reach the exact middle of the desert. Then I could return knowing I had the stamina, survival instincts and the courage to tackle the desert with nothing more than what an Indian of two hundred years ago might have had.

For the first hour I was full of energy, and though I knew I would be tired and must pace myself, I would still leap over a rock just for the pleasure of feeling the strength of my legs. But as time went by, with the sun higher and brighter, me dripping sweat, and my mouth like a cotton ball, I stopped the leaps and slowed my trot down to a steady walk. After about two hours of steady moving I took my first rest. There were no rocks or bushes large enough to throw a shadow, so I spread my jacket over two small sage bushes, giving me enough shade to cover my face as I took a ten-minute breather, ten minutes in which I sweated more profusely than when moving. During that ten minutes, I cussed myself for leaving the canteen. To play it like the Indians, I located a pea-sized pebble and put it in my mouth. At first it didn't seem to help, but within a couple of minutes, the cotton seemed to dissipate and some slight moisture returned. At about midday, I still had a long way to go before equalizing the distances between the two ranges. I had serious thoughts about heading back the way I had come, but stubborn pride and my personal commitment made me head farther into the desert. With each step my stride became more like a flat-footed wino's and I slowed to a walk again.

My second rest stop was forced on me by cramps in the back of my legs. I had thought that all the climbing and running around that I had been doing for the last month had kept me in condition, but those leg cramps gave me some bad pain. I sat down in the hot sand so the heat would loosen up the knotted muscles. By licking the sweat from my arms, hands and what was dripping from my face I managed to get some salt into my system.

Around three o'clock the desert is at its hottest, and by that

158

time, maybe by cheating some on the distance, my eyes told me I had reached the halfway point. Heading back I wasn't the energetic person who had challenged the desert earlier in the day. Between blurry eyes and a light head, I had to fight off fainting spells, and I gathered a few rocks and built a marker, like a prospector staking a claim. I wasn't claiming anything, only leaving a symbol that I had journeyed through the heart of the desert without food or water or the conveniences of modern man.

By six o'clock, it seemed just as hot as when I had started the return hike. I'd walked steadily for the last three hours and yet the range of mountains seemed just as far away as ever. My tongue was so swollen I could no longer work the pebble around to keep the saliva going. There wasn't any liquid left in my mouth anyway. Nor was I able to sweat any longer. I would fall every few steps, and it took so much energy to get up that I tried crawling, but the sand and rocks were hot and hard, and my skin got so raw, I couldn't crawl. If I was to make it at all, I had to get on my feet and walk. I tried to ignore the fatigue of my body, but my head ached so much from the exposure to the sun and from hunger, I couldn't focus my mind.

Many times in my life I had been hungry enough to cry, my head aching and my body void of all strength, but never during those times had I thought of death. In a normal environment, or even in jail, there was always that morsel of food or drink of water needed to pull you through. But I wasn't in a normal environment; I was far from any ear that would hear my cries for help. As foggy as my mind was, I realized that to shout or cry would be just wasted energy. Save it, I told myself, get up, get up, you can make it, you can't die here. Several times I did get up and move forward a few steps. But, finally, there was no strength left, my lips were parched and my tongue so swollen there wasn't room for it in my mouth. I fell and my arms did not have the strength to keep my face from striking the gravel and sand. I couldn't move my tongue or moisten my mouth, so I cleaned my tongue and mouth with my hands. I didn't have enough strength to get up. I just lay there on my stomach with my arms under my head to keep my face and swollen tongue from touching the dirt. My eyes focused on a rock and I talked to it with my thoughts. "You lucky bastard, you don't have life, so you don't know what it's like to suffer, be hungry or thirsty

159

or worry about living and dying. You're dead, you son-of-a-bitch, dead." I rolled my body over and looked at the sun, a sun that was just starting to drop over the same mountain where I had begun my day's journey. For a few minutes I totally gave up. I knew I would never walk another step. Inside me there was some fear of dying and my thoughts registered a plea, a prayer to any God who might want to hear a dying man say, "Help me, I don't want to die yet." Then my eyes turned to the rock and again my thoughts spoke to it. "You lucky piece of earth, you don't know pain."

Then a clearer part of my mind registered that I was trying to relay my thoughts to a rock. Here I was talking to something without ears, feeling or life—was I crazy? Hell no! I wasn't crazy, and as much as the condition of my mouth and throat would allow me to, I started laughing out loud. For minutes I lay there laughing and chuckling at my stupidity. And in that laughter, I felt the moisture of tears on my face. I wiped the moisture from my cheeks and eyes away with my hand and then placed the dampness against my hard, swollen tongue. "Geez," I thought, "no near-dead person laughs and sheds tears, so get up, struggle a little bit, life ain't over yet." I lay there for some time, and with each breath I felt some strength returning to my body. I didn't rush things, but shortly I knew I was strong enough to make it back to the ranch. When I got up the earth turned around on me a few times, but when I started walking it was in the right direction. By the time I got back to the rock where my canteen lay, the sun was long gone. I sipped the coffee slowly, having presence of mind not to overdo it. The ranch was still a couple hours of uphill hiking, so like the snakes, I huddled between two large warm boulders and spent the night at the edge of the basin where I had begun my crazy journey.

Waking up the next morning was no picnic. I was so stiff and sore it was a struggle to get to my feet, and once on my feet, things didn't get any better. My muscles and bones ached so bad, walking was pure torture. Even my face was screwed. The swelling of my tongue had gone down but my damn lips were so puffy and split it hurt to wrinkle my nose or open my mouth. But hey, everything was all right; I was alive and I appreciated the aches and pains that let me know it.

When I finally got back to the yard of the house, one of the kids saw me and shouted to the rest of the group, "Hey, here he is,

Charlie's here you guys!" With that, the kids came charging from all directions and a thousand questions came flying at me. When they saw the condition of my face and realized I wasn't moving too well, all the girls started playing Florence Nightingale. I appreciated the attention I was getting even though, just the day before, I had left the house to be away from it.

We spent hours each day practicing, arranging and writing songs, and the music was often so good it gave me goosebumps, especially at night when all of us lounged around a big bonfire in the yard. The acoustics out in the open didn't compare with a studio set-up, but the quiet, open desert added its own magic to our music. Without microphones or amplifiers there was a pure, earthy quality to our instruments and voices. We were a bunch of kids sitting around an open bonfire in one of the most primitive areas in the nation, but our arrangements and lyrics were as modern and free as our philosophy. God, there was so much talent there. One of my strongest regrets is that the world didn't get to hear our music. In the two months we had been in the desert, we had reached a level of accomplishment that was amazing. Since it was all original material, I became more intent than ever about getting us recorded.

Wilson, Jakobson and Melcher were the best ones to open the door for us. So me and a couple of the kids got in the bus and headed for L.A.

PART THREE

WITHOUT CONSCIENCE

CHAPTER 7

ACCORDING TO SOME, this is when the devil started sprouting horns. Two or three of those who lived within our circle have written books contending that when they first met me I waved a magic wand of love and music. With a single wave, they came under my spell and had to be with me. While they don't say the magic wore off, they do say that around the beginning of 1969 I began undergoing personality changes that eventually caused love and togetherness to turn to evil and discontent. They say I became bitter and frustrated because I was never able to record successfully. They say I became convinced the Beatles' *White Album* with its songs of "Piggies," "Revolution #9," and "Helter Skelter" held special messages for me and my circle, that I interpreted them as signals to create an uprising between the races, and began programming everyone to prepare themselves for the shit that was going to come down.

I don't deny disappointment at not reaching my goals as a musician. Nor do I deny being impressed with the *White Album*. But I gotta say, those kids were expressing their own ideas more than what was going through my mind. Hell, those were kids of the Beatles' generation—I had at least ten years on most of them. I envied any successful musician and appreciated any best-selling album, but like most people, the music I felt close to was music I had heard when I was young. Sinatra, Crosby, Como and people of that era meant more to me than the Beatles, Beach Boys or any of the prominent groups in the 60s. The lyrics I wrote and the music I put to those lyrics identify me as not being all that wrapped up in the Beatles. Shit, it was Sadie and Little Paul who started deciphering messages from the Beatles' *White Album*. In the desert, the music I was most interested in was my own, since I knew that would interest the studio people most. After two months in the desert, the drive into L.A. was enjoyable. My head was full of

165

things to lay on Dennis, or anyone else, to convince him that we were ready to record. I had written several new songs, a couple of which I considered near masterpieces, and I was eager to have a professional listen to them.

My first disappointment came when Dennis wasn't in town. But Jakobson lifted my spirits some by saying, "Damn, Charlie, it's good to hear from you. I've been intending to get out to the desert to talk to you. Dennis and I been talking you up to some of the studios and there are a couple that are interested in hearing you play. Trouble is, you living out of town the way you do makes it hard to get in touch. Why not stay close for a while, and when Dennis gets back, we'll get something going."

It sounded great. Now that it was December, when the high desert where we were living gets cold, a temporary move back into town would be good for all of us. Of course, we still had people at Spahn, mostly girls who spelled each other looking after George. But things at Spahn were too disorganized for us to do any serious rehearsing. Finding a place that would accommodate fifteen or twenty kids wasn't an easy task. I finally found a house on Gresham Street in Canoga Park. It sat on about an acre of ground, had four bedrooms, two baths, a big kitchen and a large front room that made a great studio for our music sessions. It was only about a thirty-minute drive from Hollywood, and only a few miles from Spahn's, which was a convenience in itself. Because of its bright yellow paint, we called the place the "Yellow Submarine." For all the ups and downs we had there, we should have named it "Roller-coaster."

The ups began with Dennis' return. He and Jakobson immediately came over and paid us a visit. After hearing us play, they were enthused about the new music and how far we had progressed.

One of the songs they liked best was, "Look At Your Game, Girl." The lyrics were:

There's a time for livin', time keeps flyin.'
You think you're lovin', baby, when all you're doin' is cryin'.
Can you feel? Ask yourself, are your feelin's real?
Look at your game, girl.
Just to say you love me is not enough if'n you can't be true.

166

You tell all those lies, baby, but you're only foolin' you.
Can you feel? Ask yourself, are those feelin's real?
Look at your game, girl.
Go on, look at your game, girl.
If'n you can't feel and the feelin's not real,
then ya better stop tryin' or you're gonna play cryin'.
That's the game.
That's the game, the sad, sad game.
Look at your game, girl.

Dennis, Jakobson and Melcher scheduled two recording sessions, the first at a studio in Westwood Village. About fifteen of us invaded the place. Right away the guy who ran the studio started telling us what we could and couldn't do, where to sit, where to stand and which way to face, even how to hold the microphone. We started out doing as he said, but the girls wanted to be looking at me while doing their background vocals. When they started moving away from where he had placed them, he came unglued. We made two or three more starts, each ending up worse than the first as far as the guy was concerned. In the end, the whole scene was a repeat of my first session with Universal. They didn't want us to perform as I felt we should. Between the studio manager telling us to get out and us telling him to get fucked, that session was a bust.

Later, Dennis tried to pull my coat, saying, "Look, Charlie, those guys who handle a studio know what they're doing. They know the best effect for sound separation, how to run everything together. So when you're doing a session, do it their way. Hell, man, even our group follows their advice." I said next time I'd do it their way.

The next time was at Dennis' brother's home studio, which was larger than a lot of the commercial studios. This time we did a pretty fair session, putting down about ten songs. But getting some money out of it and getting us on the market was still going to take some time.

In the meantime, there was the rent and the utilities, plus food and all our other needs that had to be taken care of. All of which cost money. There were still those out at the Barker place to care for, and the few out at Spahn's needed looking after, too. To use

167

the words of the media, I had a "Family" to take care of. A family in which, it seemed, no one would do a damn thing as far as working or bringing in some money was concerned unless they were told what to do and how to do it. So, though I was happy about finally getting our songs on tape and was confident the music would eventually take care of all our needs, we needed expense money now.

The situation at the Barker Ranch was especially pressing. Way out there, those kids no longer had a nearby market for purchasing or helping themselves to the discarded produce. Food had to be bought in large quantities, and we needed generators for electricity, propane appliances and plenty of reserve supplies. Because I looked at the desert as a place where I wanted us to spend a lot of time, I wanted to start making things as comfortable as possible, including having a lot of vehicles to cover the mountain and desert terrain.

With no one geared to hold down a steady job, myself included, we looked for other ways to get the needed dollars. One possibility was my prison background and all the ex-convicts I knew. In what I thought was our hour of need, I wasn't above forgetting my vows not to challenge the system anymore.

In the past, I hadn't sought the company of my old convict friends except for a select few who I liked putting on the dog for. Now I became less selective about who visited and stayed with us a while. I even made a few phone calls to some of the money-making thieves I knew. With fifteen or twenty young lovelies in my household, getting a few thieves to lend a helping hand wasn't a problem at all. The best part was, with all the willing and skilled help I came up with, I didn't have to be at the scene of the crime. Nor did I have to set up scores or give orders. An occasional suggestion usually resulted in the goods being delivered.

Within three or four weeks of moving into the Yellow Submarine, it had become a concert hall for musicians, a porno studio for kinky producers, a dope pad, a thieves' lair, a place to dismantle stolen cars and just about everything but a whorehouse. Not a body was sold! Shared for favors returned maybe, but not sold for dollars. And during it all, we still kept our faces straight for Dennis, Jakobson, Melcher and anyone who could do us some good in the music world.

It wasn't long before the acre at the Yellow Submarine became

168

too small. We were growing in numbers, and car parts were starting to pile up and attract the attention of neighbors and police. So I went to see old George. A couple of his horse wranglers weren't happy at seeing me drive up, but George and I got along just fine.

I left with George's, "Sure, son, there's always room for another critter or two. You'll have to do with where you started before, though, 'cause some new people are in the other house." "That's all right, George, it's spring. We don't have the bus anymore; it gave up on us in the desert. We'll put up a tent or two and make it just fine. Thanks." To put in the clincher, I added, "The girls been taking good care of you, George?" "Sure have, I love having them around." His wink and pleased grin said more than his words.

Giving up the house on Gresham Street wasn't easy, since it gave us living quarters, a studio and a two-car garage for dismantling stolen vehicles. Some of the girls weren't thrilled at the thought of moving from a comfortable home to the open air, or at best, a tent. Their words irritated me and I shouted at them, "What's your fucking story? Ever since we been together, we been living on the road, in buses, on beaches, in the desert in tents, everywhere. What's happening to you? Can't you see this move is for our future? Christ, four months ago you'd have moved anyplace without all this static. What's different now?"

Later when I realized how strong I'd got down on them, I also realized I should have been asking myself what was happening. Every one of us was going through some pretty heavy changes, because of the struggle for dollars. Dishonest dollars. Though most of the group weren't against petty thievery for survival, they were seeing a side of me that they'd never seen before. Now I was the con, a conniver, a thief out to make money no matter how. The simplicity of our previous life, the love and thoughtfulness for each other, was being replaced by the greed for possessions. I consoled myself and condoned my actions by telling myself that all this bad shit would end just as soon as our records got on the market. In the meantime, it had to be this way until we were totally set up in the desert.

A month later, most of us were entrenched back at Spahn, though we didn't have the main ranch house. We did have the full use of the movie set, but even with all of the six structures that represented the mock-up western town, we didn't have room for our numbers and activities. Including those still in the desert, we had over thirty-five people wandering around. So over the hill and along the creek we made several parachutes into large canopies to serve for sleeping and living arrangements and to shade a small assembly line where we modified vehicles for desert use. There were two or three stolen vehicles for every legal one we converted. We mostly concentrated on converting Volkswagens into dune buggies, but jeeps, motorcycles and four-wheel drive trucks were also in our plans. For power to operate the assembly line, one of the more talented thieves in our midst had stolen a truck with a large gas generator and arc welder. The generator also provided light for night work.

Of the thirty-five, about twenty were of our circle. The rest were a combination of ex-convicts, bikers and one or two young kids who were just drifting. For their contributions in stolen goods and labor, they had space to live, food to eat, dope to smoke and, if they lucked out, sometimes a girl to sleep with.

For added attraction, and to keep the crew content, we enlarged and remodeled the old saloon. It looked the same on the outside, but inside it was a spacious, updated go-go entertainment center. For everyone not working on the desert vehicles, it was a fun place to hang out and soon became a place for full-fledged performances. Even without outsiders, there were enough people around the ranch so that we were never playing to an empty house. With strobe lights, dancers and an avid audience, it felt very professional on the bandstand.

Word of good music, nude dancers and a variety of other pleasures quickly spread throughout the valley, and before too many nights passed, we were getting people from Hollywood, San Fernando, Malibu and elsewhere. The place got popular, and we sold no booze, so we weren't out of line in charging a cover. Special customers could buy an assortment of pills, grass or hashish.

The ranchhands at Spahn's were no dummies, and some of them were disturbed that we got away with the things we did. Especially Shorty Shea. Shea was all right when we first showed up; he smoked some grass with us and got his kicks eyeballing the girls. But when vehicle parts, obviously stolen, started showing up, he threatened to call the cops. By flashing a couple of legal pink slips in his face and saying I could prove nothing was stolen—at the same time threatening that some evil might come his way if any of us got busted—he kind of backed off. Johnny Swartz, whose old Ford we often used, was into sharing some of our party time. Juan Flynn got so hung up on being around the girls, he helped us out with just about anything we asked of him. And Steve Grogan became one of us the day after we first drove into Spahn's.

For a while there, everything was really coming together for me. There was promise of a soon-to-be released album, I had a small nightclub in operation for which I wrote the songs and led the band, I had able bodies putting together vehicles for the desert, and it was general knowledge that twenty or so of the girls did only what would be pleasing to me. Things were good. I felt proud and moved around with my head up and chest out. But that kind of good thing never seemed to last for me, and when things stopped working out, it all seemed to fall right back in my lap. Then the head starts reeling, pressure mounts, tension increases, frustration starts and there ain't no rhyme or reason to a fucking thing.

The go-go club was the first to go. Under-age kids were showing up and their parents notified the police. The police came storming in one night, rousted everyone and threw a bunch of charges: contributing to the delinquency of a minor, possession of illegal substances and operating a nightclub without a license. Old George had to bear the brunt of the police action because he owned the property. They slapped him with a healthy fine and told him it would be in his best interests to get us off his property. To keep peace with George and hold on to our place to stay, at least until we had everything together for the desert, I paid the fine and told George we'd be moving on soon, but we still needed a few weeks there at the ranch. He grumbled a taste, but didn't pressure us to move on.

Pacifying George was the least of our problems. Once in our face, the police never let up. The kids started getting rousted everytime they stepped off the property. Our vehicle operation slowed down until it seemed we were never going to get the needed items for the desert. With the heat around, some of the drifting kids left and so did some of the ex-cons. What was great only days before was now shit. And seeing nothing moving us toward the desert, maybe I got

171

a little surly with the kids. I started using anything that might convince them the desert was the only place for us.

Some of the kids were as pumped up about getting out of the city as I was, but several still frowned on being out in the desert. Their argument was, "Geez, Charlie, except for a few places like Barker's there's hardly no water or shade. It's too hot in the summer and too cold in the winter. There ain't no protection from nothin'." "Are you kiddin'," I almost screamed, "that desert's got everything. Hell, the whole desert ain't nothing but an upside down river. Water's running under every inch of it. How do you think those springs stay full? You just have to know where it's at. I've come across places out there where the sun don't beat down on you all day and it never gets cold in the winter, and water's everywhere. It's underground. I haven't explored it yet, but I sat on the edge of the hole and watched the water flowing underground. Man, the possibilities of that place are endless. And we'll find that hole again and build our own city.

"Why do you think we been breaking our asses to put together all this equipment? The dune buggies, the generators, the supplies all the gas we been stashing out there are going to make that desert into a paradise. Barker's and the Myers place ain't nothing compared to what we'll have going for us. When our records hit the market, we'll build our own town. In the meantime, if we put our act together, we can make the desert just as comfortable as we want it to be. Think about it: no rent to pay, no laws to obey and no cops on our asses. Hey, we'll be one step ahead of anything that goes on in this world.

"Look around you, the worm's turning on the white man. Him and his pigs have put the dollar in front of everything. Even his own kids. Blackie's tired of being the doormat for the rich man's pad. So while the white man's locked into his dollars, blackie's balling the blond, blue-eyed daughters and making mixed babies. It's all leading to bad shit. Real madness is going to explode soon— everything is going to be Helter Skelter. But that won't affect us, 'cause we'll be in a beautiful land that only we know how to survive in. To be ready, we need equipment and supplies by the tons. If we have to do a little stealing and hustling to get what we need, let's do it."

In days to come, and even now just about everything I said got so

172

twisted and exaggerated that none of it sounded like what actually came out of my mouth. If saying I would find the hole in the desert where I saw water means building a city under ground (as the DA said), then I don't know how to speak or hear. And if in expressing my opinions about the whites and blacks and wanting to be away from their hassles means I wanted to start the war and straighten out the world afterwards, then I'm not the only one with a huge imagination. The whole thing about the desert was that I loved being out there and so did some of the kids. The hassles we were getting from the police, my rap about possible trouble between the races and the picture of a better place to live put the kids into a game-for-anything frame of mind. Even those who showed some reluctance in the beginning were now game and daring. Actually, they were too daring at times, and drew more heat our way—not all of it from the police.

Susan, for example, was the kind of girl who would split from the ranch with the intention of doing something to benefit our cause. Once away from us, she'd get so wrapped up in what she was doing she wouldn't get anything done—or else, she'd burn whoever she had been sleeping with and come running back to the ranch with her trick right behind her. One time after she had been gone for several days, she came back and handed me about two lids of grass, which might net us thirty dollars, and said, "Here, Charlie, this is all I could score, but I'll do better next time." Twenty minutes after she handed me the grass, three big suckers, two Mexicans and a white guy, come driving into the yard. One of and the Mexican guys started shouting, "I'm looking for Sadie, Susan Atkins, she here?" I met him about halfway between his car and the front of the saloon, asking him why he was looking for the girl. "She's my woman and I know she's here. Tell her to get out here!" I hollered at Susan to come out of the saloon. Reluctantly, she came over to where the four of us were standing. The guy that was doing all the talking grabbed her by the shoulder and said, "Come on bitch, get in the car and don't be splittin' anymore." Susan pulled back and told the guy, "I'm not going anyplace with you, man. Now get out of here and leave me alone. Charlie's my old man, and this is where I'm staying." The guy then gave me all his attention, saying, "That's my bitch and I'm taking her with me." "Okay, pal," I told him, "do you see any fences here? Take her if she wants to go with you. Nothin's holding either one of you from doing what you want to do." The guy again reached out for Susan, but she backed away, telling him she wasn't going anyplace with him. "Then I'm going to kick your old man's ass and get my two pounds of grass back," the guy said as he made a move on me. I didn't have anything in my hands but my guitar, so I evaded his first move and told him, "Now, man, don't make me break my guitar over your head. If the girl wants to leave with you, you got her. If not, she stays and you go. But if you insist on sticking around, I'm going to pull my gun out of my pocket and blow your motherfucking head off."

The guy shook me down with his eyes and, since I was wearing jeans and a tee shirt, he could see I couldn't have been packing a gun. "You little asshole, you got no gun. I'm taking that broad out of here and my two pounds of grass." He brought a switchblade out of his pocket and made a move at me. I jumped back and pulled a larger hunting knife from my boot. The guy hesitated and I told him, "Look, man, there's two lids of grass in the house. It's yours if you'll just get all this shit out of your head and leave. Now it ain't two pounds like you said, but if it will make you happy, take it and leave and both of us might get out of this situation without getting cut." "I ain't settling for no two lids and being made a fool of by that bitch," he said, and lunged for me with his knife. I side-stepped him and put a small slice in his arm as he went by me. "Now see what you did to yourself. I didn't want to cut you, but you forced me to. Now you got nothing coming. Not the girl or the two lids." "Fuck you," he said. He tried to stab me and I shifted out of his way, this time cutting his other arm. His two partners were on the verge of making a move on me, but seeing that help was coming out of the saloon and they were now out-numbered, they just watched. After I cut the guy for the third time, I told him, "Look, guy, you can't win here. You can't touch me with your blade and you keep getting yourself cut. The girl done told you she don't want to leave with you. I've told you there ain't no two pounds of grass and now that you've made an ass of yourself, I'm not into giving you the two lids I offered when you drove up. Now the best thing for you to do is let your friends drive you someplace where you can get them cuts sewed up." Muttering that he'd be back to even things up, the guy and his partners got in their car and left.

Susan came running toward me, asking, "You all right, Charlie? The lying bastard didn't cut you did he? He's a liar! I didn't take his two pounds." "Susan," I said, "you got no reason to explain things to me. I've told you a thousand times: what you do, you do for you, not me. But I'm getting pretty fucking tired of your shit always coming back on the rest of us. One of these days, you're going to have to settle up on all you owe."

Naturally, even with the urgency to get out of the city, I was still after Dennis, Jakobson and Melcher to come through with something good for us. At Jakobson's insistence, Melcher and a guy finally came out to Spahn's and did some video cassettes. But evidently Melcher wasn't impressed enough to try to move the material. All we got were promises that we'd do it again. Not being able to live on promises, we continued stealing, selling dope and hustling in any way we could to help the cause.

Susan Atkins and Tex Watson have both written books declaring their rebirth as born-again Christians. In their books, they cop to being into drugs, vice, and complete opposition to the law long before they met Charles Manson. If, in fact, they are as sincere about Christianity and as strong in religion as they were sold on drugs and deceit during the time our lives ran parallel, then God has got two very devoted disciples. But if, on the other hand, they are with their God as they were with me, they are still going to do just as they please. I'd like to emphasize that those two, who screamed the loudest and cried the hardest that I influenced their lives and actions, were themselves instrumental in what I feel was the biggest blow to the life we were living and led to murder and chaos.

Even before that blow, the whole atmosphere at the ranch had been drifting from love and games to tension and discontent for several months. I guess I have to pick up that load, for instead of following my own advice of "be your own person" and "live and let live," I was pushing to get things done and pretty heavy into being the voice of authority. It was a thing that crept up on me. Even at the Spiral Staircase, when I first realized that someone had

175

to hold things in check, I never meant to play boss or keeper. But as the numbers grew, so did the responsibilities—and the pressure. I may have tried to direct our goals as a group, but I never locked anyone to me. In spite of what has been said since, everyone was always free to come and go as they pleased or hit the road for good if that was what they wanted. So, even with the change, I wasn't into hurting anyone except in self-defense. Never, at any time, did I feel our actions could push us into taking a human life. And I still don't believe any of the violence would have erupted if we had controlled the drugs instead of letting them control us. But who can say where we would have ended up if it had not been for the ensuing incidents?

One day Indian Joe, a biker who often hung around the ranch, was hiking around the canyons a mile or two from the ranch houses when he stumbled on some telatche (belladonna) plants. He brought them down to the kitchen and explained to Brenda how to trim the plants, boil the roots and make talatche tea. The plants were potent and poisonous and it wasn't advisable to cook them indoors because of the fumes, but Brenda trimmed the roots to about medium-sized onions and began boiling them in the kitchen anyway. Tex walked in and wanted to know what was in the pot. He was told, "This is what belladonna is made from." With that, he picked up a large root and started scarfing it like he was eating an apple. Before the full effect hit him, Tex caught a ride into town.

I wasn't in the kitchen, nor did I know what was going on. I had seen Tex come out of the building and waved goodbye to him as he left the ranch. He waved back saying, "See you later." I think it was the last time until the trials I saw Tex in what might be called his right mind.

Several minutes after Tex left, Brenda came staggering out of the kitchen and collapsed on the porch. I ran over and picked her up. She didn't know who or where she was. She would open her eyes, mutter incoherently and then pass out. I hollered at T.J. who I had seen coming in and out of the kitchen several times. T.J. was pretty stoned himself, but he was coherent enough to tell me what was going on inside the kitchen. One look at T.J. and Brenda told me Tex was in no condition to be away from the ranch and in town where he could get into trouble and get busted. I shouted at

Squeaky to come and take care of Brenda and then took T.J. and threw him under a cold shower. After the shower and some coffee got his head straight, I sent him to find Tex and keep him out of trouble. As it turned out, T.J. got to Tex's place in town too late. Tex had already been dropped off, gotten on a motorcycle and split. Later that evening Tex crashed the bike into a parked car. He then climbed into the car and passed out. The next morning the owner of the vehicle, unable to awaken Tex, called the police. They booked him for being under the influence of narcotics. Three days later Tex returned to the ranch, and as I said, never seemed the same again.

All this took place in the early part of June, 1969. Though Tex now spent almost all of his time at the ranch, he still came and went as he pleased. He was engaged to a girl who had an apartment in Hollywood; it was there that a dope burn involving a black guy, Bernard Crowe, took place. And the repercussions of that dope burn began the violence which would eventually surround the Family.

Tex had taken his girlfriend's Volkswagen into a shop to have it converted into a dunebuggy. The tab was to be around five-hundred dollars. To get the money, he was going to turn over some grass. He went to the black guy's pad with the girl and got twenty-four-hundred dollars front money, promising to return with the grass before the day was over, but after getting the money, Tex decided to screw the nigger. He never did score the grass and he never returned the money.

Late that same night, the phone rang at the ranch. T.J. answered the call on a phone that was by the corral and shouted, "Hey, Charlie, it's for you." I was in George's house at the time and picked up the extension there. A girl's voice, crying, said, "Charles, you've got to come back with the money or the grass. Crowe's here at my place and says he's going to kill me if he don't get his money." About that time another voice came on the line, "Okay, you smart motherfucker, I got your old lady here and if I don't have my bread back inside two hours, I'm going to cut her up and dump the pieces in your front yard." I didn't know what either one of them was talking about, and I shouted into the phone, "Hey, wait a minute, what old lady, what money? Who is this and what the hell you talking about?" The voice answered, "Don't give me that

177

shit, you know who this is, it's Crowe and I want my bread or the stuff—two hours, Watson, or the broad's dead!" "Hey wait a minute, pal," I said, "this ain't Charles Watson, I'm Charles Manson. Hold on man, Watson's not here right now but don't be talking about cutting some girl up, we can straighten this thing out. Where you at?" The voice told me he was at the girl's apartment. "Okay," I answered, "Tex isn't here and I haven't got much bread but I'll be right over."

T.J. had listened to the whole conversation on the other line, so when I went down to the corral, he was already telling Danny De-Carlo and two other bikers about it. I filled them in and added, "I'm going over there and would appreciate some help, you guys game?" Danny and the other two suddenly found other things they should be doing, like shoveling some shit and checking on the horses. It was one o'clock in the morning, these bastards had never done a lick of work around the ranch, and all of a sudden their concern for the horses was more important than helping me out. "Okay, T.J., it's up to you and me. Are you going with me?" I could see his heart wasn't in it, but he said, "Sure, Charlie, I'm with you. But wait a minute, we might need some persuasion." With that he disappeared and returned with an old Buntline .22 revolver. Seeing the gun and realizing I might have to use it should have opened my eyes about how drastically things had changed in our group. But since we had gone into all-out thievery, guns were as common with the bikers and ex-cons who hung out with us as the knife I always carried.

We took Johnny Swartz's old Ford and headed toward Hollywood, the gun lying on the seat between us. When we got to the apartment, T.J. picked up the gun and stuck it in his belt. On the way up the stairs, I stopped, turned around and asked T.J. what he was going to do if he had to use the gun. He gave me a blank stare. "Hell, man," I said, "if it takes you that long to decide, you aren't going to be very useful, give me that gun." I stuck it in my belt behind my back. While on the way over, I had been trying to imagine what we might be getting into and how I was going to handle it. I felt Crowe and I could come to some agreement without a fight if I'd promise to be responsible for the money. And I hoped he'd give us a few days to come up with it. So when I knocked on the door, I was still into bargaining and not fighting.

After the first knock, the door opened a few inches and a big white guy peeked out at me saying, "You Charlie?" I nodded and he opened the door. Besides the guy who opened the door, there was another white guy in the room, but no black. I was told Crowe had left for a few minutes but would be right back. The girl, bound and gagged, was lying on the bed. The guys didn't seem too hostile and there wasn't any tension. I made light of the situation and started clearing off a very cluttered table. The two guys remained as they were after letting me in. T.J. had found himself a spot against the wall by the front door and remained standing. Seeing the guys weren't uptight, I went over and started untying the girl. One of the guys spoke up, "Crowe said to keep the girl tied." "Come on, man," I replied, "where's your manhood? This girl can't out-muscle both of you. Besides, we need some coffee and she can make it for us." I finished untying her and told her to go to the bathroom and wash her tearstained face and then make us some coffee while we waited until Crowe arrived, as he soon did.

Crowe, known as "Lotsapoppa," weighed close to three hundred pounds. He sized me up, gave T.J. a look and shouted, "What's that broad doing up walking around? I told you guys to keep her tied! What's the matter with you fuckers? And you, you smart little bastard, where's my money and that other bastard?" "Look, man," I told him, "things aren't any different than when I talked to you an hour ago. Tex ain't nowhere around. If he's still got your money, I can't find him. And until tomorrow or the next day, I can't come up with that much bread. But let the girl go. I'll stand good for the money." Crowe didn't say anything until after he had walked over to a padded chair and sat down like some king on a throne. Then, in a louder than natural voice, "I gots'ta answer to some more people"—he was tied up with some more black dope dealers—"so I'm gonna give you four hours to raise the bread. The broad stays, and if I don't fuck her to death in the meantime, you can have her when I gets my money."

I begged and promised I'd deliver the money but needed more time, and asked him to let the girl loose. The more I begged, the more vicious and threatening he became. We weren't getting closer to any terms and the girl started crying and pleading with me to do something and get her out of there. Crowe seemed to delight in our dilemma and became even more arrogant, finally saying, "Get out

179

of here, punk! Now you got two hours. Go get my money!" I dropped to my knees in front of his chair. "Look, man, I'm on my knees to you, please don't hurt the girl. I promise to get your money. Just let the girl go." He laughed at me and said maybe he'd just rather kill the girl and watch her die instead of waiting for the money. Still kneeling, I took the gun from behind my back and held it butt first out to Crowe and told him, "Here, man, if you have to take a life, take mine." He looked at the gun for an instant before reaching for it. When he reached, I twirled it around so the handle rested in the palm of my hands and sprang to my feet. I stepped back and said, "All right, you motherfucker, I've begged, kissed your ass and promised—now I'm taking the girl out of here, and you can say goodbye to her, me and your dollars."

Crowe stood up and showed a lot of heart, saying, "You little white trash bastard, you ain't got the balls to shoot anyone. I'm going to take that gun from you and shove it up your ass. Then I'm going out to that commune of yours with all my partners and screw all those white trash bitches. And if I have to, I'm going to pin your eyes open with toothpicks and make you watch while your white whores suck my black dick." He was taking steps forward as I backtracked. After a couple of steps, I pulled the trigger. CLICK, nothing happened. Crowe smiled and I thought, "Oh fuck, what now?" Crowe laughed and put his meaty hands around my throat. By now my back was up against the wall. He started squeezing and lifting me from the floor. I pulled the trigger again and got just another click—"Oh shit"—then once more I yanked on the trigger. Buried as it was in his stomach, the gun didn't make a loud report, but it was enough to change the whole atmosphere of the room.

Crowe raised up on his toes, his fingers tightened on my neck for the slightest instant, then relaxed as he slid down my body to the floor. The guy closest to me lunged toward me, but T.J. finally came to life and grabbed the guy around his neck and threw him back against the wall. He made no more efforts at being a hero and neither did the other guy. The girl let out a weak scream and started crying again. I hadn't moved. Crowe's body, lying at my feet, had me pinned to the wall.

I looked down at the body and though there wasn't any blood showing, I knew he was dead. I pointed the gun around the room

180

and told the other guys I hadn't come there to hurt anyone but had been forced into it. "Now, if either of you have an argument with me, let's hear it." Their faces were drained of color and their lips seemed too dry to speak. They just stood there staring at the body on the floor. As I stepped over Crowe, I was aware that I had just killed a man, but had no feeling of remorse. I wasn't sick or, at that moment, concerned about what the consequences of the shooting might be. Actually, all the pressure and tension left me; a feeling of strength surged through me. I felt good! Looking at Crowe's friends, I could see fear in their faces, as if each expected to be the next victim. I delighted in their fear.

One of them had on an expensive doe-skin pullover shirt. The guy was tall, about six-foot-four and had to weigh at least two-twenty. I complimented him on his taste in clothing and asked if he would give me the shirt. Without hesitation, he slipped out of the shirt and handed it to me. To put it on, I had to lay the gun on the table. Surprisingly, neither of them made a move. The shirt came well past my knees and the sleeves were so long they covered my hands. I had T.J. roll the sleeves up, and then reached over and picked up the gun. I waved it around a few times and told the guys to clean up the apartment and get rid of their friend. They seemed to breathe a sigh of relief and some color returned to their faces. T.J. and I left, sure that the girl would be safe now that Crowe was out of the way.

Back in the car and heading toward the ranch, T.J. was staring at me. He was quiet and there was a slight trembling in his body. Finally he said, "Geez, Charlie, did you have to kill him?" I told T.J. I hadn't planned on killing anyone. I just did what, under the circumstances, had to be done. "Besides, T.J., it was you who brought the gun. And I don't remember you making a move when the black bastard had his hands around my neck."

It was a thirty-minute drive back to the ranch, and after the one exchange of words, we didn't talk anymore. T.J. had his thoughts and I had mine. Things were racing through my mind and the seriousness of having killed someone was starting to come home to me. Like, "Well, you little bastard, you have done it all now—stolen, cheated, raped, and now you've done the big one. You're going to end up dying in the joint." Still, I felt no remorse for taking that life. I had been forced into it. Pulling that trigger didn't

181

mean any more to me than watching a cops-and-robbers movie, and if the police came after me, it was self-defense. I was sure the police would be coming to the ranch for me within hours, and for that, I had a score to settle with Tex. It was his burn, he got the money and it was a cross he belonged in, not me.

When I got back to the ranch, I didn't look for Tex, but went straight to bed. The next morning T.J. woke me up to tell me he and Brenda had just heard the news. The feature story was that a high-ranking member of the Black Panthers had been shot. The body had been dumped on the lawn of a hospital in Beverly Hills. "Wow," I exclaimed, "do you think it was our guy?" "It had to be!" said T.J. Paranoia immediately set in. The police I had answers for, but the Black Panthers weren't about to let some score go unsettled. It meant war. Guns and learning how to use them instantly became a part of getting things together for the desert. Finding a hole in the desert also became more important.

Even while T.J. was telling me the news, I was walking out to find Tex. The news was a little on the startling side, and I had some anger to vent on the responsible party. I found him curled up in a sleeping bag with Little Patty. I woke him up, took him out of Patty's hearing and laid it on him about the previous night. He went back to where he had been sleeping, brought back a wad of money and handed me what was left of the twenty-four hundred. I pushed the money back at him and said, "I don't want the money, you dumb fucker. What you have done is to bring the Black Panthers down on us." From where I was standing, I could see the highway, and though I was talking to Tex, my mind was visualizing cars filled with blacks driving by on that road and taking shots at us. I hurriedly ended our conversation with the words, "What I did for you last night put our whole circle in a cross with the blacks. I saved your life by putting mine on the line. Now it looks like all of us are in for it because of your shit. You owe us, brother!" I started to walk away, and as an afterthought, I turned to him and said, "On second thought, give me some of that money." He put fifteen hundred in my hand.

I went directly to the saloon and told everyone present, "We are going to have to change the way we have been living around here. We have to be more observant. More than just the police, the blacks are raising up. With the police, we don't have to fear sniper shots, but the blacks will be coming with guns. There might be some shots from the main road, so from now on, keep the buildings between yourselves and that road."

Severe changes had to be made. On my instructions, we started setting up look-outs and became more of a military encampment than a bunch of kids playing at fun and games. Life was no longer sex, drugs and doing whatever each of us had a desire to do. Our joys were already on the decline, and now there was a need for constant vigilance and deep concern.

I was worried and suspicious of any new face that appeared. I became a person with ever-changing moods, and what I felt was reflected in the kids. To compound things, three carloads of blacks pulled into Spahn the very next day. The cars were a mixture of men, women and children who just toured the ranch with normal tourist curiosity, but in our paranoia we suspected them of being a scouting party for the Panthers. Those of our group who may have doubted my words the previous day now believed the blacks would be back in force with guns and violence.

I think it goes without saying a lot of the stuff I was putting down to those at the ranch amounted to my personal fear of repercussions from the shooting of Crowe. And if I had known that he wasn't dead, or even the Black Panther we thought him to be, the scene at the ranch might not have been so uptight. It was almost a year before I learned that Crowe wasn't dead. In the meantime, the coincidence of a Black Panther being killed with a single shot and left on the lawn of a hospital was unimaginable. So during that time, I was convinced I had initiated a war with the blacks. The kids at the ranch caught the worst of my paranoia.

With the Panthers weighing heavily on my mind and with all the hassles from the police, I had visions of bad shit coming down and me waking up one morning with my ass back in prison. I often had the urge to get my things together and head for unknown places, but I was so caught up with those kids and the role I played in their lives, to leave would have been like ripping my heart out. Something inside me needed them, more than they thought they needed me. To overcome the bad vibes, I thought, "Once out of the area, nothing will come down." The need to get out of the city and back to the desert became more urgent than ever before.

For months we'd been screwing around putting together equipment and vehicles for the move when we could have completed things in just weeks. For that, I have only myself to blame. I always had too many irons in the fire and never wanted to miss out on anything. It was my nature to start something with a ton of enthusiasm and drop it just as soon as something else attracted my attention. But now, thanks to Tex and his drug burn, my back was up against the wall. We had to stay on top of everything that would get us where we wanted to be.

First things first; I went looking for some money I was owed for lyrics I had helped Dennis and his group with. Before this, it was like money in the bank. Now that there was a need, I went to collect. Dennis' agent didn't want to see me and I had to force my way past his secretary to get into his office. He felt I was responsible for some of Dennis' hang-ups, so our meeting was anything but cordial. When I first asked for the money, the guy gave me a polite, "You'll have to come back later." I was tired of everything being "tomorrow." I got chesty and tried to intimidate him by saying, "You know what, man, you owe me the money, it's a long overdue bill. Just pay up or I'm going to have to do something to make you regret it. Like one of these nights you might go home and see nothing but charred embers where your house was." My mouth blew everything, for the guy turned the tables on me by saying, "You know what, Manson, you're a flakey little nothing. You haven't a contract or any kind of an agreement, we owe you nothing. And because of your attitude, nothing is what you get. Now get out of my office, and if you want to keep playing tough guy, I'm going to make a phone call, and it's *adios* Manson. Get my message?"

The son-of-a-bitch caught me by surprise, and I left his office with some shit on my face, and a very disgusted feeling in my stomach. The police were in our faces, the blacks were on my ass and now I was getting "hit-man" threats.

Next, I went to see Melcher. I hadn't been hassling him for the last few weeks, but the recording date was still unfinished business and I had to have an answer on it. Melcher was friendly enough, but beat around the bush about another recording date. "Goddamn, Terry," I told him, "we been going through this kind of crap for the last year. Is it ever going to happen or not?" He answered, "Charlie, there's mixed emotions about promoting you. You're unpredictable. You amaze me at times, and at other times, disappoint

184

the hell out of me. Jakobson told me just this morning, you were involved with shooting some Negro, so frankly, for the time being, we are skeptical about investing any time or money in you." (Apparently one of the white guys at the apartment the night I shot Crowe was a friend of Dennis' or Jakobson's and had told them.)

Man, what a day I'd had! Leaving Melcher's, my stomach felt like it did twenty-three years earlier when I was first left at Gibault. My dream of the last ten years had gone the way of any dream when you wake up. Back to reality. I was the same grubby nothing whose mother dumped him on the State. Only this time there were no tears.

If I had left Melcher's feeling down and sorry for myself, by the time I got back to Spahn's, the self-pity was pretty well shadowed by hate and contempt. Hate for a world that denied. Contempt for people who can't see or understand.

Because Bobby was into the music and being recorded as much as I was, I found him and laid out the bad news. Some of the disappointment faded. Rolling with the punches was a way of life for both of us. So we lit a joint, played some music together, and before long we were laughing at the whole situation. Inside an hour, we both agreed, "Fuck them—who needs them? We'll do our own thing, turn our own bread and get the hell out of the phony-faced asphalt jungle."

With a disappointing damper on the prospects of becoming a recording success, practicing music no longer occupied as much time as it once did. That isn't to say we stopped playing, for the joy of music and the atmosphere surrounding it was too much a part of our lives ever to be without it. Regardless of the setback with Melcher, we still believed our talent would someday be recognized and appreciated. But for the time being, except for an hour or two in the evening, music took a back burner to more pressing issues.

Anticipating a move on us by the blacks, we collected all the guns we could get our hands on. Danny DeCarlo and some of the other guys around the ranch who were familiar with guns taught the kids to use them. In our paranoia, we relocated and separated into groups staying at different locations throughout the property. Some of the moves were for the safety of the girls and children, others for vantage points in case of an attack. We were gearing

185

strategically, physically and mentally for anything that might come at us.

In the meantime, there was progress on all the vehicles and equipment. Several vehicles had already been sent to Barker Ranch. We had a large truck and trailer being outfitted and loaded so that when we did make our final move, we could do it with everything we needed. The equipment and the money were finally coming together.

A healthy and much appreciated gift came when a new face appeared. Linda Kasabian was a pretty little girl, who at twenty years of age was no stranger to communes and drugs. Gypsy had met Linda at a guy's pad down by the beach and brought her back to Spahn's. Intending to visit for a couple of hours, she spent two days and was balled by Bobby, Tex, Bruce, Clem and Danny. After her two days with us, she returned to her pad to pick up her belongings and to say goodbye to her husband. While gathering her personals, which included a bag of acid tabs, she also ripped off her husband's friend for $5,000. I loved her and her little gift to the "desert fund."

Tex had told me she was a hell of a lay, so that night I checked her out myself. Because Linda's husband might come looking for her and the money, I had sent her, Brenda and Gypsy up to a cave to sleep. The cave was one of the "safe" spots we had been using since we began expecting trouble from the blacks. When I walked in the girls were listening to the experiences of Linda and comparing them with some of their own. I told them to keep talking and sat down to listen. Linda had been on the road since she was sixteen and had lived in several communes in various places across the US. She wasn't shy in her conversation and I knew through Tex, Bobby, Bruce, Clem and Danny she wasn't stingy with her body. Just for the joy of doing it, I wanted to see how she would react to a solo performance in front of a live audience.

It was a hot July night. I had come in shirtless, and none of the girls were wearing much. Linda had on a thin tee shirt and a pair of panties. I told her what a beautiful girl she was, and asked, "Why hide it? Take your clothes off." With a look at the girls she got up and did so. "Do you like girls?" I asked. She shrugged her shoulders, not a yes, but not a denial. I went on, "Will you make love with Gypsy and Brenda?" "In front of you?" she asked. "Including me," I said. Again the shrug of the shoulders. I told her to come

186

over to where I was standing and she waited in front of me, expecting to be kissed. Instead I put my hands on her shoulders and pressed her to the floor on her knees, telling her I couldn't make love with my pants on. She unbuttoned my pants and slid them to the floor. When she started to get up, I put my hands on her head and pulled her into me. I did not need to guide her anymore. Still standing, I motioned for Brenda and Gypsy to join us. They were already nude and crawled over on their hands and knees. They both started fondling Linda and we worked our way over to the sleeping bags, Linda accepting all their movements and caresses but not responding with any of her own. I began kissing her, and with my free hand I pulled Gypsy's head over so that she could exchange kisses with Linda. Linda's body stiffened when she realized she was exchanging tongues with Gypsy, but she was returning the kisses just as fervently an instant later. She wrapped one arm around Gypsy and I removed myself and watched the three girls do their number with each other. They had a perfect circle going, exchanging places so that each gave and received the same. I rejoined the circle, moving from Linda to Brenda and from Brenda to Gypsy. Because it was Linda's first trip with us, I ended the night buried deep inside her. It was a good trip. Linda was my kind of girl. Six months later, she became the prosecutor's kind of girl.

Bobby was bringing in a few dollars with his dope dealing but it was small-time stuff. One of the best connections and suppliers was Bobby's old friend, Gary Hinman. Gary was an intellect, a professional student and a pretty fair musician. We had known him for some time and he was a good friend. If any of the group was in his area and needed a place to crash, a ride, or a small favor, he always came through. More importantly, Gary manufactured mescaline. He had a small lab in his house, and, given enough time, he would provide us with almost any amount needed.

For several weeks, Bobby had been moving Gary's stuff off on a group of bikers, without any problems. But one morning three of the bikers came riding into the ranch and wanted to see Bobby. The bikers said the latest batch of stuff he had sold them was bad, laced with poison. Some of their own group had gotten deathly ill and some of the people they sold to were also sick. They wanted their money back. Bobby told them to give him the unused mescaline and he would return it to his connection and then give their money back. "It was bad shit and we dumped it. Just give us $2,000 back," said the leader. "Man, I can't buy that, my connection won't go for it," replied Bobby. The leader said, "Tell us where your connection is, we'll get our bread." I spoke up, "You guys know better than that. We'll see our man, if he thinks the shit could have been bad, he'll make it good for you. Give us time to talk to him." The three guys fired up their bikes and pulled out of the yard, saying they wanted to hear from us the next day. Bobby and I discussed the validity of their complaint. None of our group had gotten sick, but we weren't sure if we had used the same batch. The only thing to do was to go talk to Gary about it.

I got Gary on the phone and told him what was going on. Gary said he didn't see how the stuff could have been bad, he hadn't had any complaints from anyone else. Bring the stuff back and he would take a look at it. When I told him there wasn't anything to bring back, he said, "Hell, Charlie, I can't buy that, it's not good business." He was right, I wouldn't have gone for it myself, but Bobby and I were in a cross and neither of us had two thousand we wanted to hand over to the bikers. "Tell you what, Gary, give us enough stuff to turn two thousand, we'll pay the guys their bread and then catch up with you later." "Can't do that," he said, "I'm getting things together so that I can go overseas for a few weeks, besides, you guys still owe me some on the last stuff you got."

His refusal and reference to the money we owed made my blood surge to the top of my head. I was instantly mad and told him, "You cocksucker, you can't leave me hanging like this, your shit was bad and I got people on my case because of it. Now make it right!" I slammed the phone down and muttered something like, "I oughta kill the motherfucker." I told Bobby we would go see him later. "He's got enough money to take us off the hook, but the queer bastard's going to let us hang for his bad shit." Susan had heard the conversation and watched me slam the phone back on the hook. My anger was leaving me and I was a little amused at myself for getting so instantly hot. I winked at Susan and jokingly told her, "Go kill him for me, Sadie." The "go kill him" was said in jest. I never meant it, nor did I ever expect those words to be used against me in a court room. Hinman did die, but not by Sadie's hand and not until days later. And certainly not at my orders.

188

Later that day, Bobby and I had a talk about Hinman. I told Bobby, "It's in your hands, handle it any way you see fit, but get those bikers off our backs."

That evening, Bobby, Susan and Mary said they were going to Gary's for a while. A few hours later, the phone rang and it was Bobby wanting to talk to me. "Christ, Charlie, this asshole won't get up off of nothin'. I had to punch him out and all kinds of shit has happened." "Okay, man, just sit on it for a while, I'll get there as soon as I can," I said. I didn't know what I was going to do once I got there. But the thought hit me, "Gary's a freak behind some kind of Japanese Buddhism, so I'll take my sword along and intimidate his ass with a display of oriental swordsmanship." The sword had been given to me by a biker from the gang before all this hassle had started. I grabbed the sword and asked Bruce to drive to Gary's. When we got there, I had Bruce wait in the car. I went up the stairs and opened the door. The place was a mess and it was plain to see there had been some struggling going on. Gary had refused to come up with any money, he and Bobby had argued, Bobby hit him and threatened him with the gun. On Bobby's orders, Mary and Susan searched the house for money and valuables, anything that might cover the $2,000 that we now totally believed was Gary's responsibility. It was a waste of time. If there was any money around, it was hidden too well for the girls to find it.

Under the circumstances, Gary seemed relieved to see me, but the relief turned to despair when he saw I was there in support of Bobby. "Come on, Gary," I said, "money ain't worth all this hassle. Tell us where your stash is and we'll get out and leave you alone." Gary was livid. He wasn't showing any fear, only contempt, which at the moment was entirely directed at me. "It's all your doing, you phoney little bastard. Get out of my house and take these maniacs with you." He took a step toward me, quivering with rage, and shouted, "Get out!" I jumped back and made a sweep with my sword, cutting his jaw and ear. His hands automatically went up to cover the wound and blood dripped through his fingers. "Oh my God," he whispered, "please get out, can't you understand, I don't have any money. Just go, leave me alone." I turned to Bobby and said, "Talk to him, maybe he'll remember where his money is. Then bring him out to the ranch until he gets

189

well." Then, to Susan and Mary, "Take care of his face. See you back at the ranch," I said, and I went out the door.

Back in the car, Bruce wanted to know what had happened. "Nothing much," I told him, "just had to put some sense in Gary's head." On the way home, unlike the Crowe shooting, I had bad vibes about what I had done to Gary. After we got to the ranch, I grabbed my sleeping bag and went off in the hills. Sleep wouldn't come and my mind raced over all that had happened in recent weeks. Nothing was the same anymore. "Hurry, Charlie," my thoughts said, "get out of the city, there's too many things against you. The people, the cops, the blacks want your ass, and now you're destroying your friends—leave!" Finally I went to sleep. When I woke up, the sun was out and I walked the hills around the ranch before going back to the buildings. From one of the hills I viewed the whole setting. The make-believe western town where all the make-believe cowboys had played at being the real thing. I had played games in it, and pretended, but I had also had dreams and expectations that were real. Those dreams were fading.

Old George, besides wanting us out, was getting ready to sell the ranch. That shouldn't have mattered to me, for we were pretty close to being able to make our move to the desert. But I felt a kinship with the old movie ranch, and besides, I resented the hell out of being told or forced to do something. Fuck, it was just more pressure. I overcame my self-pity, replacing it with bitterness and contempt for anyone who disagreed with me.

When I got back down to the buildings, I went to the kitchen and asked Brenda if Bobby, Susan and Mary were back. She didn't think so. As it turned out, Bobby and the girls didn't come back until the second day. They drove into the ranch yard in Gary's VW bus, and I half expected to see Gary with them. When he wasn't, I knew, without being told, that he would not be visiting anyone—ever.

The girls went straight to the saloon and Bobby came over to me and said, "Gary's dead." According to his account, Gary had started to scream to attract some help, and to quiet the screams, Bobby stabbed him. Bobby handed me the titles to Gary's vehicles, saying, "This is the only thing of value we could come up with." I wasn't shocked at Gary's death, but I sensed a slight increase in my heartbeat as my mind flashed on, "That's two now." I'm sure

190

people would expect me to be affected differently, but emotions aren't controlled by what other people think. My only words to Bobby were, "Where's the other car?" He replied, "It's still at the house." So we went to Gary's house and brought the other car to the ranch.

The bikers had phoned while Bobby and the girls were at Gary's, and my message to them was that we were working on it, but they might have to give us more time. I told them the connection wasn't coming through, and someone might have to go north where we were sure we would come up with enough money to straighten things out. Some of what I said were lies, but I was buying time. Truth is, there might have been enough money around the ranch, but if I could come up with some more drugs for them, I wouldn't have to put out the dollars. With the mark-up for the replacement drugs, I could square things up and still be out less than half the money they felt was owed to them. I knew there wasn't much truth to their story of it being bad shit, anyway. But with the situation at the ranch being what it was, I wanted a group of bikers on my side if the blacks did come down on us.

When I lied about going north, it started me thinking. It would be nice to get out from under all the tension and be on the road for a few days, and who knows what might turn up? So I threw some gear in my truck and told the kids, "I'm taking a trip north to see what I can come up with. Be gone a few days." What I didn't say was that I wasn't feeling too cool about the Hinman thing, and once the body was discovered, there might be some evidence that would lead the police to the ranch.

I left the ranch alone, so it was over a week before I discovered Bobby's fate. When Gary's body was discovered, the police automatically put out an "all-points bulletin" on his vehicles. But two days after I left, Bobby took Gary's Fiat and also headed north. On the first day, Bobby drove as far as San Luis Obispo, where the Fiat quit on him. Too tired, or maybe too stoned, he went to sleep in the car. A highway patrolman arrested him and he ended up back in L.A. as the prime suspect for the murder of Gary Hinman.

On the road I had a slight feeling of guilt. The Hinman thing didn't enter my mind too much, but I was cutting out when so many things at the ranch needed my attention. Foremost was the project for the desert. For over a month now, everything had been

191

nearly ready. All it would take was a couple of days of effort and we could be on our way. But somehow, I always managed to find a reason not to terminate our life at Spahn, even though that life certainly wasn't what it had been in the beginning. Between the police and the anticipated invasion by the blacks, we were living in a state of fear. Fights were more common than lovemaking, and kids were drifting away. It was a situation that would have to be remedied once I got back. But for now, I was on the highway heading away from all those problems.

For the next five days, I would hardly think about the ranch, the desert or anything except what I was doing at the moment. I really didn't have a destination in mind—I was just going north. It was like all my early traveling in '67 and '68: going nowhere, looking for the unexpected.

Just out of Santa Barbara, I spent the night with some old friends. When I left the next day, it was with a supply and variety of drugs that would take the bikers off our backs and make a lot of the kids at the ranch happy. Following Highway One, my next stop was Big Sur. After I was first released from prison, I would often go there to escape from what was going on at the Haight. So, looking for that feeling of escape, I drove there now. I spent the night in my truck, and the next day, I visited the Esalen Institute to enjoy the mineral baths. It was totally relaxing and I felt refreshed when I left.

After leaving the Institute, I parked my truck by the ocean, smoked a joint, played some music and fell asleep. About two in the morning, I woke up and went looking for a coffee shop. While looking, I pulled into a service station for some gas and to take a leak. On my way out of the john, a young, pretty girl was going into the ladies' john and I lingered until she came out. When she did, I asked what a pretty girl like her was doing out so late at night—by now it was well after three. She pointed to a car with a guy sitting in it and said she was with him. "Is he your boyfriend and are you having fun?" I asked her. "Not really, he's a rube," she said. "Well then, why don't you leave him and come with me, I promise you fun." I made the pass without thinking, in fact, I wondered if I should keep my mouth shut before her friend got out of his car and wanted to fight. Her answer surprised me. She said, "I will, if you take me back to San Diego eventually." "Agreed," I answered, "let's get your things." The guy she was with couldn't

192

believe the girl was leaving him for a stranger. But he didn't give either of us a hassle. We got in my truck and were on our way to nowhere—just party time. Me and Stephanie Schram.

We spent the night on the beach. I laid some acid on her—her first. Nothing crazy happened, but the acid put her in another world. At my suggestion, she peeled off her clothes and ran and played along the beach like a young sea nymph. Through the acid she saw herself as a princess, a stripper, a witch and a whore, and we went through sex acts to accomodate each of her fantasies. When we woke up the next morning, she was in love with me and swore never to leave. She also wanted another hit of acid. I told her, "No, that's just for special occasions, and in the future we'll have plenty of those."

We headed back south to the ranch. Stephanie liked what she saw and wanted to live there. We stuck around for a few hours and then went to San Diego to get Stephanie's possessions. While at the ranch, I was told that Bobby had left and taken Gary's Fiat—at this time no one knew he was already in jail. But shortly after I left, Bobby phoned the ranch and informed Linda that he had been picked up as a suspect for the murder of Gary Hinman.

The trip to San Diego was a leisurely one. I was relieved to learn that no police had been to the ranch, so I could give my full attention to my new love, a seventeen-year-old beauty who was experiencing things she had never dreamed of. I enjoyed the showing and the teaching. Being on the road with Stephanie was reminiscent of 1967 and my first travels in northern California.

Stephanie had been living with her sister and brother-in-law. After getting Stephanie's possessions and having dinner with her relatives, we headed back to Spahn. Though we could have made it back that night, I was in no hurry. I was clinging to the pleasures of the moment and losing the tensions that had been pounding in my head for the last few months. We spent the night sleeping beside the truck. We counted stars, told stories and made love. The early morning sun woke us up. It was August 8, 1969.

Days and dates are not my thing, but the events of the following hours established this as one of the worst in the lives of many, many people. It was around noon when I drove the truck into Spahn Ranch. As I pulled to a stop, the usual "happy to see me faces" were not there. The individuals were present, but their faces showed strain and tension, not smiles and welcome. Sensing the need for some serious conversation I introduced Stephanie to those she hadn't previously met and suggested some of them take her on a tour of the ranch.

As a group, Leslie, Mary, Squeaky, Sadie and Linda informed me of Bobby's arrest. Linda repeated the phone conversation with Bobby, the charges and what he had told the police. At present, he was being held as a suspect and had not been charged with murder. After the phone call, the girls had held their own meeting and discussed the best method of assisting Bobby. They decided that if murders similar to the Hinman slaying continued to occur, the police would begin to believe Bobby was not their man. They hadn't got as far as figuring out who was going to do these copy-cat killings or who would be the victims.

I told them the plan was crazy and that the police wouldn't go for it. Sadie blurted out, "It will work, Charlie. At Gary's house, we wrote things on the wall like 'Political Piggy' and drew a panther's paw and that kind of stuff. We can do it again and they will think the niggers did it. It will be Helter Skelter." Her words were reflections of what I had been saying to the kids in recent months, but the difference was that I did feel the blacks were tiring of their suppression. They would rise up against the whites, and there would be chaos. Maybe since the shooting of Crowe, I had purposely initiated fear and resentment of blacks in the kids, but I had never wanted to start a war. My concern was for defense and awareness. Leave it to Sadie to throw my words back at me. I almost shouted, "Look, it ain't going to work! You fucking people have got me headed right back to prison. I'm not going for it! As a matter of fact, I'm getting my shit together right now, loading it in my truck and getting the fuck out of here. I am not going back to prison because a bunch of kids can't handle their own problems."

Squeaky was the first to speak up, "No, you can't go, love is one! We are one!" Again, my words came right back in my face. "If one goes," she said, "we go together!" Sadie begged, "Don't go, Charlie, we won't let you go back to jail. We'll take care of Bobby. We will do what we have to do to take care of our problems. Stay, Charlie." All the girls said the same thing. "Don't leave us, Charlie, stay here, we need you! We can do whatever is necessary and we won't send you back to jail."

194

Deep inside, I knew that if I stuck around, anything those kids did would come right back in my lap. No way could they keep me out of prison if the shit came down on us. But as I looked at them, I remembered something special about each one. The first meeting, the first romance, the first fight, the times I loved them most, as well as the times I disciplined them. They had given me the first real love and sense of belonging I had ever known. I also realized— though I would not admit it to them—that I needed them. And as far as the heavy situation surrounding us went, I was as responsible as they were. And I knew it.

"All right," I said, "I'll stay, but what you do is on your heads, not mine—understood?" Together they said, "We understand, Charlie." There were smiles, hugs and kisses.

With that, we dropped the talk of Bobby and pending plans. My days away from the ranch and the events concerning Bobby had taken a toll on the normal routine. People were bum-kicked, they were down and they needed something to raise their spirits. I told Squeaky to pull out some credit cards and send someone to town for gifts and trinkets. New items always made the girls happy and I wanted to see some smiling faces. Squeaky gave the cards to Mary and Sandy and sent them after goodies.

I went into the kitchen to see what Brenda might need to prepare an extra special meal. She gave me a list and I asked Bruce to take one of the girls and get the needed supplies. Before leaving the kitchen, I asked Brenda how she had been feeling, if the effects of the talatche still bothered her. She explained she still had slight fainting spells, but nothing weird anymore. "How about Tex?" I asked, and she replied, "You know Tex, it's hard to tell if he's on an old high or just starting a new one. He and Katie did some acid a little while ago. The last time I saw him, he was headed toward the back house."

I found Tex, as Brenda had said, stoned in the back house. When I walked in, he was sitting on an old couch, his head bobbing and his hands tapping his legs in time to some music that no one could hear except Tex. Inside his head, he was probably doing a command performance at the Hollywood Bowl. "Hey, man, how are you?" I asked. His head rolled back and his eyes focused. He jumped up, shouting, "Hey, Charlie, you're back! All right! Geez, it's good you're here. Guess you heard about Bobby?" "Yeah, Tex, I

195

heard about Bobby," I said, "It's a tough way to see a brother go down." Tex nodded his head in agreement and said, "But things are going to be all right. The girls got a plan, and now that you're back we can get on with it. Bobby will be out in no time. Did they tell you what they want to do? Have you talked to them yet?" "I just left them a few minutes ago," I replied, adding, "Thing is, partner, I told them what they do, they do on their own. I ain't ready to go back to jail." "I hear you," he said, "Jail's not where it's at!"

I knew Tex was wiped out, but I also knew that he could function pretty well while on one of his trips. Tex had good retention of what he said and did until he reached a state of complete unconsciousness. To make sure, I asked him, "How's your head, Tex? I mean are you together, do you know what I'm saying to you, can you hold on to it?" "Sure, Charlie," he said, "you know me, sometimes I go overboard and lose a day or two, but if I'm on my feet and talking, I can stay with it." Satisfied he wasn't that far gone, I went on with what I had to say. "Tex, you remember the black and what I told you when I came home after killing him?" Tex was very quiet and thoughtful. It wasn't as though he hadn't heard or understood, it was like he knew what was coming next and wanted his head to be ready to take it. And he was right, some heavy things were going to be laid on him. "That life I took for you was your life. Bobby is my brother. He is your brother. And to save our brother, I'm asking you for the life you owe me." Tex pulled himself to his full height, looked me in the eyes and solemnly said, "I can handle it, Charlie. What have you got planned?" "I don't have any plans," I told him, "it's the girls' thing. I just know they can't take care of it by themselves. Whatever they decide, they're going to need a man to carry it out."

I left Tex and headed to the boardwalk. Stephanie and the girls had returned from their tour; they were laughing at Clem, who was imitating some of the people he knew. Stephanie somehow seemed different from the typical girl who ventured onto the ranch and remained. She didn't have the resentment and hostility toward authority the rest of us shared. She was kind of a class broad, and I wondered how long she would stay with us.

As I walked toward the group, she broke away and ran up to me. She was impressed with the ranch and the people who lived on it. "Which house are we going to live in?" she asked. I hadn't yet told

196

her that I didn't belong to anyone and that she wouldn't belong to just me. Why say anything now, I thought. So I took her by the hand and we walked away from the others. "Well now, my pretty little thing," I said, "I really haven't decided which of these stately mansions I want to make into a palace for my queen. Maybe we'll just use a different place every night. When we've made love in every one of them, we'll decide which place is the best for us, and that will be our castle." "Okay then," she said, "let's get in the truck and go back to Big Sur." We both laughed, remembering the beach and her acid trip.

I thought, "Charlie, you are a rotten bastard! Why don't you take this girl back to her righteous home? You like her, and today you might love her, but you know that tomorrow or the next day, you're going to pass her on to someone else. Why fuck up another life?" But those were weird thoughts for me. What was happening to my head? Was this little girl getting her claws in me? Aloud, I said, "I think, for tonight, we will sleep in that little trailer right there. Did you get your things out of the truck?" She answered that she had, and Squeaky had been given everything, so I arranged to see her at dinner. I needed time to think.

That evening, I sought out Squeaky. I wanted to check on the other girls, but the important issue was what to do about Bobby. My first step on the porch of George's house brought her to the door, and her first words were, "I've been waiting for you." She brought out two cups of coffee and we sat on the porch. "Have you heard from Mary and Sandy?" I asked. "No, not yet," she replied, "it really isn't that late so we shouldn't worry. But I have the strangest feeling. Maybe it doesn't mean anything. We'll know in an hour or so."

With that out of the way, I got on with my real reason for coming to Squeaky. "Have the girls made any plans? I mean when and where?" She said, "Charlie, you know Susan doesn't plan anything. If somebody doesn't guide her, tell her or push her into something, she isn't going to get anything done. If we wait for her to make a decision, Bobby will be in the gas chamber and Susan will be saying, 'Don't worry, I'll take care of it.' You know that! And Katie is trying to run away from it, she's on an acid trip right now. Linda is into any kind of thrill. She'll probably go along, but she isn't going to originate anything. They're going to need help. You're going to

197

have to handle it, Charlie, they'll need a man with them." "Girl," I said, "I told you kids, I do not want to go back to jail! Tex owes me—he will be the man. But I'm out of it!" Squeaky smiled and said, "Okay, Charlie, we'll see. It's time to eat. You go ahead, I'll be right there."

I walked to the main cluster of buildings and into the saloon. There were about fifteen people there, but on special occasions such as I had meant this meal to be, there were normally twice as many. Bobby, T.J., and several others were gone. Damn it, things were changing. Depression swept over me. But I didn't have time to let it get the best of me. Everyone was waiting and they were hungry and anxious to hear about my days away from the ranch. I went into one of my happy, "everything is okay" routines and said, "Let's eat! Mary and Sandy will soon be here with gifts for every-one. And here on my right is the newest member of our happy group, Miss Stephanie Schram, most recently from San Diego and given to us by a tab of acid and a moonlit beach at Big Sur." Steph-anie's face flushed as she nodded to the applause from those present.

Brenda had done a masterful job with the vegetables and other "throw-outs" from the local supermarkets. During the meal, I told of my experiences while away from the ranch. The conversation was light and joyful and I projected the same joy, but inside I was very troubled.

During the month of August, the days in southern California last until nine-thirty or ten o'clock in the evening. By the time we fin-ished our dinner, it was almost dark. Mary and Sandy were still not home. A look at Squeaky told me she was also worried about the two shoppers. Being the first to travel with me, Squeaky and Mary shared things many of the others didn't. Though Squeaky was younger than Sandy, she very much mothered by her. It was natu-ral Squeaky would show deep concern for her two favorite people.

Shortly after ten o'clock the phone rang. It was Sandy. She and Mary had been arrested while shopping with the stolen credit cards. Squeaky took the call and relayed the bad news to me. She was upset, but I was in a rage. I walked away from the buildings, stood beside a tree and pounded my fists against it until the shak-ing rage left my body, but my head was still pounding. I forgot that the girls were doing something illegal, forgot the murder of Hinman and the shooting of Crowe. All I could focus on was, "What the fuck is happening here? One by one this fucked-up society is stripping my loves from me. I'll show them! They made animals out of us—I'll unleash those animals—I'll give them so much fucking fear the people will be afraid to come out of their houses!" These thoughts might sound like pure insanity, but every abuse, every rejection in my entire life flashed before me. Hatred, fury, insanity—I felt all of these things. "Get a hold of yourself, Charlie," I thought. "Slow down, be cool, think this thing out." My head stopped throbbing, but no self-analysis could drive me away from the thought of revenge. I went looking for Sadie and Tex.

Sadie and Linda were in front of the old movie set with some of the other kids. I motioned for them to take a walk with me, and when we were out of hearing range I said, "It's time to do something to help our brother. Have you thought about it?" Linda just looked at me and shrugged her shoulders. Sadie hesitated and then said, "Well, yeah, like I said, we'll do it witchy and then make it look like the same person that did Gary in is still out and doing it again." A little irritated, I asked, "I mean, Sadie, do you have a plan, do you have a house picked out?" "Well—no but . . ." she stammered. "But, my ass, Sadie. I'll talk to Tex. You just do what Tex tells you!" I was getting angry at her so I left, telling her to get her things together.

Looking for Tex, I ran into Stephanie. "When are you going to take me to my palace?" she asked. I wasn't in the mood, but I didn't want Stephanie to be aware of what was going on. I put my arm around her shoulders and walked her to the trailer, took her inside, gave her a couple of kisses and a pinch on her tit, and then told her, "Look, I've got some important business to take care of for the next hour or so, and then I'll be back, okay?" I left, thinking I would be back in a short while.

I went through the back house looking for Tex, but ran across Katie instead. She was lying down, trying to shake the effects of her afternoon acid trip. I nudged her with my foot, saying, "Katie, Katie, get up. You're going for a ride with Tex and Sadie." She was still groggy when I walked away, but I knew she would get up and do what she was told. As I left the back house, I spotted Tex walking toward the boardwalk. I gave him a call, he stopped, and we

199

had a talk near the corral fence. I did most of the talking. "It's time to get something done for Bobby. The girls are ready to do whatever is necessary. They don't have a plan or a place picked out, so it looks like it's going to be pretty much up to you. But I think it would be best to hit some of the rich pigs' places. Get some bolt cutters or something you can cut a phone wire or gate chain with. You know what else you need, so put it all together and get going." He said, "Geez, Charlie, my mind's not working, I can't think of a house." "Come on, Tex," I said, "you've been to a lot of those rich guys' places. You know the neighborhoods—someplace like where Terry used to live. Just make sure the girls do it like Gary's house was done. Maybe even take some rope and hang somebody, like a reverse of the Ku Klux Klan thing; that way it will put the heat on the blackies."

Twenty minutes later, the old Ford and its crew of four pulled out of the dirt driveway.

Watching the car leave, my mind flashed on the events of less than twelve hours ago, when I had pulled into that same driveway and declared I would leave the kids, the ranch, and the lifestyle rather than be part of something that was sure to put me back in jail. Now I was so much a part of it, I might as well have been in the car with the others, knife and gun in hand. I knew that each suggestion dropped to Tex would be followed as a course of action. Whatever they did, it would be the same as if I had done it with them. For one short moment, I had an urge to overtake the car and bring them back. Instead, I turned and walked in the direction of the trailer where Stephanie waited.

The thoughts that were flooding my head wouldn't allow for any tender lovemaking. The devil needed time to himself. So I turned away from the trailer and Stephanie and took a long walk. Maybe sometime during that walk I thought of how wrong it all was. Personally, I had never believed any tactics, copy-cat or otherwise, were going to get Bobby off the hook. Yet I had let the kids run with their scheme, and just minutes ago, I had put the clincher on it by saying, "It's time to go!" I had shared in the madness. I had a moment or two of regret, but for the most part, bitterness and contempt for a world I didn't give a shit about allowed me to go along with anything that might come of the night's activities.

I felt Tex had forced the Crowe incident on me, and that act had put us up against a wall of fear and paranoia that was reflected in all the changes that happened since. As for Hinman, even though I had lifted a hand against him, in my present frame of mind it was easy to lay the blame on the three who had botched a simple job going to the guy for money. I felt that these two incidents were more behind the direction the old Ford was headed than any beliefs of Charles Manson. I hadn't twisted any arms. I wasn't sitting behind anyone with a gun next to their head, giving directions. Yet, I can't deny making some of the suggestions that led to the events of that night. Nor can I deny that I was the one person who could have prevented that car from leaving Spahn Ranch. But—so goes the feeling of power when coupled with hatred.

CHAPTER 8

O<small>N THAT EVENING</small>, August 8, 1969, I was aware of being totally without conscience. Though I have pointed to numerous circumstances in my life that may have turned my head in the wrong direction, I can't put a finger on when I became devoid of caring emotion.

While waiting for the kids to return, some of my thinking went back to the day in 1967 when I walked out of prison. At that time I resented the law and the system, but I respected the people who abided by the laws and supported the system. During those first months after my release, I knew a love and a sense of belonging that was the greatest reward of my life. I remembered the time I had taken the guns and thrown them in the bay because of the violence they represented. I found myself thinking, was that only two years ago? It seemed like another lifetime. Here I was, waiting for a report of murder to come back to me, not caring who had died or how many victims there were. And the closest I could come to disliking myself was, "Charlie, you are your mother's son—one dirty bogus bastard."

Thinking of my mother quickly altered any softness that may have been creeping into my mind. I saw my mother guiding me through the court room door, and heard her speak the words, "Yes, your Honor, I want my son, but I just can't afford to support both of us at this time." I remembered the argument she had had with her boyfriend a few nights prior to that day in court, and I heard him saying, "I don't give a shit, I'm leaving, I can't stand that kid. Get rid of him and we can make it just fine." I saw four larger and older guys beating the hell out of me and wrestling me to the floor, and I remembered them holding me while one ripped my ass with his big cock and then the others took their turn. I thought of good old Mr. Fields, in charge of all the boys and paid to teach us the responsibility of being honest citizens, lubricating my asshole with

202

tobacco juice and raw silage and then offering me to his favorite pets.

My head was straight now. Fuck this world and everyone in it. I'd give them something to open their eyes, and then take our group out into the desert.

I saw the headlights and recognized the old Ford before it pulled in the driveway. By the time it stopped, I was almost to its parking place. I wasn't sure what time it was, but it had to be around two in the morning, and I was ready to hear the details of the night's activities.

Sadie was the first one out of the car. She was beaming with excitement as she ran up to me and threw her arms around my neck, saying, "Oh, Charlie, we did it . . . I took my life for you!" "Girl," I said, taking her arms from around my neck, "what you did, you did for yourself! What you've done is lock me to you." I pulled away from her and walked toward the car. Tex was getting out and favoring his leg. My first thought was he had been wounded, but he had only bruised his foot while kicking one of the victims. He was glassy-eyed and grinning, and while not as high as Sadie, he was not suffering from remorse. To the contrary, other than his limp, he was moving around with an air of arrogance. We clasped hands and exchanged a brotherly hug. I told him, "Don't go away, I want to hear about it." Linda and Katie were slowly getting out of the car and I wanted to have a look and a word with each of them. Both indicated they were not feeling too good. I told them to make sure the car was free of any possible evidence and then to go to bed. Sadie, having noticed some blood on the exterior of the car, was already on her way out of the saloon with the needed items to thoroughly clean the vehicle. Sadie Mae Glutz was completing her night's work without orders from anyone.

The car cleaned and inspected, Tex, Sadie and I sat down in the bunk house so that I could get a complete run-down on all that had happened. Sadie was really fired; she couldn't sit still unless her mouth was going so she did most of the telling.

Tex had straight away driven to the house Terry Melcher had once lived in. He was familiar with the place, since Tex and I had both visited when Melcher lived there. It was a wealthy neighborhood, Bel Air, and the seclusion of the house was a major consideration. Once there, they drove uphill toward the dead end at

203

the top of Cielo Drive. Then they went past the driveway, turned the car around and parked it facing downhill, ready for a quick escape. Before the girls got out of the car, Tex climbed a telephone pole and used the bolt cutters to cut the lines leading into the house. Avoiding the driveway and gate, the four of them entered the yard by climbing over the fence. As they walked up the driveway, lights flashed from a car coming down in the opposite direction. The four immediately dropped to the ground and the car came to a halt so the driver could open the gate. When the car stopped, Tex approached the driver, a teenage boy (Steven Parent) and shot him several times with the .22 Buntline revolver I had used to shoot Crowe. The four of them then pushed the car back off the driveway.

They waited until they were satisfied the shots had not alerted anyone, then went on to the house, a ranch-style dwelling with a large lawn and a swimming pool. The girls stood at a rear door while Tex cut through a screen and entered the home through a window. Opening the door, he asked Sadie and Katie to come with him, telling Linda to remain outside to warn them if she saw or heard anyone approaching.

As they quietly entered the living room, they saw the first of the four individuals who were in the house. A man [Voytek Frykowski] had fallen asleep on the couch with the lights on. Motioning for the girls to circle from behind, Tex approached the sleeping man and stuck the gun in the sleeper's face, saying, "Wake up!" The man opened his eyes to see the barrel of a pistol less than six inches away. Startled, he tried to get up, but Tex put the gun against the man's forehead and told him to stay where he was. Sadie excitedly described the first encounter, "Oh, Charlie, you should have seen it. Here's Tex standing over the man with a gun in one hand and a knife in the other, and with the coil of rope over his shoulder; he reminded me of a Mexican *bandoliero*. And when the man asked what he was doing there, who he was and what he wanted, Tex told him, 'I'm the Devil and I want your money.' Tex really *looked* like the Devil." Tex then sent Sadie to look for something to tie the man up, because he had other plans for the rope he was carrying. She brought back a towel and she and Katie used it to tie the man's hands behind his back.

Sadie then went through the house, checking for other occu-

204

pants. Going down a hall she passed an open bedroom door, and inside, lying in bed reading a book, was a young lady [Abigail Folger]. "It was the funniest thing," described Sadie, "it was like the lady almost expected me to be there. She glanced at me and said, 'hi,' so I waved at her and said 'hi' back. Then I went on past her room until I came to another door. Looking in I saw a pregnant lady lying on her bed [Sharon Tate]. She was beautiful Charlie, you'd have loved her. A guy [Jay Sebring] was sitting on the edge of the bed holding her hand and talking to her. Neither one even looked up. I went back and told Tex about the other three people."

Tex told Sadie to bring the other three into the living room. Sadie was very proud that, armed only with a knife, she had intimidated the three so convincingly. Once they were all in the living room, Tex started giving orders and demanding money. He gave the rope to the two girls and told them to tie it around the prisoners' necks. The untied man (Sebring) made a lunge at Tex, and Tex pulled the trigger of the gun. Sebring fell to the floor wounded, looking up at Tex with an expression of fear and disbelief. Tex planted a foot in his face, injuring himself in the process.

Until this point things had been going smoothly for the invaders, but with the shot and the first injury, fear and hysteria prompted the victims to struggle for their lives. But those kids had come to kill and they were bent on doing so in a shocking, sensational manner. The desperate struggles of their victims only intensified their acts of violence.

Sebring still lay on the floor. Tate and Folger screamed, but fell silent after being threatened with knives by the girls. A rope was then placed around the necks of the two women and Sebring. The prisoners wanted to know the intentions of the invaders, and Tex informed them they had to die to save his brother. Hysterically, the women pleaded for their lives. Sadie went over to add more bonds to the already-tied Frykowski. As she began her task, Tex said, "Kill him!" Sadie raised her arm to plunge with her knife, but Frykowski managed to free his hands and grabbed Sadie by the hair. They struggled, and Sadie stabbed away while Frykowski pulled her hair and tried to ward off the thrusts of the knife, finally causing her to drop it somewhere near the couch. Severely wounded, Frykowski broke loose and headed toward the yard. Tex left Katie holding the rope attached to Sebring, Folger and Tate, and ran to catch the fleeing man. Frykowski, now in the yard, struggled and fought desperately as Tex administered the final knife wounds.

Tex's final thrusts were suddenly interrupted by a frantic shout from Katie. While Tex and Sadie had been focusing their attention on Frykowski, Folger had freed herself from the noose and was making an effort to escape. Katie caught her, but was losing the battle until Tex got there. He clubbed Folger with the pistol and then stabbed her until he thought she was dead. Between his dash from Frykowski to Katie, Tex saw Sebring moving, and paused long enough to make several knife thrusts into Sebring's body. Once Folger was down and apparently dead, Tex returned to finish the job on Frykowski.

Tate, meanwhile, frozen in fear, had not made an attempt to flee until now. The three kids were still outside with Frykowski and she made a run for it in the opposite direction. Katie saw her and alerted Sadie, and the two girls easily caught Sharon and brought her back into the living room. Sharon, still unharmed, now had the full attention of all three killers. Ignoring her pleas for her life and the life of her unborn child, Sadie held her while Tex stabbed. But at some point, Sadie must have borrowed someone's knife, because she said she also had stabbed Sharon.

The kids then went about adding their witchy "get Bobby out of jail" decoration to the premises. Using Sharon's blood. Sadie wrote the word "PIG" inside the house. They abandoned the idea of stringing the victims from the rafters, explaining, "Everything was too messy and we were too tired." Linda had left the property and had the motor running by the time the others reached the car. On the drive back to the ranch, they discarded their clothing and weapons at various points along the way by throwing them over embankments from the moving car.

A normal person would find the details of the night's events shocking and horrifying, but I had long ago stopped measuring myself by society's standards. The story I was hearing from Tex and Sadie did not shock me. I did not feel pity or compassion for the victims. My only concern was whether it resembled the Hinman killing. Would the police now have reason to believe that Bobby was not the slayer of Hinman? And were the kids, loaded with drugs, clever enough to avoid leaving prints or evidence of their identities? Knowing Sadie and Tex, and their flair for dramatic exaggeration, I doubted the slayings went down as they had described. Most importantly, did they leave a trail that would lead to the ranch? Concern for clues compelled me to get in the Ford and head for Bel Air. I took another member of our circle with me.

Returning to the scene of any crime is risky business, so instead of turning up Cielo Drive, we drove past and looked up the hill to see if there was any activity that might indicate the police had arrived. Everything was quiet. Still not wanting to be too obvious, we parked the car a short distance away and walked to the premises. We entered the grounds by climbing over the fence, as the kids had done. As Sadie and Tex had said, the first victim's car was off the driveway a short distance from the gate. Going by Tex's description of how he had approached the car and how he had pushed it, I carefully wiped the car clean of possible finger prints without disturbing the body of the boy who lay dead inside.

Approaching a house where you know there are dead bodies has a spine-chilling effect, and I think if I had been alone, I might have forgotten about continuing any farther. My partner probably felt the same way, but neither of us spoke and we did go on to see the whole gory mess. Tex and Sadie's description had been accurate. What I was seeing was not a scene from a movie or some horrible acid fantasy, but real people who would never see the morning's sun. I'd had thoughts of creating a scene more in keeping with a black-against-white retaliation, but in looking around, I lost the heart to carry out my plans. The two of us took towels and wiped every place a fingerprint could have been left. I then placed the towel I was using over the head of the man inside the room. My partner had an old pair of eyeglasses which we often used as a magnifying glass or as a device to start a fire when matches weren't available. We carefully wiped the glasses free of prints and dropped them on the floor, so that, when discovered, they would be a misleading clue for the police. Within an hour and twenty minutes after leaving Spahn, we were back. The sun was already bringing the light of day as I crawled in bed with Stephanie.

I slept until well past noon and by the time I walked out of the trailer, the deaths had been discovered and were the major topic of all news broadcasts. Sadie, Linda and Katie had been waiting for me to appear and immediately gave me a word-for-word update on

207

what was being reported on the radio and TV. It was through the broadcasts that we first learned the names of the victims.

The three girls—Tex slept most of the day and wasn't around—spent their day with each other, doing a lot of whispering and getting close to a radio or a television when it was time for a newscast. They seemed to have taken on an air of superiority over the rest of those at the ranch. As for myself, I was surprised at how prestigious three of the victims were. Tate had been extremely popular in the celebrity world. Folger, heiress to the Folger coffee fortune, had been rich beyond the average person's dreams. Sebring had been a hair stylist of international fame.

In learning of the popularity and wealth of the victims, I suddenly felt cheated that the kids had come away from the scene with less than a hundred dollars in cash. Later newscasts reported that a variety of drugs was found by the police and I felt added disappointment in myself and the kids for not searching the place for valuables and narcotics. Whatever else went on in my mind regarding the previous night, remorse or compassion did not affect me. I did, in days to come, have my private laughs at the theories and speculations of the police and reporters as they announced possible motives for the slayings, but I was disappointed that no connection was made between the recent murders and Hinman's death. While rumors were still flying and the police still scratching their heads, I had visions of another night that would add to the confusion and make the affairs of that night look like more than copy-cat murders. We'd make it appear as though a full-scale war was being waged against the whites.

Leslie Van Houten was a girl Bobby had been traveling with for several months. She was very concerned about Bobby's being in jail and was willing to do anything to help get him out. After dinner that evening, she and six others—Tex, Sadie, Linda, Katie, Clem and myself—stuffed ourselves into Swartz's old Ford and went searching for victims, random victims, so many of them that the deaths would shock not only the area but the whole world.

All of us had taken mild hits of acid; not enough to space us so far out that we would leap off buildings or jump in front of speeding cars, but enough to make us feel invincible, enough to make us feel the world was totally ours and that there was no right, no wrong. We felt free of guilt. During our search for the right place to

208

continue spreading fear and panic, we were not a bunch of uptight kids, but a singing, laughing group who might have been on their way to a party.

We did a lot of driving that night. From the ranch, we toured San Fernando Valley, Santa Monica, West L.A., Hollywood, Pasadena and everywhere in between. Several stops were made to check out houses and occupants, with me doing the checking. We stuck mostly to homes that indicated wealth. The first couple of homes I cased looked middle class, so I told the kids to drive on. At one point I had them stop in front of a church. As I started out of the car, Linda said in a surprised voice, "We aren't going to kill a priest are we?" "No, *we* aren't, but *I* am," I responded. "Besides, what's so fucking different about a priest? They eat, shit and tell lies just like you and me." Actually, I had just stopped the car because I had to take a piss. But to keep her thinking for a minute or two, I walked to the side door of the church, took a leak out of sight of the car and stood there for a couple of minutes. When I returned to the car, I told the kids the priest had lucked out, no one answered the bell.

After over two hours of driving with nothing coming down, I thought of an area out near Griffith Park. In the past we had partied at a guy's pad in that neighborhood. It was a pretty ritzy area with some pretty big homes. A couple of the kids recognized the house, and said again, "We aren't, are we?" "No," I said, "I'm thinking about the house across the street. Wait here, I'll be right back." [*The house across the street was the home of Leno and Rosemary LaBianca at 3301 Waverly Drive. —Nuel Emmons*]

I walked up a long driveway and looked in a window. The only person I could see was a heavy-set guy about forty-five years old who had fallen asleep while reading a newspaper. Satisfied that this was where the night's work would start, I went back to the car and got Tex. The two of us, me with a gun and Tex with a knife, went to the back door. It was open. A big dog met us as we entered, but instead of barking or growling he licked my hand. We went into the living room. To wake the sleeper up, I nudged him with the gun. His eyes opened to see a pistol pointed at his face. With a startled look and an equally startled voice, he asked, "Who—who are you? What are you doing here? What do you want?" "Just relax, pal," I said. "We're not going to hurt you, just be cool. Don't be afraid." He was honest in his reply: "That's easy enough for you to say, but how can I help but be afraid when you've got a gun pointed at me?" "It's all right man, nothin's going to happen to you, all we want is your money. Is there anyone else in the house?" "Yes, my wife's in the bedroom, but don't bother her. I'll give you all I have," he answered.

I handed Tex a leather thong and had him tie the fellow's hands behind his back while I went into the bedroom after his wife. Like her husband, she was asleep. I pulled the covers off of her and touched her shoulder, saying, "Wake up, lady, you got company." Her sleepy eyes focused on me. Then, with a start, she sat up and grabbed for the covers in an effort to hide her body. She had a nightgown on, but to assist her in her modesty, I handed her a dress that was folded over the back of a chair. She quickly pulled it over her nightgown, and said, "What are you doing here? What do you want?" She was a pretty lady, close to forty, and very composed, considering a stranger with a gun pointed at her was in her bedroom. "Don't be alarmed, lady, no one's going to get hurt," I said. "We're just after some money." With that I moved her into the living room. "Okay, where's your money?" I asked them both. "In my wallet in the bedroom," her husband answered, "and some more in my wife's purse." I sent Tex to get the wallets. They contained less than a hundred dollars. "Is that it?" I asked. "Yes, that's all we have here, but if you'll take me to my store, there's more. All you want."

I thought about leaving Tex and some of the girls to guard the wife while the guy took me to his store. Hell, I thought, if he owns a store and has offered me anything I want, maybe there were big bucks there. But then I thought, he's just buying time. Maybe there was a store and maybe there wasn't. He might just be looking for a way to trap us. No, what I had in hand would have to do.

When we left the ranch, I had been geared to handle some of the dirty work. The kids had done their thing last night, and I was going to perform for them tonight. But these two people were not panicking or doing anything that might set off a surge of temper that would make me strike out at them. Somehow I couldn't make that first move. Thinking that if just the husband and I were head-on I could initiate an attack, I told Tex to take the lady back to her bedroom. I purposely turned my back on the guy to watch Tex and

210

the lady go out of the room, thinking he would make a lunge at me and in defense I could do what had to be done. He didn't, and when Tex came back, I told him, "Guard them, I'll send the girls back."

I walked to the car and told Katie and Leslie to go give Tex a hand. "Do it good! Make sure it's done so the pigs will put it together with Hinman and that pad last night. We're going to find another house. When you finish up, hitch back to the ranch and we'll see you there."

I got in the car with Sadie, Clem and Linda, saying, "Okay, it's our turn. Who's got someone on their shit list?" Linda spoke up. "There's this dude over in Venice, thinks he's the world's greatest stud. We made it together once and the asshole couldn't even bring me." We headed toward Venice. On the way, thinking we were passing through a black neighborhood, I had Linda take the lady's wallet into the john of a service station and leave it there. That way the blacks would get the heat for what was going to happen on Waverly Drive.

When we got to Venice and the apartment house Linda directed us to, I had come off the acid and wasn't feeling all that confident we were invincible. When we stopped, I handed the gun to Clem, saying, "You're the stud, help these girls do their thing. See you when you're finished." I sat in the car for a few minutes trying to picture what had happened on Waverly Drive and imagining what was going on in the apartment here in Venice. I realized I was just sitting there waiting for the police to come, and if they showed up, I was on my way back to the joint. I started the car, drove to Santa Monica, stopped for some breakfast, then went back to the ranch to wait.

I started worrying about what the kids might bring down on themselves and what kind of attention they might bring to the ranch. I didn't want to be a sitting duck, so instead of hanging out around the buildings, I grabbed a sleeping bag and headed for a spot where it would take some searching to find me. Just in case. Sometime in the afternoon, I went back to the buildings and was relieved to see some of the kids from each group. Sadie was off sleeping somewhere, but Clem and Linda let me know what had happened in Venice. Nothing! The three of them had gone to the apartment Linda identified and knocked on the door. When no one answered, they gave up the night's effort and hitchhiked back to

211

the ranch. Several months later, Linda spread the story she had decided she didn't want to see the guy dead, and had purposely taken Clem and Sadie to a different apartment.

As for Katie, Leslie and Tex, they reported they had done the "number of numbers" at the LaBianca residence. Stab wounds were as plentiful as those administered the previous night. To add to the horror, a knife was left in the man's throat and a carving fork in his stomach. As at the Hinman and the Tate scenes, they had used the victim's blood to print out messages—"RISE," on one wall, "DEATH TO PIGS" on another and "HEALTER SKELTER" on the refrigerator doors. Katie, doing the printing on the fridge, had misspelled it.

In twenty-four hours, seven of the most brutal murders in Los Angeles' history were committed. The media got on top of it, and before a week had passed there were many different versions of the reason for the slayings. Fear and paranoia had spread from Spahn's to all of Los Angeles. Neighbors stopped trusting neighbors. Everyone in L.A. began double locking doors, looking over their shoulders, panicking at every sound and carrying guns. And the more the media sensationalized the crimes, the wider the grin got on my face. Yet for all the publicity, the similarity of the blood-written messages on the walls and the savagery of the slayings, the Tate-LaBianca murders were never compared to Hinman's. Bobby was still the prime suspect in the Hinman case, and we had not taken any of the heat off him. For that, I felt some disappointment. I was also disappointed that my ploy for dropping the suspicion on the blacks didn't work. The wallet wasn't discovered for four months, and the district that I thought was predominantly black, I later found out, wasn't black at all.

At the ranch, a circle of people who had always been one now became two: those who knew and those who didn't. Katie, Linda, Leslie and Sadie had their secrets, and they would whisper among themselves and stop talking when some of the other kids appeared. That started a little wave of, "What's going on that I don't know about? Why aren't I included? Are they talking about me?" Some complexes started showing. I wasn't fond of the situation, but how the hell can a guy blurt out to twenty-five or thirty kids, "Hey, don't feel like you're being left out of anything. All those girls are whis-

212

pering about has nothing to do with you. It's just that eight people are dead and the rest of you aren't supposed to know about it."

For two or three days after the murders, I was constantly watching the roads. I couldn't shake the feeling that, any minute now, a bunch of police cars were going to come racing to the ranch to gather us all up and book us for those slayings. The long-delayed move to the desert now became extremely urgent. I sent several kids and some vehicles with supplies out to Barker's, where some of us had stayed, and, except for some time out for music and sex, we worked at getting ready for the final move.

After a couple of days and no police, my vigil on the road eased off. There was a lot of organizing and stealing to be done before we pulled out of the ranch, and my attention was on getting those things done. About the time I totally had relaxed from the tension of having murders hanging over my head, they nailed us. And man, it was the raid of raids. Al Capone, Pretty Boy Floyd, Ma Barker or Creepy Karpis never got half the action or attention the Los Angeles Sheriff's Office showered on us.

It happened early one morning about a week or ten days after the two nights of murder. The evening before the raid, there was a party that lasted until two or three o'clock in the morning. It seemed like I had just closed my eyes, when all of a sudden there was so goddamn much commotion a dead man would have come awake. Helicopter motors roared, doors were kicked in, and there were shouts of "Freeze! Hands up. Don't move. All right, get out of there." Instinct more than thought caused me to react. Without taking the time to say "come on" to Stephanie, I grabbed my clothes and split out the back door. Helicopter lights had the whole area lit up like a football stadium, so running across an open area was out. I dove under the porch and bellied my way as far out of sight as possible. Lying in the dirt, I worked my way into my clothes. From where I was, I couldn't see anything but feet and shoes. Because of the 'copter noise I couldn't hear what was said, only the shouts. "Stop. Stand still. Hey, George, grab those two. Freeze." It seemed like every cop in L.A. was there. Feet were coming from every direction as the cops herded the kids out of the buildings. Those bastards even knew our hiding spots away from the buildings. Somebody had supplied them with information on all our habits. We'd been snitched on.

213

I knew this was it: they had busted the murder cases and come out in full force to capture the killers. It was like seeing my world torn apart. I lay there for fifteen or twenty minutes. As the time went by, I began to hope I'd get away, but as soon as the hope was born, a booted, fatigue-clad bastard flashed a light under the building. "Okay, you, out of there," he shouted. To back up his order, two guys with rifles dropped to the ground like soldiers in combat.

When I was within reach, two of them grabbed my arms and pulled me the rest of the way, finally jerking me to my feet. "Here he is! Here's Manson. He's the guru of this bunch of hippies," they crowed. Handcuffing my hands behind my back, they carried, shoved and kicked me into the group of captives. Some of the kids, the ones who didn't know anything, were laughing and submitting to arrest without much concern. But I saw some pretty serious faces on those who had been part of the slayings. Tex was out in the desert at Barker's and had escaped the bust.

The cops were having a field day. With guns at the ready position, they posed with their trophies and captives. They ransacked all the dwellings, tearing everything up and scattering it around like they were part of a demolition crew. When the place was a complete shambles from their search and destruction, they took pictures of the mess and debris. Their hostility left marks on some of us. But while none of their swinging clubs or kicking boots was on film, the results were. Some of those pictures were published later, indicating that we always lived in this way and were responsible for all the litter. The cops confiscated everything of value, some of it as evidence and some for their own private use. I watched them, resenting every move they made but at the same time thinking, "What difference does it make, I won't be around to use the place or enjoy the things. So come on, bastards—you're making history, but let's get through your moment of glory and get on with the charges."

When they finally got around to reading us our rights and telling us the charge—auto theft!—I almost laughed in their faces. I couldn't believe it. Katie and I looked at each other with smiles of relief. We would have shared a few hugs and maybe done a little dance to express our happiness if the handcuffs hadn't stopped us.

Out from under the heavy load, all the other minor charges they started throwing against us didn't mean a thing, and the whole

214

scene became amusing as hell. Here were at least a hundred cops, all decked out like they were on a commando raid and geared to kill or die in their efforts to arrest twenty-five kids on auto-theft charges. Some of us laughed and sang all the way to the Malibu police station. If a guy can enjoy being arrested, I did, but the biggest joy came two days later, when all the charges had to be dropped because of an invalid search warrant. It was like I was some god who could do no wrong. More proof of my invincibility came a couple of days later.

Stephanie and I were back in the old outlaw shacks. We'd been making love for a couple of hours and were now just lying there relaxing, when two cops came busting in with guns drawn. Our clothes were lying on the floor. Going through my pockets they came up with a half-smoked roach, so they charged me with possession and her with indecent exposure, because her tits weren't covered. They drove us to the Malibu station and booked us.

I was pissed; someone at the ranch had to be snitching. The cops hardly knew about the outlaw shacks, much less when I was going to be in one of them. And when Stephanie and I had gone in there, we weren't smoking, and I damn sure didn't have anything on me. When the police lab ran a check on the roach, it wasn't even grass, so whoever had tried to set me up had blown it. We were cut loose. The charge against Stephanie was dropped because the cops couldn't find a law prohibiting a bare top inside a house. I left the police station feeling I was above ever getting nailed for anything and having it stick. I was chesty about that, but the snitch had to be found and got rid of.

After the big raid I knew that whoever was going to the police knew nothing about the bad shit. And at no time did I think any of the kids in our circle would call the cops. It had to be one of the ranch hands. Juan Flynn was into all of our games. John Swartz enjoyed all the fringe benefits that came his way. My attention then focused on Shorty Shea. Shea was a frustrated movie actor waiting for his chance to become the next Hopalong Cassidy. He'd liked us well enough when we first moved in at Spahn's, but in recent months he'd had a lot of differences with us. Since old George was thinking of selling the ranch, Shorty was kissing a lot of ass with the people who were thinking of buying. He and I had already had a confrontation about how much longer we would be there. He told me, "It's all over for you, Charlie, when the new owners take over. They've already told me they don't want you and that gang to be here." I answered by saying, "Shorty, you know what? You got no call to be playing policeman with us. And if you keep on trying to be the fuzz, you'll wish you had minded your own business instead of sticking your head someplace where it doesn't belong." Walking away from me, he said, "We'll see about that, Charlie. You might tell some of those kids what to do, but not me. I know how to handle you."

Leaving the Malibu station for the second time, I had no doubt about Shorty being the snitch. I shared my conclusion with several of the kids. They didn't need convincing, for while I was locked up, Shorty had been bad-mouthing me, telling the kids, "Charlie's bad news. If you stick with him, you're going to end up in jail for long terms. Get away from him."

Much later, Bruce Davis, Steve Grogan and I were convicted for the slaying of Shea. At the time of our conviction, no body had been discovered. Since that time Clem has confessed, and he directed the police to the spot where the body was supposedly buried. The report I got on the first effort to locate the body was that they didn't find anything. A later report came to me that a second attempt did unearth Shea's body. Not to deny that dead is dead any way you look at it, I have to say we were convicted on circumstantial evidence at the time of the trial. That evidence came from several people who said the body was totally dismembered. Head, arms, legs and body were said to have been chopped into bits and pieces. When Shea's body was found, it was intact. Testimony also indicated that numerous members of our group participated in the slaying, but somehow the prosecuting attorney saw fit to ignore that part of the evidence. Inasmuch as he ignored it, I can't clear up anything on Shea without being a snitch. But I will say that the DA, caught up in his theory of "Helter Skelter" and obsessed with making the world believe I was a satanic pied piper, overlooked many participants, accessories, and conspirators. Someplace out there in that society he protects so well, he has left several killers to prowl the streets.

216

CHAPTER 9

THE MESS the cops had left at the Spahn Ranch and the loss of our worldly possessions put a crimp in the joy we had been feeling after the charges had to be dropped.

Besides all the stolen stuff, they had confiscated four legal dune buggies, televisions, radios, musical instruments, camping gear, knives, guns, food supplies and even some clothing. We were left with little more than the clothes on our backs. We tried reclaiming our legitimate belongings, but the cops weren't about to give us anything unless we had positive proof of legal purchase. The way we lived, we didn't have a receipt for a damn thing.

It didn't make any difference to us that most of the stuff was stolen to begin with. What mattered was that the pricks had included even our legitimate possessions. Our natural contempt for the police turned into a unanimous, "Fuck you, you bastards, we'll get it all back and then some." And we did! And everything we stole went immediately to the desert.

Thanks to all the hassles, even those kids who weren't previously keen on moving to the desert were now so resentful of the police and the restrictions of the city that the desert looked good to them.

Considering I had been trying to put together a permanent move to the desert for the last year, I should have been in some kind of seventh heaven. And I did drive out of L.A. thinking, "At last! We're on our way, everyone is happy. We are headed toward a world of our own. Plenty of space to live by our own rules." But I wasn't as content on the inside as I tried to project on the outside. The police, in coming down on us so heavy, were cheating me. The circumstances now left me with a feeling of being pushed out. It wasn't the same, and maybe because of it, I became more of a tyrant. The old understanding Charlie, who once held the right an-

217

swers and offered the alternatives the kids sought when leaving their homes to travel with me, was disappearing.

In 1967, I had been like a baby, eager to join the easy and irresponsible lifestyle the kids enjoyed. I now found myself at the head of the pack, with everyone looking to me for all the decisions. Our fun and games and all the drugs had put us in more serious trouble than those kids believed was possible. Because they didn't know what to do next, they put their trust in me. Well, the truth was that I didn't know what the next move should be either. Out in the desert, I tried to live up to their expectations by doing what I thought best, but some of the kids started looking at me with hard eyes.

Beginning with the murders, I allowed things to happen that I could have prevented. And I did, in fact, initiate the scene on Waverly Drive. The kids had their own purposes and motives for going to the Tate-Polanski house, but, once done, the responsibility of it fell on my shoulders, like everything else. I don't mean just what the police eventually dumped on me. I mean the burden of carrying the weight of murder charges around in my head. The kids seemed to push it out of their minds easily enough, but I couldn't shake the constant pressure. I'm not saying I was feeling sorry or suffering from remorse, but I knew sooner or later the cops and the whole establishment were going to come down on us for those murders. Because of that knowledge, I pushed at being combat-ready. I pushed for vigilance, secrecy, mobility and contempt for anyone outside.

In the middle of gearing for combat and building awareness by promoting hate and distrust, it was hard to continue practicing love and playing music as we once did. Even our sex became more of an angered lust than the natural free-flowing pleasure of love and togetherness. Now it was all digging bunkers and establishing storage places for reserve gas and supplies. It was hate the pigs and learn to protect yourself.

On our return to Barker Ranch, there were heavy clouds hanging over us. Our music had not made it past a recording studio. Love had given way to mistrust. Our own violence threatened our freedom. After just a few days back in the desert no one had to be a genius to realize being there was a mistake. For that matter, even remaining together wasn't wise. But a number of us leaned on each other so strong that we could never consider a permanent separa-

218

tion. That wasn't true of everyone, and several of the kids did head for other places. I had mixed emotions about those who left. On the one side it was, "Good for them, they're out of it." On the other side, "You chicken-shit bastards, where's your loyalty?" And what plagued me most about those who left was my fear of them running to the police.

As the weeks passed, I think we all grew wilder. Our instincts became more animal than human. We hid by day and did our moving around by night. It wasn't long before some of the local people and police began to notice and resent us. One day in October, a bunch of cops surrounded Barker's and arrested twelve or thirteen of the kids. I had gone into L.A. for supplies and to hustle some money. One of the kids phoned from jail and caught me at Spahn's. When he first mentioned he was phoning from jail, I had that sinking sensation—but after being told that the charges were auto theft, possession of firearms and other petty charges, I wasn't alarmed, just irritated at the police for continually fucking with us.

I stuck around L.A. for another day gathering supplies and looking for money, then headed back to the Barker place wondering what it was going to take to get the kids out of jail. From the phone conversation, we weren't suspected of anything other than the charges mentioned. The murders had happened over two months ago, and even with Bobby in jail for Hinman's death, the cops hadn't questioned any of us about that. I wasn't worried about showing up at the station to try to get all those I could out of jail. I was even thinking that perhaps in my paranoia I had been a little too heavy on everyone in the last few weeks. Maybe I had gone overboard on stressing the need to be ready to defend ourselves. "Okay," I thought, "I'll get the kids out and we'll ease off on all the get-ready-for-war shit and get back to the things we once enjoyed." Besides, to desert any of them now would have been to deny the togetherness I had been struggling to hold on to.

I got back to the ranch in the late afternoon. Several kids who had escaped the bust were still in the area. When they saw me, they all came out of hiding and joined me in the house. By the time the sun had gone down, about eight or ten of us had been in the house for a couple of hours, and we had lit a candle for light. They were busy telling me what had happened, and I was deep in thought about the best way to approach the police about getting the rest of us out of jail. All of a sudden, up jumped the devil. "Freeze! Hands up! All right, now one at a time, back out the door," shouted the officer who had thrown the door open. I dropped to the floor as soon as I heard the first word and bellied it into the bathroom. Figuring the place was surrounded, I didn't see any way out. The only refuge possible was a small cabinet beneath the wash basin. Somehow, I managed to squeeze inside that cabinet and get the door shut. I was so cramped it was almost a relief when about ten minutes later the door was opened and a voice said, "All right you, out of there." It seems that when I had closed the door some strands of my hair were visible. Had it not been for that hair sticking out, the officer later stated that he would never have looked in that cabinet because it seemed too small to hide in.

We were taken to the Inyo County Seat, Independence, California. With those previously arrested, plus two more of the girls who were arrested on their way to the ranch as the cops were taking us away, the Independence jail was now bursting at the seams with twenty-five members of the so-called Manson Family. I think the date was October 12, 1969.

At the time of the arrest I thought most of us, including myself, would be back on the streets in a matter of days. But the worm had finally turned. Except while being transported from one jail to another, I haven't seen the streets since.

The first day in custody, we were only questioned about the charges the California Highway Patrol and the local cops were interested in. So I was still resting easy about those L.A. happenings. One night's contented sleep is all I got. The very next day some of the L.A. Police Department showed up and I realized we had more serious problems than what we were booked for. I waited for them to call me out of my cell for questioning. When the day was almost over, I thought I was on the verge of getting another pass—until I heard that the L.A. investigators had left, taking Sadie, Lyn and Katie with them. With that, I knew the police were at last closing in on those who had put fear and panic in the homes and on the streets of Hollywood some two months ago.

Some heavy scheming and a lot of communication had to be done. The police made both avenues possible when charges on several of the kids were dropped. With their release, I had the means to spread the word, "Clam up, no talking! Find out where the cops are getting their information." The warning came too late. Almost immediately, word got back to me that Kitty Lutesinger, a biker named Al Springer, Danny DeCarlo and Little Paul Watkins were not only telling what they had heard, but were spicing things up with imaginative input of their own.

Springer and DeCarlo had pending beefs they were trying to beat. Telling their tales about me and the rest of our circle got their charges dropped.

As for Little Paul talking to the cops and later writing a book, that was his desire to be noticed and looked on as someone special. His rap to the police, like the book he wrote, was so full of lies, I'm surprised he has the balls to ever look in a mirror again. Kitty was a pregnant little girl who got threatened with the gas chamber just for knowing us. She, of the four, was perhaps the most authoritative person to be repeating things she heard. She was close to Katie, Sadie and Linda, two of whom were always running off at the mouth.

When Lyn, Katie and Sadie were taken to L.A., Sadie was booked as a suspect in the Hinman case. Katie and Lyn were both released, and Katie split out of the state. Lyn and Sandy, a girl who had been released earlier, came to Independence and got an apartment. They were my link to everything that was going on. Though in jail some six or seven hours' drive from L.A., I had Lyn and Sandy burning up the highways and telephone lines with daily reports on who was saying what, and to whom. And with each report, Charles Manson was getting buried deeper and deeper.

Sometime in early December, I was moved to L.A. and formally charged as the one responsible for the Tate-LaBianca slayings. Sadie, it seems, had blabbered to a couple of her jail-house roomies. In her bid for immunity, Sadie delivered the final blow. She and her attorney put her version of all the happenings in the DA's lap. A few days later, Sadie, through her attorney and some writers, sold a story, "Two Nights of Murder," for the whole world to read. *The Los Angeles Times* published it on December 14, 1969, and other publications picked it up quickly. This girl, who had perhaps taken more drugs, created more scenes, inflicted more stab wounds, possessed the most perverted imagination, and desired more attention than anyone among our circle, told a story that projected me as love itself, magic musicmaker, a devil, a guru,

221

Jesus and the man who ordered her and others to kill. Her story gave the newsmedia the material for any fantasy of death and perversion they cared to print. If I hadn't been the guy they were writing about, I'd have laughed at every word printed, but being in the spot I was in, laughter didn't come that easy. Still, some of the stories were so ridiculous, I was amused.

I was a half-assed nothing who hardly knew how to read or write, never read a book all the way through in my life, didn't know anything except jails, couldn't hold on to my wives, was a lousy pimp, got caught every time I stole, wasn't a good enough musician to hit the market, didn't know what to do with money even if I had it and resented every aspect of family life. But a week after Sadie's story, I was a charismatic cult leader with a family, a genius who could program people into doing whatever I asked of them. Shit, if there were any truth to what I was said to be capable of, I'd have been sitting in Hearst Castle with stereos in every room, listening to my own platinum albums.

Sadie's story was so widely accepted by the public that the other kids involved could use it to escape or minimize their roles. The DA grabbed Sadie's sick version, capitalized on the publicity, and ran all the way through the courtroom with it. By the time I made my first court appearance, the myth of Charles Manson had taken root and was spreading clear around the world.

After reading or hearing someone tell me what I was supposed to be, I'd lay there in my high-security cell wondering, "Wow, am I really all they say?" And the more I read and heard, it wasn't too many days before I was half way believing the shit myself. Half way believing it, and yet knowing that I was truly a nothing, I let the girls feed me the myth until it has finally burned me so bad, I'm not sure what face I should be wearing.

Actually, the way we started adding to all the hype came through a bad visit with Lyn and Sandy. The two girls had come to see me and I was feeling it was the kids' and the world's fault that I was in jail. During that visit, Lyn and Sandy took the full brunt of my bitterness. I told them, "See where it's ending? I told all of you months ago you had me headed right back to prison. I knew I should have packed my shit and hit the road. But, 'No,' you said, 'please stay, Charlie, we'll take care of everything, we won't let you go back to jail.' Well, here I am, and in deeper trouble than I've ever been in my life. So now what?"

Both girls were crying and suggesting different things that might keep me from going back to prison. "Charlie," said Lyn, "you weren't in the houses when any of those people were killed. They will have to let you out. We'll tell the whole world about your good, your love. We'll make them see that you're not responsible."

When they left, none of us had any idea what their method of getting a message through to the world would be. But Lyn, the little girl who was always at the end of the line, the one who seldom made herself noticed, came right to the front with what she thought would do me some good. She and some of the other kids started spending their days on the street corner next to the jail. They weren't bashful about anything they did or said, and everything they did made for more hype about the power I had over my followers. But it wasn't me or my wishes that put them on a street corner and kept them there. It was Lyn's strength and devotion that engineered and kept that scene going. And the longer they stayed, the more publicity all of us and the trials received. And with all the publicity, more people came into the fold and wanted to be part of the "Manson Family."

When the girls first hit the corner, I guess I was somewhat on the proud side. Every other time I hit jail, everyone I knew or depended on left me before the ink got dry on my prison number, including a wife and another girl I'd had a kid by. So when a bunch of girls started living on a street corner to profess my innocence and their love and loyalty for me, it was a big switch from all the other times I had gone to jail. A couple of tabloid publications interviewed the girls and printed stories suggesting we weren't as callous and cold-blooded as the straight papers indicated. Remember, this was the 60s, and when they called me a revolutionary martyr, I thought, "Hey, there might be something to all the charisma, love and magic trip Sadie was rapping about. Now if the bitch will just retract her statement of, 'Charlie instructed us to,' there's no way these people are going to convict me of killing anyone."

As the trials progressed, Sadie did do a turn-around and got on my side again. At one time she, Katie and Leslie even wanted to

223

cop to the whole thing so I'd be off the hook. But it was too late for that, because, the way I see it, Linda and Mary picked up Sadie's old stand and testified against me to get immunity for themselves. Their stories were almost a word-for-word repeat of what Sadie had said. I can't help but wonder how they would have laid out their clean-ups if they hadn't had Sadie's words to guide them.

Anyway, as the weeks and months passed, any thought of beating the case sank. Nothing was going my way, and the only voice I had was those girls on the corner. The attorney the court gave me was full of motions, but all his motions were with his hands. Nothing that might carry some weight in a court room was ever heard. I kept asking for a chance to be my own attorney, but every time I asked or made a scene to represent myself, I was denied, and sometimes even removed from the court room. So, if over the years, I have screamed about the injustice of the system, it's not because I'm without guilt. It's because I don't feel I got a fair shake in the court room according to the laws and codes of justice as written in the books.

When those of us facing murder charges were found guilty, Lyn and the rest of the kids on the street corner stopped promoting love and innocence and started mouthing threats and violence. For the most part, the threats were nothing more than a bunch of kids wanting to be heard, but the media grabbed them and frightened the whole world. And Charlie Manson was that much more a monster.

A few of those kids, in their own frustration, did commit robbery for the purpose of raising money and arms to take me out of jail by force. They got nailed robbing a sporting-goods store. When some of them started rapping to the police, it was as though I had engineered that, too. Shit, by then I'd been in a high-security cell for over a year and a half. I didn't even know half the people involved. The guys that had come into the picture and carried the guns weren't there because of me, but because publicity had alerted some sex-hungry, thrill-happy guys that there were some pretty, young girls available on the street corner. The girls did the rest of the maneuvering. From where I was sitting, I had no control over anything that went on outside my cell.

When the judge finally laid the death penalty on us, I wasn't shocked—just resentful. I'd been on the wrong side of the law too long not to realize, "if you get caught doing the crime, you gotta do the time." The resentment and denials I've expressed over the years stem, not from being convicted and sentenced, but from the way things got totally turned around, and from the manner in which I was convicted. I mean, the deaths happened, so someone has to pay. It's obvious the right people are locked up, but the motives used to convict us, especially me, were absurd.

The media, film directors and book authors took a mole hill and made it into a mountain. The myth of Charles Manson has twisted more minds than I was ever accused of touching. Hell, in that book the DA got rich on, he's got me so powerful that a look from me stopped his watch. In one movie, they had me making the hands of a clock spin by giving it a glance. The only way I ever stopped a watch is by stepping on it. Since the movie I've been staring at every clock I see. And you know what? As hard as I try, the clock neither stops or spins. But all the bullshit has people believing I hold some kind of magic.

And if there is some doubt about that statement, I've got tons of mail to prove the fact. Mail from every country, from all ages and both sexes, sent by people totally unknown to me. Their awareness and interest are strictly the result of books and other forms of public exposure. The letter-writers believe I have the power and charisma that status-hungry journalists have put in their eyes. The twister is that about fifty percent of the people who contact me are offering me their lives to instruct and deal with. Some want to pick up guns and knives for me. Some just want my love and attention. Shit, I could have been on the streets a hundred years trying to lure people into my fold and I'd never have come up with more than those who were with me at the time we were arrested. But thanks to all the sensationalism, there are thousands out there who want to be associated with me and a part of what I've been promoted as being.

Now I ask you, is my charisma, my power, my love or my madness drawing those people to me? Or is it an attraction caused by writers so obsessed with proving themselves to the public, they created a monster and fed a myth to establish their own names?

When I first hit Death Row I wanted to be a forgotten person with a normal prison number. But that hasn't been the case. I've spent eighteen years trying to make it to the general prison popula-

225

tion and be just an everyday number in the yard, but the authorities won't let it happen. Nor will the media let up.

There are days when I get caught up in being the most notorious convict of all time. In that frame of mind I get off on all the publicity, and I'm pleased when some fool writes and offers to "off some pigs" for me. I've had girls come to visit me with their babies in their arms and say, "Charlie, I'd do anything in the world for you. I'm raising my baby in your image." Those letters and visits used to delight me, but that's my individual sickness. What sickness is it that keeps sending me kids and followers? It's your world out there that does it. I don't solicit any mail or ask anyone to come and visit me. Yet the mail continues to arrive and your pretty little flowers of innocence keep showing up at the gate. Hell, they don't know me. They only know what your world has projected and won't let go of.

Truth is, the load is too heavy to carry this many years. I want out from under it. I ain't never been anything but a half-assed thief who didn't know how to steal without getting caught. The only home I've ever known is one of these concrete and steel prisons. How I was raised, what I actually am and what all your printed words have made me is on your head. I'm not sorry or ashamed of who I really am. I'm not even sorry for the myth of Manson that your newspapers, books and television keep putting in front of your faces. My disappointment is that so many of you are so gullible, that you eat everything you are fed.

Even the system lends to the madness. Your world requires the California Board of Parole to call me before them for release consideration. On my recent appearances they have had the room full of TV cameras so that everyone can go through their act of justice and efficiency for anyone that wants to watch. But it's a game with two sides, theirs and mine. They know they aren't about to let me out. And to make them feel good about their foregone conclusion, I play the fool for them and their cameras. And even if they should say, "Okay, Manson, you can go home," I'd have to ask, Go where? You gave me this cell when I was twelve years old. I've become as much a part of the cells as the bars on the windows and doors. This is my home. You kicked me out in 1967, gave me your kids, allowed me a little space on the desert and then took it all away from me. I got nothing out there. If you did kick me out, I'd just have to find some place to hide. Truth is, I'm tired of hiding. I've been hiding under the myth and using it for protection ever since I've been here, but I'm tired of playing that game that was created in 1969. Like me, it's growing old.

So for you people who are filled with the fear that I might some-day be released: breathe easy, I don't see it happening. And for you people who are victims of all the hype that portrays me as a charismatic cult leader, guru, lover, pied piper or another Jesus, I want you to know I've got everything in the world, and beyond, right here. My eyes are cameras. My mind is tuned to more television channels than exist in your world. And it suffers no censorship. Through it, I have a world and the universe as my own. So, save your sympathy and know that only a body is in prison. At my will, I walk your streets and am right out there among you.

Conclusion

by Nuel Emmons

Charles Manson is currently confined in San Quentin Federal Penitentiary, outside San Francisco, where he was first imprisoned after his conviction in 1971. In 1972, after California abolished the death penalty, he was transferred from San Quentin's Death Row to Folsom Prison, and in 1976, he was transferred again to Vacaville Medical Facility (where I renewed my acquaintance with him) for treatment. In both institutions, he was kept in segregated housing (isolated from all but a few other inmates and under constant supervision) and denied the privileges commonly granted the general prison population, until 1982.

From 1982 through 1985, Manson received some work assignments at Vacaville that permitted him to work among the other inmates, although he was closely supervised and allowed only limited contact with others. It was during these periods that the most constructive work on this book was done.

Unfortunately, his relative freedom ended in 1985, as a result of his own actions. Among other incidents, Manson recorded some of his music and smuggled the tapes out of Vacaville. Friends of Manson's then mailed the tapes to someone who was to market and distribute them. However, when a dispute arose between the friends and the would-be distributor, the latter began receiving threatening telephone calls. Perhaps recalling Terry Melcher, he notified prison authorities and was allowed to speak to Manson, who responded, "If you've lied and broken someone's trust, I have no control over what happens. I didn't send you the tapes. Your fear is of the people who did, not me."

A few days later Manson was on his way to San Quentin. During a routine body search on his arrival there, a four-inch piece of hacksaw blade was found in his shoe. He was immediately placed

228

in administrative segregation, where he remains. Manson knew that the metal hacksaw blade would not pass the electronic device used in searching inmates. He carried it in order to make certain that he would be placed in a segregated unit until he was familiar with the institution and the convicts he would be associating with. As he told me, "Sure, I knew the blade would be found, but I had to be in a safe place until I found out who I could trust."

Prison personnel say that Manson constantly tests the staff and abuses most of the opportunities given to him. Manson says, "That's bullshit. Like at Plainfield when I was a kid, I'm still the whipping post for anyone who wants to feel important, and the guy to use when an example is needed. If I demand to be treated like any other convict, some guard writes me up as threatening him or her, and I go back in the hole. Those suckers don't know what truth is, and when I try to hold them up to their rules, they turn it around on me and I'm written up as arrogant and defiant."

Prison psychiatrists diagnose Manson as suffering from paranoia and schizophrenia, and Manson himself accepts that diagnosis, explaining, "Sure I'm paranoid. I've had reason to be ever since I can remember. And now I have to be, just to stay alive. As for schizophrenia, take anybody off the streets and put them in the middle of a prison yard and you'll see all kinds of split personalities. I've got a thousand faces, so that makes me five hundred schizophrenics. And in my life, I've played every one of those faces. Sometimes because people push me into a role, and sometimes because it's better being someone else than me."

Manson's many faces were never more apparent to me than on a day very early in our working relationship when I brought with me the young woman mentioned in the Introduction who wanted to interview him for a local newspaper. When we arrived, Manson was already in the room provided for us. Either because he knew I would be taking photographs, or because the interviewer was a woman, he had changed his appearance significantly. His full beard was gone, reduced to a square goatee that covered only his chin. He was dressed immaculately, in pressed blue jeans adorned with symbolic patches embroidered by his two favorite girls, Lynette Fromme and Sandra Good. He wore a blue-grey velour shirt that was handstitched by Fromme.

At first Manson virtually ignored the woman, but as he showed

229

us his photo album and identified those pictured he became a charmer. The interviewer was in her late twenties, neither a beauty nor homely, but by the time Manson had talked to her for a while, she must have believed she was the most attractive woman on earth. Since I was now the one being ignored, I had ample opportunity to observe Manson's performance, and I was fascinated by it.

When he spoke to her, he was polite, courteous and complimentary. His normal profanity and prison slang had disappeared, and in fact, he was more articulate than I would have believed possible. Very soon he was holding her hand and caressing the skin of her bare arm while she listened intently to every word he said.

He stood up and began massaging the back of the interviewer's neck and shoulders. She closed her eyes and smiled appreciatively. Then, continuing the conversation, he casually reached across the table and picked up the cord of the tape recorder we were using. He looked at me and winked. Suddenly and menacingly, he wrapped the cord around the woman's neck. Her eyes opened wide, filling her glasses, and she looked at me pleadingly. Manson applied some pressure on the cord and in an intimidating voice said, "Whatta ya think Emmons, should I take this little bitch's life?"

The woman was terrified, and though Manson's wink had indicated he was not serious, the pressure of the cord on the woman's neck gave me cause for a moment's real concern. Just as I was contemplating a rescue effort, he laughed and loosened the cord, saying, "See bitch, you never want to trust a stranger." To this day, I don't know why Manson decided to frighten the woman, but his sudden mood changes and drastic attempts to impress or intimidate those around him have become familiar to me.

Gaining Manson's trust and keeping it was one of the constant struggles I fought in our relationship, and Manson continually tested me. He would often say "You could get me out of here if you wanted to," and then give me detailed escape plans, including what someone on the outside would have to do to help him get out. In the beginning, wanting to build his confidence in me but hoping to discourage him, I would point out flaws in his plans. However, my continued evasions eventually became transparent, and one day he confronted me. "You know what Emmons?" he said. "You're not my friend. You haven't got the guts to help a brother when he's down. All you're after is to get rich like the DA and all those other assholes who wrote books about me. Shit, now that I've told you things I'd never tell anyone else, I'm worth more to you dead than alive. When are you going to send someone in to do a number on me?"

"That's not true, Charlie!" I replied vehemently. "I don't want to see you dead. And if those are your true feelings, we can stop working on this project right now. I'm a firm believer in the guilty being punished, and I think you got what you deserved. So if all I am is a tool for you to make a break, I'll leave now and never come back. But if we continue to visit, you'd be doing me, and maybe yourself in the long run, a favor by never mentioning your schemes again."

Our eyes were glued to each other's and I seriously thought my words might terminate our relationship, which was the last thing I wanted, even though I knew I had to make the point. But Manson smiled and said, "You know what, man? That's pretty straight and I don't blame you. I wouldn't put my life on the line for any son-of-a-bitch either. I did in '69 and look what it got me. Anyway, don't stop showing up. You're about the only sane person I get to talk to. They keep telling me how crazy I am, but the guys they got me locked in seg [segregated housing] with still believe I'm everything Sadie said I was. They are worse than those kids out there wanting to believe I'm some kind of God. I hear it so much, sometimes I believe it—believe it so strongly that I think the world should bow down to me and ask forgiveness. Not forgiveness for what they did to me, but forgiveness for what they do to themselves.

"Maybe this book of yours was meant to be. Maybe some kind of God out there cut me loose to live the life I lived and brought you into the picture to write a book about it so the world could look at itself. I'm nothing but the reflection of evil that goes through the minds of all those people who created the monster and keep pushing the myth to kids who don't know any better."

As inflated as such statements are, I believe they betray something of the reason Manson allowed this book to be written. Behind his feelings of obligation to me for our past association lies his desire to let others see him as he sees himself. For that reason, this book may be as close to the "real" Charles Manson as we may ever get. In the course of gathering material for this book, Manson has often said to me, "I owe this to you because you let me live." In saying "you" Manson was probably referring not only to me, but to society as a whole, for not having executed him.

Even so, Manson is still not sure which "Charlie" he wants people to know. He has said to me, "Man, you didn't have to write everything I told you. You're pulling the covers off me. All that stuff the DA fed the world has been my shell. It immortalized me and gave me something. It's my protection. You've been in these hallways, you know the convicts I'm living with—they don't respect nothing but the meanest and baddest." I told him that he was the one who felt the shell had become too heavy a load to bear, and that he was tired of carrying it. "Yeah man," he replied, "but sometimes I was God to some of those kids."

The "God" he perhaps was to his followers was turned into a monster for the rest of us. Yet Manson has no superhuman powers, neither divine nor demonic. The image of "the most dangerous man alive" bears little resemblance to the man I have been visiting these past seven years. Perhaps the myth of Charles Manson satisfied our hunger for sensationalism, but certainly it also absolved us of the darker side of the humanity we share with him.

What made Manson what he is? The unbroken chain of horrifying abuse and neglect from early childhood on doesn't explain it all, for others with an equally unhappy past have managed to escape his fate. Ultimately, the mystery of Manson's life and the man he became is a complex one that doesn't yield easily to examination. But somewhere in this story and his own words, some of the answers may begin to emerge, allowing us to see him, and perhaps some part of ourselves, more clearly.